FROM REBEL TO HERO:
The Image of the Highlander, 1745–1830

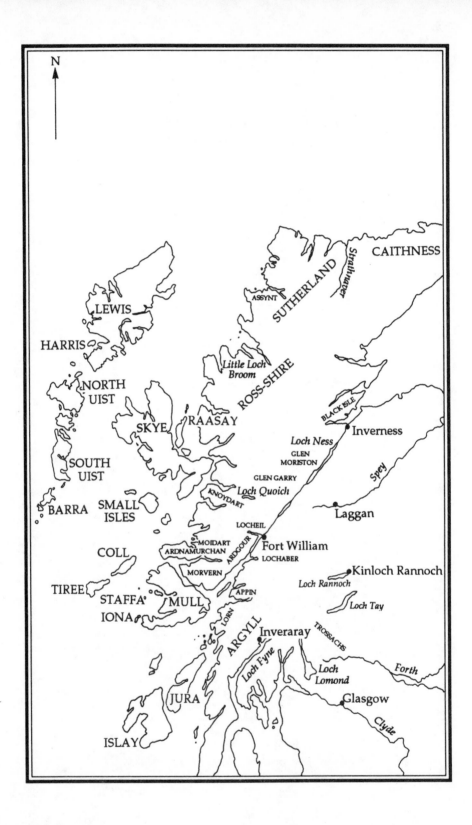

FROM REBEL TO HERO

The Image of the Highlander, 1745–1830

Robert Clyde

TUCKWELL PRESS

ACKNOWLEDGEMENTS

Thanks are due to the staffs of the Scottish Record Office, the National Library of Scotland, and the Libraries of the Universities of Glasgow, Edinburgh, and Aberdeen for their courtesy and assistance in facilitating research. I am grateful to family and friends in Texas for their love and support; to Allan Macinnes for his expert advice; to all in North Carolina; and to friends in Scotland for making me feel at home.

First published in Great Britain in 1995 by

Reprinted in 1998

Tuckwell Press Ltd
The Mill House
Phantassie
East Linton
East Lothian EH40 3DG
Scotland

The publisher acknowledges subsidy from the Scottish Arts Council towards publication of this volume.

Typeset by Hewer Text Composition Services, Edinburgh
Printed by Biddles Ltd, Guildford

CONTENTS

Acknowledgements
Foreword

1.	Whig Polemicists	1
2.	Improvers	21
3.	Civilisers, Educators, and Evangelisers	49
4.	Travellers	97
5.	Romanticists	116
6.	Militarists	150

Conclusion	181
Bibliography	189
Index	199

FOREWORD

The purpose of this book is to explore the rehabilitation of the Scottish Gaels from the time of the Jacobite Rebellion of 1745 to 1830. 'Rehabilitation' is a subjective term with a number of connotations. In the present case, it refers to the change of attitudes towards the Highlander, from the rebellious barbarian of public image to that of model British subject. This transformation from rebel to hero – or from threat to pet – as revealed by those involved in the process is remarkable and involves the replacement of myth with myth. The views expressed by such commentators only occasionally took notice of the true nature of the crisis that faced Gaeldom in these years. That the people of the Highlands and Islands had shed their unsavoury image should not be taken to mean that they were the better for it. At the end of the process, they were on the brink of disaster. Famine and mass emigration were the realities of the Highlands in the nineteenth century, but tartan-kitsch imagery formed the public perception of the day.

I

Whig Polemicists

FOLLOWING THE REVOLUTION in 1689, the Highland supporters of the Stuart cause found themselves in conflict with a distant Government which knew or cared little about their region but was prepared to use any means to gain obedience. The Glencoe massacre of February 1692 may have hardened attitudes against William, but it demonstrated that the long arm of the Hanoverian establishment could reach into the Highlands to smash those suspected of Jacobitism. After the massacre a new fort was built at Inverlochy and subsidies were paid to Jacobite chiefs to keep the peace,[1] but these measures failed miserably; all attempts to 'pacify' the Jacobite element in the Highlands were to be unsuccessful until after the battle of Culloden.

The inheritors of William's policy towards the Highlands were the Whigs, a political and intellectual grouping that stood for reform in the eighteenth and early nineteenth centuries. Whigs were staunch supporters of the Hanoverian establishment and were therefore utterly opposed to Jacobite aims; in Scotland, Whigs were for the most part Lowland and Presbyterian, and naturally suspicious of the Gaels. Much of the hostility shown by Whigs towards the traditional order in the Highlands and Islands can be attributed to resentment dating from the use of Highland troops (as well as some Lowland militia) to subdue Covenanters in the south-west of Scotland for two months in 1678, and from the time of the Revolution, when some clans rallied to the cause of James VII and II and thereby threatened the Presbyterian ascendancy. The Gaels were not popular in the Lowlands at any rate; those Lowlanders who lived in areas bordering on the mountains were often the victims of the criminal element in the Highlands, and people of Covenanting stock hated them 'as the children of Israel hated the Philistines'.[2] The Whig agenda to 'reform' the Highlands and Islands, aside from the political necessity of pacifying the region (and perhaps a desire to settle old scores), originated from an underlying aim of Whig ideology: the replacement of traditional social roles with commercial ones. Whigs viewed the clan system not only as conducive to Jacobitism but also as an insurmountable obstacle to law and order and economic advancement. As one commentator puts it, 'the improving spirit of the age – the prevailing Whig concept that material and cultural progress through the acquisition and exploitation of property entailed the replacement of customary by commercial relationships – identified the eradication of clanship in the aftermath of the Forty-Five with the 'civilising' of Scottish Gaeldom'.[3]

While the reputation of certain clans for Jacobitism was well known in Whig circles, the Government did remarkably little to contain the threat in the years following the Glencoe massacre. The rebellion of 1708 had drawn attention to the considerable support for the Stuart cause in the Episcopalian north-east of Scotland but the situation in the Highlands remained unresolved. The Government's intelligence-gathering network in the region was almost non-existent; in the build-up to the rebellion of 1715 it had only two agents beyond the Highland line, and they were self-appointed.[4] That rebellion was inconclusive in the military and political sense, but the Government felt its position was secure enough to disband the pro-Hanoverian Highland companies in 1717. It soon became apparent that only the 'loyal', Whig clans were complying with the Disarming Act of 1716, leaving the rest equipped for another attempt.

A small number of papers began to circulate in London and Edinburgh after the rebellion which advocated the education of the Gaels in the habits of industry and proper (Presbyterian) religion, and the abolition of the trappings of Highland feudalism; one argued for 'the completion of the Union' by abolishing superiorities, which the writer believed would make the Gaels 'free' and end clanship.[5] The rebellion of 1719, which was quickly neutralised by Government forces, did not cause much worry in London as it was localised and clearly a Spanish initiative; nevertheless, the rebellion resulted in the flooding of the north-west Highlands with Spanish arms.[6] In the 1720s, rumours (as well as more polemics) circulated about the Jacobite threat. Many proposals for taming the Highlands were too radical for consideration and involved the reform of land law, criminal courts, local government, and the redistribution of parliamentary seats which the political system at the time could not accommodate.[7]

Evidence that the Government had after three rebellions finally embarked upon a plan of action can be found in General George Wade's appointment as Commander-in-Chief in Scotland in 1724. He was given the huge task of pacifying the Highlands and had at his disposal, in addition to British army regulars, six Highland companies raised in 1725 to police the region. Between 1725 and 1738, Wade presided over the construction of a road system in the central Highlands; this was done not to improve the economic infrastructure of the region but to make it more accessible to Government forces in case of rebellion. Despite this effort, which involved the construction of about 250 miles of road and 42 bridges in rugged terrain, despite the addition of four Highland companies to the original six to form the Black Watch in 1739, and despite the supremacy of the Whigs in Britain in 1745, the rebellion of 1745 caused great discomfiture (and fear) until it was defeated in April 1746.

While the conflict was still in progress, Whig commentators offered their interpretation of its causes and implications. After the battle of Culloden, when Whigs realised that the Highlands and Islands demanded immediate attention, the trickle of suggested remedies to the 'Highland problem' became a flood. Some Whig polemicists concentrated upon the reputation of Gaels for criminality and drew the connection between lawlessness and support for the Stuart family. Others were concerned about clanship and argued for the abolition of its trappings, such as the speaking of Gaelic, the use of Highland dress, the wearing of arms, and the system of heritable jurisdictions.

Heritable jurisdictions (rights of legal jurisdiction attached to land ownership and transmitted by inheritance) were abolished by Parliament in 1747 in an attempt to separate the chiefs from the common people, but the authority of a chief was personal rather than legal, and as a result the act had little effect. The 3rd Duke of Argyll, who dominated Scottish politics after the death of his brother the 2nd Duke in 1743, also held the country's largest heritable jurisdiction, and was understandably unenthusiastic about their abolition, perhaps because of the considerable electoral influence that went with them,[8] but eventually yielded for party-political reasons. However, the chiefs and clan gentry in Gaeldom as a whole had long before the defeat of the Jacobites viewed their management of human and land resources increasingly in the light of commercial interest rather than their traditional obligations to their people. Whigs wanted to obliterate any vestige of feudalism, and a number of them focused on the issue of heritable jurisdictions to bring about change. In time, the Highland chiefs were happy to be unencumbered with such an unprofitable responsibility.

The Rise of the Present Unnatural Rebellion Discover'd, a tract written anonymously in 1745 when the outcome was still in doubt, placed the blame for the upheaval upon the system of heritable jurisdictions, which the writer claimed made the Gaels 'slaves' to the every whim of their despotic chiefs. He argued that the Highlanders should not be condemned as rebels and enemies; instead, 'we must Pity their Misfortune, and regret that so many brave Men are Slaves to Arbitrary Power'.[9] The common people were 'in such Subjection to their Chief, that they dare not if they had the Inclination, disobey their orders'. But they had been subservient for such a long period of time, they 'have lost almost all Sense of Liberty, and given up their Understanding and Will, to follow blindly the Dictates of Tyrant-Chiefs'.[10] The Gaels themselves, despite their condition, were.

> ... Men brave to Temerity; open hearted and hospitable in their Disposition; with as large a Share of Honesty, and Sagacity as any common People on Earth, but miserably that they are strangers to Liberty.[11]

The writer believed it was heritable jurisdictions that gave the chiefs their power, and until these were at least regulated, 'these People will always prove troublesome to any Government: Its no matter of what complexion, if ambitious Heads go to work with the Chiefs, they are easily wrought upon, the Commons must obey'. But once forced into battle, he wrote, 'they will surely fight, whatever the Cause is they are engaged in', adding that the Highlanders valued their reputation for courage, 'and to support that I believe is all they fight for'. He went on to suggest a scheme for regulating heritable jurisdictions (he did not think their abolition possible), and advocated a pardon for 'the common Highlanders' participating in the rebellion'.[12] The writer did not accuse the Gaels of barbarity as did other Whig commentators, but in claiming that the persistence of Jacobitism could be attributed to a single factor such as heritable jurisdictions, he overlooked vital social, religious, and political considerations.

Following the failure of the Forty-Five, a number of writers offered histories of the rebellion, complete with analyses of its causes. These were typically Whiggish, and attributed the blame to the 'backwardness' of the Highlands and Islands, the religion and customs of the Gaels and, quite often, the region's reputation for lawlessness and violence. Jacobitism and banditry were believed to be inextricably linked. Andrew Henderson's *History of the Rebellion, 1745 and 1746* was typical. Henderson named a number of Jacobite clans whose alleged savagery and lust for plunder had led them to fight for the Stuart cause. Donald Cameron of Lochiel was 'a very humane Gentleman' who had given 'great Proof of his Inclination to civilize those of his Name, who had been odious some time past for a thievish Disposition, which frequently shewed itself in open robberies'.[13] Likewise, Donald MacDonald of Clanranald 'is reckoned a very good Gentleman',

> ... but the Misfortune is, that his Clan, who live with him-self, and are Roman Catholicks, have little or no communica-tion with the Continent (except once a Year, that some Drovers transport their black Cattle) which makes them utter Strangers to civil Policy. Their Religion recommends an Abhorrence of the ecclesiastical Constitution; no Arts or Sciences prevailing among them, their Exercise is the Sword, and Education the Accounts of

their Sea-fights with the Mac Leans, and their Rebellions since the Revolution.[14]

MacDonald of Clanranald's men were, according to Henderson, 'generally of very low Stature, speak the Irish Tongue, and despise our Laws'. The Macdonells of Glengarry were 'of a good Size, but very poor, and addicted to Theft and Robbery: If any Religion be among them, it is Popery', and for their part, the MacDonalds of Glencoe were 'drowned in Ignorance, and like many other of the Rebels, were ready to engage in the most desperate Cause, when a Prospect of Plunder was before them'.[15] Not only was the Jacobite cause scorned, but its adherents were depicted as morally bankrupt. Henderson wrote:

> Such were the Abettors of this Insurrection! These were the Men the young Pretender brought with him for reinstating the British Isles in their Religion, Laws, and Liberties, to remove the Incroachments made upon a free People, and secure them in the enjoyment of their valuable Rights![16]

In support of its position both during and immediately after the Forty-Five, the Government published a number of broadsheets which combined caricature with polemical verse; these were anti-Jacobite but carried an explicit anti-Highland message together with a more vague anti-Scottish tone for consumption south of the border. One such broadsheet published in London in 1745, entitled 'The Chevaliers Market or Highland Fair', warned what a Jacobite victory would mean, i.e. domination by Gaels and Catholics.[17] Another broadsheet included an illustration of a number of tartaned figures surrendering to Government troops, with polemical verse published in the *London Courant* newspaper during and after the rebellion.[18] A poem dated 10 September 1745, before the eventual Hanoverian victory had been secured, asserted that 'Rebellion' had emerged from 'Northern Caves' to 'Behold her Banners wave in Scotia's Air'. Britons were roused to purge the country of 'these infectious Pests' who had been 'Nurtur'd in Climes where Pow'r Despotic reigns / and shackles the free mind in slavish Chains'.[19]

A caricature circulating in Edinburgh in 1745 depicted Charles Edward Stuart as a Highlander, a portrayal that would not have warmed its Lowland viewers to the man or his cause. He wears a distinctly effeminate form of Highland dress which resembles a twentieth-century miniskirt. He discards his manifesto, which says little for his political steadfastness. A caption at the bottom of the caricature reads, 'A likeness notwithstanding the Disguise that any Person who Secures the Son of the Pretender is Entitled to a Reward of 3000 L'.[20] The Jacobites were not to be outdone, although understandably they avoided the anti-Highland approach. A poster held by the National Library of Scotland features comments allegedly made by Charles Edward Stuart and General Sir John Cope of the British army before the battle of Prestonpans. The poster asserts:

CHARLES PRINCE REGENT,
His SPEECH to His Army,
When He began His March to meet
General John Cope at the Field near
Dudiston, September 20th, 1745;

The prince being clothed in a plain Highland
Habit, Cocked His Blue Bonnet, Drew His Sword,
Threw away the Scabord, and Said,
GENTLEMEN, Follow Me, By the Assistance
of GOD, I will, this Day, make you a Free and Happy People.[21]

The alleged speech of 'Sir John Cope General of The Usurper's Army' shortly before the battle carried a different message:

GENTLEMEN, You are just now to Engage with a parcel of Rable; a parcel of Brutes, being a small Number of Scots Highlanders. You can expect no Booty from such a poor despicable Pack. I have Authority to Declare, That you shall have Eight full hours Liberty to Plunder and Pillage the City of Edinburgh, Leith, and Suburbs, (the places which harbour'd and succor'd Them) at your Discretion, with Impunity.[22]

After the failure of the Forty-five, Whigs set the agenda in Scotland. Whig ideology found powerful proponents in two chiefs of Clan Campbell, the 2nd Duke of Argyll and his brother and successor the Earl of Islay. These men were in their turn the political managers of Scotland whose control of patronage gave them almost dictatorial powers as the preferred tool of the Government in London. Their position in the southern Highlands was very strong – the Duke of Argyll was hereditary sheriff and Lieutenant of Argyll, and also controlled the Commissioners of Supply, the main element of county administration, as well as the power of appointment of Justices of the Peace, who would have been clansmen, as well as having the largest and most productive estate in the Highlands.[23]

The two Dukes also formed close working relationships with Scottish law officers. Duncan Forbes of Culloden served the 2nd Duke as estate manager and advised him on the abolition of the traditional tacksman system on his estates. (Tacksmen were the 'middlemen' of the old order: often closely related to the chief, a tacksman leased large tracts of land

and sublet them to tenants, receiving rent in money, goods or service and paying some to the chief, the remainder being his income.) As a political agent, Forbes helped the Duke to manage the Scottish political scene; the 3rd Duke had a similar relationship with the Lord Justice Clerk, Lord Milton. As Rosalind Mitchison wrote, 'no decisions made by them on estate policy can be divorced from questions of government'.[24] The two Dukes of Argyll believed that careful handling of the political scene would ensure the dominance of Whiggism and the liquidation of Jacobitism, just as astute estate management would accelerate the decline of clanship and bring about a more profitable, market-oriented system. From 1737, the policy on the Argyll estates involved the raising of rents and the selling of tacks to the highest bidder. The House of Argyll clearly practised the Whig tenets it advocated.

Duncan Forbes of Culloden (1685–1747), a staunch supporter of the Government during the Forty-Five and Lord President of the Court of Session, dissuaded a number of clan chiefs from joining the Jacobites, spent a great deal of his own money in aid of the Hanoverian cause, and as a polemicist wrote several essays on 'civilizing' the Highlands and Islands.[25] In one such essay, written shortly after the failure of the rebellion, Forbes described the Highlands as 'that large tract of mountainous Ground to the Northward of the Forth and the Tay, where the natives speak the Irish language'.[26] The people living in the mountains, according to Forbes, tended to be savage:

> The inhabitants of the mountains, unacquainted with industry and the fruits of it, and united in some degree by the singularity of dress and language, stick close to their antient way of life; retain their barbarous customs and maxims; depend generally on their Chiefs, as their sovereign Lords and masters; and being accustomed to the use of Arms, and inured to hard living, are dangerous to the public peace; and must continue to do so, untill, being deprived of Arms for some years, they forget the use of them.[27]

Forbes wrote, not quite accurately, that there was no court of justice beyond the Highland Line, nor were there any inns or other accommodation for travellers except for the few erected by General Wade. He wrote that in the Highlands there was little land under cultivation and the people had to depend upon their cattle for their nourishment, and described the shielings where the Gaels tended their livestock in the summer as 'the most miserable huts that ever were seen'.[28]

According to Forbes, the existence of the clan system made enforcement of the law difficult, if not impossible; he held the Whig belief that the Gaels were by nature lawless. 'As those Clans or Kindreds live by themselves, and possess different Straths, Glens, or districts, without any considerable mixture of Strangers, it had been for a great many years impractical (and hardly thought safe to try it) to give the Law its proper course amongst the mountains', because, he explained, 'it required no small degree of Courage, and a greater degree of power than men are generally possessed of, to arrest an offender or a debtor in the midst of his Clan.' This difficulty led to the persistence of heritable jurisdictions, which in Forbes's mind had caused untold trouble. For all these reasons, he wrote, at a time when the rest of the country was generally improving, the Gaels continued to be 'the prey of their accustomed sloth and barbarity':[29]

> The Want of Roads, excepting the King's Roads already mentioned, the Want of Accommodation, the supposed ferocity of the inhabitants, and the difference of language, have proved hitherto a bar to all free intercourse between the high and low lands, and have left the Highlanders in possession of their idle customs and extravagant maxims, absolute strangers to the advantages that must accrue from Industry, and to the blessing of having those advantages protected by Laws.[30]

Before the Highlands and Islands could be improved, the Whigs believed, the people there had to be deprived of the weapons of war. The Disarming Act passed in the wake of the rebellion of 1715 imposed fines for possessing arms and encouraged their surrender to the authorities; and the Disarming Act of 1725 provided for the search and seizure of weapons. The Hanoverian clans, chiefly the Campbells, Grants, and Munros, naturally complied, but those with Jacobite inclinations kept their weapons and some even arranged to procure old and broken arms to be turned in for reward. According to P. Hume Brown, the main result of the acts was that by 1745 'the loyal clans were without weapons while the disloyal were comparatively well armed'.[31] After the Forty-Five, the disarming of the Gaels became a vital part of the Whig agenda in the Highlands. 'Arms in the hands of men accustomed to the use of them,' Forbes wrote, 'are dangerous to the public peace, and must therefore be taken from them.' But even if there were not a single sword or firearm in all of Gaeldom, 'the Government would not be absolutely secure, so long as the present race, acquainted with the use of Weapons, exists', simply because, his reasoning went, France or Spain could simply supply them with more. On the other hand, if the Gaels could be disarmed until they forgot how to use weapons, 'their successors . . . must be as harmless as the commonality' in the Lowlands. When the Gaels 'could no longer live by Rapine', Forbes wrote, they would be forced to 'think of living by Industry'.[32] Enforcement of the disarming acts would not be difficult amongst the 'loyal' clans, but Forbes anticipated trouble from the remaining Jacobites.

Past experience had shown that the Jacobites would not willingly comply with any order to surrender their arms. To overcome this difficulty, Forbes proposed the founding of five or six garrisons in the Highlands, to be manned by ten to twelve companies each.[33] In addition to enforcing the new Disarming Act, these troops could prevent contact between the people and 'attainted persons', in other words, Jacobites condemned as rebellious and still at large. Forbes further proposed that craftsmen working for the garrisons be given property on which to set up shops. In addition, spinning schools should be established 'to draw the idle females of those Countries into that Manufacture'.[34] At the King's discretion, these military settlements could be designated burghs of barony to be held directly from the Crown. With these proposals Forbes suggested the long-term occupation of the Highlands by Government troops.

Nothing on the scale of Forbes's scheme was ever adopted, but the Government did accelerate its road-building programme in the Highlands, as well as erecting the large and expensive Fort George near Inverness, begun in 1748 and completed in 1769. Forbes believed that the clan system had to be broken whatever the cost, chiefly in the interest of British national security, but also for the good of the Gaels themselves. He wrote that if the benefits derived from economic progress could persuade the Gaels to attach importance to property 'more than they at present do, it is to be hoped the enthusiastic regard for their Chiefs will subside, and some regard for the Security of their property, the Laws, may take place of it'.[35]

It was remarkable, Forbes noted, that in the areas bordering the Highlands where the people had once spoken Gaelic, worn Highland dress and carried arms, upon the 'accidental' introduction of industry 'the Irish Language and Highland dress gave way to a sort of English, and lowland Cloathing; the Inhabitants took to the Plough in place of Weapons', and although not disarmed by an Act of Parliament, they were 'as their Low Country neighbours'.[36] He described the people of the areas adjoining the mountains, in the shires of Perth, Forfar, Kincardine, Aberdeen, Banff, and Moray 'where some sort of Industry has prevailed, and where the soil is tolerable' as having for many years abandoned the use of Gaelic, Highland dress and the wearing of arms; as a result they could no longer be regarded as threats to public order.[37] This is interesting, for considerable Episcopalian and Jacobite sympathies existed in these areas.

An anonymous writer who in common with Duncan Forbes of Culloden viewed the 'Highland problem' primarily as a law and order issue wrote the essay 'Some Remarks on the Highland Clans, and Methods proposed for Civilizing them' shortly after the end of the Forty-Five.[38] The writer, manifestly of the Whig persuasion, argued that the King's loyal subjects 'now groan under the Oppression of the Clans', but that it was 'unquestionable' that 'great advantages' would come to them by 'civilizing' that barbarous people'.[39] To realise this, one needed only 'to Examine into the Thefts and Depredations daily Committed by that lawless people' and to make

> . . . a Serious Consideration upon, and retrospection, into the Monstrous progress of the late Unnatural Rebellion, the Devastations then Committed; The tremendous Convulsions into which our happy Constitution was thrown; and the several Manifestations of the like restfulness of Spirit, that Eminently appeared in the Clans on Antecedent Occasions to the great Disquiet and Detriment of the State.[40]

Before the writer would propose any methods for bringing the clans to heel, he wished to explain 'why Theft and Depredations, which above all things Cherrish the Spirit of Jacobitism and Rebellion are more luxuriant of Growth amongst the Highland Clans' than amongst other Scots. Based on his own observations and 'the best Information I could expiscate from the honester Sort of Natives', he attributed 'the latest springs of theft & Depredations' in the Highlands to 'the Exorbitant lawless power Exercised by the Gentry over the Commoners'; the encouragement they gave to their clansmen 'to Commit all manners of vice' by giving them support and protection 'when guilty of the most flagitious Enormities'; and to the dangers faced by informers or givers of evidence if discovered by their clans.[41] Not one given to understatement, the writer repeated the prevailing contemporary myth that the clans were by nature criminal organisations with the chiefs acting as 'bosses', who directed and profited from the crimes perpetrated by their clansmen. This misconception may have arisen from the fact that Highland marauders (or 'caterans') acted in groups rather than as individuals. Because the rule of law hardly existed beyond the Highland line, the writer asserted,

> . . . the poor people are quite left a prey to the Merciless Tyranny and Government of their Lawless Leaders, and Oppressive Taskmasters, who thereby have gained such an absolute dominion over them, as at pleasure to mould them into any fashion, Even so far as with a single word to Cause them Committ, the most Excessive Cruelties, and swear to the most abominable falsehoods without hesitation.[42]

'The Commoners are as Cunning lazy and Vindictive as the Gentry are,' the writer stated. He believed the reason for this was the alleged fact that they never had leases but had to depend upon the good will of their chief and his tacksmen, 'who thereby have it in their power to fleece them as they do their Sheep, and keep them in the abject State of Slavery and Dependence', and as a result, 'every kind of Industry was Industriously discouraged; and Laziness, that Delusive mother of Vice and source of Dependency, was the Chief things aim'd at'.[43]

The writer was eager to point out that not all Gaeldom was a den of thieves, and desired to name 'the Quarters that are justly Chargeable': Morvern, Sunart, Ardnamurchan, Moidart, Arisaig, Kingairloch, Glenmoriston, Ardgower, Glenfinnan, Morar, Lochaber, Knoydart, Glengarry, Badenoch, Rannoch, and the Highland regions of Perth, Stirling, and Dumbarton shires.[44] It is no coincidence that these were the districts most notorious for Jacobitism. The writer proposed a series of measures to bring law and order to Gaeldom. He began by arguing that the Government should take over the land of 'disaffected' clans, and at the same time establish colonies in the 'thieving countries' composed of those 'well affected to His Majesty's person and Government'. The success of these measures would depend upon the complete disarming of the local people and the arming of the colonists, he wrote, in order to protect the lives and property of the incomers 'from the fury and resentment of the Natives, who no doubt will look upon them as Invaders of their Rights, spies on all their actions, and Informers Established to lay open all their evil practices'.[45] He continued:

> It is Easy to perceive by the General Savage Character of the people that the thoughts of such Evils, must Kindle in their Breasts the blackest flames of Malice and Despair, and hurry them on to the perpetration of all the Evil Suggestions of their Barbarous inclinations, which According to Ancient Customs will be the murdering of people of all Sexes and Ages, the Burning of Houses, and Cutting of Cattle to pieces, with Swords and durks or Knives. . .[46]

On the legal front, the writer proposed that protection be given to informers of crimes and givers of evidence, and that oaths administered in court be given as 'solemnly' as possible, in order to provide a contrast to oaths made between Gaels. Further, he argued that the execution of condemned persons from Highland areas be carried out in the neighbourhoods from which they came, in the presence of the local people (presumably to put the fear of authority into them). He also believed that the Government should more adequately fund criminal prosecutions in the Highlands, and made the rather impractical suggestion that accurate registers of cattle be compiled to deter 'lifting'. To provide more vigorous law enforcement, troops stationed in the Highlands needed to be made available to civil officers if force was required; sheriffs had to be qualified, of the 'right' class and well paid (probably to put them beyond the temptation of bribery); each Highland parish needed two or three justices of the peace, and each JP needed to have three or four constables at his disposal.[47]

On the social front, the writer recommended the draconian policy that 'all vagabonds, Sturdy Beggars Gipseys and other Idle and suspected people, old or young, that are likely to be able to Earn their Bread, ought to be taken up and put into Workhouses or Banished'. He argued for the erection of new churches and schools, and more and better ministers in particular, on the grounds that 'the influence of the Clergy in Scotland over the vulgar Laity is pretty well known'.[48] The writer was careful not to offend any English readers by explaining the essentially anti-Episcopalian outlook of the Kirk. He was on safer ground when he argued that it was essential that 'all Lawful means' be used to eliminate the Roman Catholic church from the Highlands:

> The Opportunitys like Priests have to tamper with the people, and Instil into their minds such Hellish Tenets as may Invigorate the Spirit of Jacobitism that already too much prevails, Enervate the good Endeavours of the King and Government for Establishing Order, and good harmony amongst the People, and Inflame the Breasts of their votaries with Detestable Notions and abhorrence of both.[49]

The writer argued further that 'stewards' be placed amongst the Gaels to teach civility, reason, loyalty (to the King), industry, and good manners. Not wishing to appear neglectful of economic concerns, he stressed the importance of encouraging manufactures and fisheries,[50] and he believed that leases should be 'clogged with clauses obliging the people to make agricultural improvements'.[51] Before it was apparent that Jacobitism was a spent force, however, the concern of Whigs was always the 'civilising' of the Highlands and Islands rather than the economic development of the region.

This is evident in *The Highlands of Scotland in 1750*, a dossier believed to have been written by Edmund Bruce, a Lowlander and Government agent who travelled through the Highlands and Islands *incognito* to gather information on the political situation there.[52] Bruce praised the 4th Lord Reay, chief of the MacKays, whose loyalty to 'our Happy Constitution' was well known. According to Bruce, the MacKays were 'the most Religious of all the Tribes that dwell among the Mountains, South or North', were 'short of none in their Zeal and Affection to His Majesty', and 'abhor Thieving'. At one time they were 'reckon'd the most Barbarous and Wicked of all the Clans' but were reformed by Lord Reay, who had 'the Civilizing [of] his Clan so much at Heart, that he made application to the General Assembly, for a Collection through all Scotland', by which he was able to create two new parishes on his lands and supply them with schools and ministers (of the Established church); the chief thereby 'encouraged Religion, Loyalty, and Industry among his People, both by his Authority and Example . . .'[53]

In September 1746, by which time the horror of Cumberland's post-Culloden pacification was a fact, Lord Reay wrote to member of the Government and suggested that the estates seized from Jacobites should remain the property of the Crown not only in the interests of the Government but also to 'establish these wild people in peace'. The granting of long leases, the promotion of industry, and plantation of old soldiers would, Lord Reay believed, make the Jacobite clans 'taste the sweet of being free of tyrannical masters', and the erection of new parishes would 'prove in time a means to civilize barbarous people'. However, he expressed the hope that the Duke of Cumberland would take steps to make 'these ignorant people useful subjects', an achievement which would make the victor of Culloden 'famous to posterity, as it is easier to conquer than to civilize barbarous people'.[54]

Bruce thought it especially praiseworthy that the chief of the MacKays had not only civilised his people but 'improv'd his own Estate to above the Double of what he found it, tho' it is not yet near L. 1000 p. Annum'.[55] He commended the Rosses of Balnagown, 'a Loyal and Religious Family for some preceeding Generations', adding that 'how zealously the master of Ross and his Tenants joined the Loyal Party in the Defence of their King and country in time of the Late Rebellion is well known'. The common people of the clan, he stated, were 'a Well affected Honest Industrious and Religious People', which explained why the Jacobites could raise only 30 men from the clan in 1745. (The fact that any clansmen joined the rebellion, however, might be taken as evidence of internal dissent.) Bruce wrote that the chief and gentry of Clan Munro 'are all Firm and Steady to a man, and the Commons are well-affected Honest Industrious and Religious People', and 'those who call them Enthusiastical, Revengefull and Lazy do not know them, or are highly prejudiced against them'. The MacKenzies and the other Jacobite clans, he added, bore the clan 'an Inveterate Hatred and Illwill for their Loyalty'.[56]

According to Bruce, the Munros shared little in common with the MacRaes of Kintail, who were 'by far the most Fierce, Warlike, and Strongest Men' under MacKenzie of Seaforth, and up to the last thirty years had been 'little better than Heathens in their Principles, and almost as unclean as Hottentots, in their way of Living . . .' But after the Kintail estate was confiscated by the Government in the wake of the 1719 rebellion, 'Ministers and Schools were planted . . . which has made a Surprizing Alteration in the People even in point of Common Civility

Decency and Cleanliness'.[57] Whether the Macraes had been civilised or not, the clan participated little in the Forty-Five.

Bruce vented his Whiggish wrath on the MacDonalds, whom he ridiculed for believing themselves to be descended from a king of Athens who after many heroic acts came to Scotland and as Lord of the Isles 'owned' half of Scotland.[58] While the chief and gentry of the MacDonalds of Sleat had 'in great Measure recovered the common People on their Estates from their Folly and Idleness', and the MacDonalds living in Kintyre had learned industry from the Campbells,

> ... great numbers of the Keppoch, Glengarry, and Clanranald Families, tho' not worth a Shilling, would be ashamed to be seen at any Kind of Labour tho' they think it no Shame to Steal or go through the Country asking assistance of their Neighbours (which they call thigging) or living upon free Quarters wherever they happen to be, and they Reckon it an Honour to other people that they should be entertained by them.[59]

'In all the countries I have yet travel'd through,' Bruce wrote, continuing the equation of Jacobitism with banditry, 'the People Live by their own Labour and Industry and are no more given to Theft than the Lowland Countries, but as I proceeded on the Coast Southward I came to Knoidart which is a perfect Den of Thieves and Robbers.' Knoydart was held by the MacDonells of Glengarry, who were 'all Papists' and had always been 'Wild Rapacious and a plague and Disturbance to their Neighbours ...' And he went on to charge the MacDonells with a catalogue of crimes.[60]

Bruce was happy to justify the Glencoe massacre of 1692, asserting that it freed the law-abiding people of the Highlands from 'that Nest of Rebels Thieves and Cutthroats'. He wrote that 'the whole Neighbourhood looked upon this as a Judgement from heaven on so wicked a Crew'; however, the Jacobites never failed to regard the massacre 'in the most Odious Light, in order to throw Dirt upon the Memory of King William. That Glorious Restorer of Our Liberty and Religion must never be forgiven because a few Rebels and Thieves who had shut themselves out from the Protection of the Law were destroyed in his Reign', while Charles I was forgiven for the 'upwards of 150,000 Valuable Protestant Subjects [who] were barbarously Massacred in his Reign'.[61] Law and order were a precondition for the success of the Whig strategy for the Highlands and Islands, and any means were justifiable to reach that end. In Bruce's mind, criminal activity had not ended with the massacre but remained endemic in the Highlands.

He related that 'thieves in other parts of the country, especially the

Camerons', were kind to strangers, but that the inhabitants of Glengarry 'are quite a Different Disposition, Churlish and Inhospitable to the last Degree, and never admit a Stranger within their Doors'. He must have had a bad experince whilst among them. 'In short,' he concluded, 'they are the very Dregs and Refuse of Mankind and it is no small Reproach to Great Britain to have allowed such a Sett of Villains to trample upon the Laws for so many Ages.'[62]

Were thievery eliminated in the Highlands, Bruce wrote, industry could become established in the region. Fisheries, wool and kelp manufacture could give the Highlanders a sound (and legal) economic base, and 'planting potatoes would both supply their Scarcity of bread and be an Excellent Method to Cultivate Wild and Barren Soil'.[63] Before improvement of that kind could occur, however, the Gaels had to be 'bridled':

> That the Disaffected and Savage Highlanders need to be Bridled and kept in awe by Garrisons and Standing Forces, 'till the present Generation wears out is Evident to all Men of common understanding, and that those unhappy and infatuated People will still Continue Savages if nothing else is done to recover them from their Ignorance and Barbarity seems as Evident; but as the rest of the People of Britain who are now Civilized were once as Wild and Barbarous as the Highlanders, I think it is not to be doubted but that proper measures would Civilize them also.[64]

Bruce did believe the Gaels could be tamed, but he admitted that it would require a great deal of money, 'perhaps £5,000 a year'. Had the Highlands and Islands been 'civilized' after the rebellion of 1715, 'the Pretender would not have had the least reason to Boast of his faithfull Highlanders'. Bruce attributed the so-called absolute power of the clan chiefs to the 'Poverty, Barbarity, Theft, and Popery that prevail among the Common People . . .':[65]

> Has not Britain laid out much Greater Sums on Colonies abroad of not half the Importance of civilizing and Improving this part of Britain itself that has been so long a Nuisance and Reproach to the Nation? Besides when the Country is improved and Trade and Manufactures are thoroughly Established, it will repay with Large Interest any Expence laid out at present.[66]

The Forty-Five supplied Whig polemicists with subject matter for years after the event. John Home's *History of the Rebellion in the Year 1745*[67] was published in 1802, and with more than a half-century of hindsight Home came to understand what modern historians accept but commentators at the time of the rebellion could not — that

Jacobitism had *bona fide* causes and was not simply the political extension of barbarity and banditry. By the beginning of the nineteenth century, the Highlands and Islands had become a Romantic ideal in the arts and the popular imagination in general, and the virulent anti-Highland tone of earlier years was absent; but the belief that Jacobitism had posed a great danger to British society remained. Home referred to supporters of Charles Edward Stuart simply as 'the Highlanders', rarely drawing a distinction between the 'loyal' and Jacobite clans.

Home believed that following the Union of Crowns in 1603, the Scottish Lowlanders and the English had 'at once' ceased to keep arms. However, 'the Highlanders continued to be the same sort of people they had been in former times: Clanship flourished, depredation and petty war never ceased'. During the Civil War in Scotland, Montrose's success 'raised the reputation of the Highlanders, and fixed them in the interest of the family of Stuart, to which they were naturally inclined'; because, Home explained, they were 'ignorant and careless of the disputes, civil and religious, which occasioned the war, Charles the First appeared to them in the light of an injured chief'. At the time of the Revolution, 'the Highlanders took up arms against the government of King William', and after the death of James VII and II, the Highlanders 'continued their correspondence with his son'.[68] Despite the persistence of Jacobitism as demonstrated by rebellions in 1708, 1715, and 1719, 'no measures were taken to reconcile them to government'.[69] In the intervals between the rebellions,

> ... the arts of peace were successfully cultivated in Britain, and the national wealth was greatly augmented; but of that wealth, no part or portion accrued to the Highland Chiefs, who still kept their people upon the old establishment ...[70]

While replete with bigotry and triumphalist posturing, the arguments expounded by these and other Whig polemicists formed the basis of 'official' attitudes towards the Gaels in the decades following the defeat of Jacobitism. Although they occasionally disagreed on specific policies, they shared common ground in most of their proposals for reforming the Highlands and Islands. After the Forty-Five, their greatest concern was that Jacobitism had not been exterminated at Culloden, and so they advocated a number of policies designed to complete the 'pacification' begun by the Duke of Cumberland. As the 'Highland problem' was perceived to be one of law and order, Whigs urged the complete disarming of the Gaels and the stationing of troops at strategic points throughout the region in order to crush any future rebellion, and the strengthening of the legal system beyond the Highland Line to deal more effectively with cattle-lifting and other crimes. Until it became evident that Jacobitism was a spent force, this emphasis upon military measures outweighed other considerations. Whigs also believed that in order to ensure that Gaeldom could no longer pose a threat to the British state, the character of the Gaels themselves had to be reformed. As they were perceived to be barbarous and pagan, measures aimed at 'civilizing' them were proposed. These included the establishment of schools and churches which would teach the English language and promote the Presbyterian faith in order to spread Lowland/English values. In addition, the Whigs attacked the social system in the Highlands and Islands, believing the clan system to lie at the root of the region's alleged backwardness and rebellious tendencies. The clan chiefs, excepting those loyal to the Government, were believed to behave like feudal tyrants, each with a standing army ready to steal and murder at his command. To break the power of the chiefs over the common people, or more to the point, to introduce a market-oriented economy into the region, Whigs pressed for changes to free the chiefs from their traditional responsibilities towards their clans in order to allow them to assimilate with the rest of the British aristocracy and to manage their estates more along the lines of a commercial enterprise. Only then could 'improvement' come to the region.

Whig ideology greatly influenced the course of events in the Highlands and Islands in the crucial years that followed 1745. Improvers who sought to integrate the region with the rest of the British economy were naturally of the Whig persuasion, and the replacement of traditional with more modern (commercial) methods was at the heart of their beliefs. The Presbyterian establishment represented by the Church of Scotland would use the changes that came to the region to establish itself there as never before; the apparent connivance between a number of Kirk ministers and Highland estate managers to contain resistance to clearance suggests they shared a common interest in the success of the Whig agenda. The displacement of people that was an inevitable outcome of Whig economic strategy made possible the recruitment of large numbers of Gaels for British military service, and ironically, the destruction of the traditional way of life in the Highlands and Islands made the Gaels a focus for the ideals of the Romantic movement. Their reputation in the Lowlands and throughout Britain reached its lowest point during the Forty-Five, but following the changes that came to Gaeldom, most of them introduced from the outside and most of them traumatic, their image would be rehabilitated.

NOTES

1. Rosalind Mitchison, 'The Government in the Highlands, 1707–1745', in *Scotland in the Age of Improvement*, N.T. Phillipson and Rosalind Mitchison, eds. (Edinburgh, 1970), p. 24.
2. William Ferguson, *Scotland 1689 to the Present* (Edinburgh, 1965), p. 16.
3. A.I. Macinnes, 'Scottish Gaeldom: The First Phase of Clearance', in *People and Society in Scotland*, vol. I, T.M. Devine and Rosalind Mitchison, eds. (Edinburgh, 1988), p. 71.
4. Mitchison, p. 30.
5. Ibid., p. 32.
6. Ibid.
7. Ibid., pp. 33–4.
8. Ferguson, p. 155.
9. Anonymous, 'The Rise of the Present Unnatural Rebellion Discover'd; and the EXTRAORDINARY Power and Oppression of the HIGHLAND CHIEFS Fully Display'd. Being an Attempt to prove, that the Common HIGHLANDERS act by Compulsion, and not by Inclination.
    TOGETHER With some Proposals for encouraging these unhappy Men, to return to their Duty; and screening them from the future Resentment of their Chiefs' (London, 1745), National Library of Scotland (hereafter NLS), ABS.1.86.46, p. 11.
10. Ibid., pp. 21–2.
11. Ibid., p. 22.
12. Ibid., p. 23.
13. Andrew Henderson, *The History of the Rebellion, 1745 and 1746*. Containing, A Full Account of its Rise, Progress and Extinction; The Character of the Highlanders, and their Chieftains; ... By an Impartial Hand, who was an Eye-witness to most of the facts (London, 2nd ed. 1748, reprinted from Edinburgh ed.), p. 5.
14. *Ibid.*
15. *Ibid.*, p. 6.
16. *Ibid.*, p. 7.
17. NLS PDP 10/23 (8): 'The Chevalier's Market, or, Highland Fair' (London, 1745).
18. NLS R.B.1.60: John Duick, 'A Memorial for Britons' (London, 1746).
19. Ibid.
20. NLS P/BW/17: 'Bonnie Prince Charlie', caricature by Richard Cooper (Edinburgh, 1745).
21. NLS PDP 10/23(4) (1745).
22. Ibid.
23. Mitchison, p. 26.
24. Ibid.
25. For a full account of Forbes's role during the Forty-Five, see George Menary, *The Life and Letters of Duncan Forbes of Culloden* (London, 1936). Forbes used his influence with Highland chiefs to deter a number of those with Jacobite sympathies from joining the rebellion. According to John Home, Forbes wanted 'to reconcile the Highlanders' to the Government; he told Lord Milton in 1738, 'You know very well, that I am like you, a Whig; but I am also the neighbour and friend to the Highlanders; and am also intimately acquainted with most of their chiefs' (John Home, *History of the Rebellion in the Year 1745* (London, 1802), p. 21).
26. H. Robert Duff, *Culloden Papers* (London, 1815), No. CCCXLIII, p. 197.

27. *Ibid.*, p. 298.
28. *Ibid.*
29. *Ibid.*, pp. 298–9.
30. *Ibid.*, p. 299. General (later Field Marshal) George Wade (1673–1748) became Commander-in-Chief for Scotland in 1724 and was given the task of pacifying the Highlands. His road-making programme was concentrated around the Great Glen and was intended to facilitate the movement of Government troops in the Highlands in quelling any rebellion. Thomas Telford believed that Wade's roads had been built 'with other Views than promoting Commerce and Industry . . . and were therefore generally in such Direction and so inconveniently steep, as to be, nearly unfit for the Purposes of Civil Life' (*Survey and Report on the Coasts and Central Highlands of Scotland, Made by the Command of the Right Honourable the Lords Commissioners of His Majesty's Treasury, in the Autumn of* 1802; by Thomas Telford, Civil Engineer, Edin. FRS. (P.P. 1803, IV, p. 4).
31. P. Hume Brown, *History of Scotland* (Cambridge, 1911), III, p. 261.
32. Duff, p. 299.
33. *Ibid.*
34. *Ibid.*, p. 300.
35. *Ibid.*, p. 301.
36. *Ibid.*
37. *Ibid.*, p. 298. A.J. Youngson estimated that between ten and twenty per cent of the Jacobite army came from the largely Episcopalian areas around Aberdeen and Banff (A.J. Youngson, *After the Forty-Five* (Edinburgh, 1973), p. 21).
38. NLS Adv. MS. 16.1.14: Anonymous, 'Some Remarks on the Highland Clans, and Methods proposed for Civilizing them' (no date).
39. Ibid., p. 1.
40. Ibid.
41. Ibid.
42. Ibid., p. 2.
43. Ibid., p. 3.
44. Ibid., p. 5.
45. Ibid., pp. 6–7.
46. Ibid.
47. Ibid., pp. 9–17.
48. Ibid., pp. 17–18.
49. Ibid., p. 19.
50. Ibid., pp. 19–20.
51. Ibid., p. 8.
52. Andrew Lang, ed., *The Highlands of Scotland in 1750* (Edinburgh, 1898).
53. *Ibid.*, p. 9.
54. Quoted in Ian Grimble, *The World of Rob Donn* (Edinburgh, 1979), p. 70, from *Book of Mackay*, pp. 456–7.
55. Lang, p. 18.
56. *Ibid.*, pp. 18–23.
57. *Ibid.*, p. 31.
58. *Ibid.*, pp. 49–51.
59. *Ibid.*, pp. 52–3.
60. *Ibid.*, pp. 59–61. Bruce wrote that the MacDonells had 'within these few years exceeded their ordinary Bounds which was Occasioned thus: Coll McDonald of Barisdale, Cousin Germane to Glengarry, took up his Residence here as a place of undoubted security from all Legal prosecutions, he entered into a Confederacy with McDonald of Lochgarry and the Camerons of Loch Arkeg with some other as great Villains in Rannoch, a part of Perthshire.

This famous Company had the Honour to Methodize Theft in to a Regular Trade, they kept a number of Savages in dependence for this purpose whom they Outhounded upon the Sutherlands, Rosses, Munroes, and McKenzies to the North, the Frasers, McIntoshes, Grants, Roses of Kilravock, Brodies, Gordons, Farquharsons, Forbes, and Ogilvies to the East; and the Shires of Perth, Stirling, Dunbarton, and Argyle to the South' (*Ibid.*).

61. *Ibid.*, pp. 78–81.
62. *Ibid.*, p. 108.
63. *Ibid.*, pp. 143–4.
64. *Ibid.*, p. 144.
65. *Ibid.*, pp. 159–160.
66. *Ibid.*, p. 160.
67. John Home, *History of the Rebellion in the Year 1745* (London, 1802). Home wrote the play *Douglas*, produced in Edinburgh in 1756, encouraged James Macpherson to embark upon the Ossian saga, and went on to become secretary to the Prime Minister the Earl of Bute (*Dictionary of Scottish History*, Gordon Donaldson and Robert S. Morpeth, eds. (Edinburgh, 1977), p. 99).
68. *Ibid.*, pp. 13–16.
69. *Ibid.*, p. 19.
70. *Ibid.*, pp. 19–20.

2

Improvers

THE 'IMPROVEMENT' OF the Highlands and Islands was ostensibly the introduction of new methods and systems in a bid to replace the 'outmoded' and 'antiquated' ways of an area that was left behind when economic growth and development came to the rest of Britain. The story was not simply one of rapacious landlords and self-seeking opportunists; a number of Improvers were driven by humanitarian motives and sought to bring about an economic revolution for the Gaels and thereby prevent large-scale emigration. But as it became understood that a great deal of money could be made by uprooting the old and transplanting the new, the voices that pled for the Gaels' interests were soon forgotten.

Improvement was more than the reform of agricultural practices or the encouragement of fisheries. By 1830, the Highlands and Islands had been transformed. Not only was the old order destroyed, but new imperatives controlled nearly every aspect of life. The rights of property had supplanted the ties of clanship, and new cultural values were imported from the Lowlands and England. Before 'improvements' could begin, however, the Highlands and Islands had to be tamed as a political threat.

Reforming the Highland character

Following the battle of Culloden, the Government's plan for the Highlands was 'pacification' – the rooting out, by violent means, of the danger posed by Jacobitism to the established order. The Duke of Cumberland's role in achieving this end earned him the title of 'butcher', but it was soon realised that the sword was not the best means of inspiring loyalty to the House of Hanover. With the Act of Attainder of June 1746 (19 George II c. 46), heads rolled; the Disarming Act (20 George II c. 52) of the same year forbade the Gaels to possess arms; the wearing of Highland dress was outlawed in 1747; and heritable jurisdictions were abolished (20 George II c. 53). In 1747 the Vesting Act (20 George II c. 41) was passed, in which everything that belonged to those attainted in the rebellion was turned over to the Crown, to be administered by the Barons of the Exchequer Court in Scotland. But it was not until the passing of the Annexing Act of 1752 (25 George II c. 41) that a reformation of sorts was begun in the Highlands.

The Act was passed 'annexing certain Forfeited Estates in Scotland to the Crown unalienably; and for making Satisfaction to the lawful Creditors thereupon; and applying the Rents and Profits thereof, for the better civilising and improving the Highlands of Scotland; and preventing Disorders there for the future'.[1] A total of thirteen Highland estates were named in the Act, to be managed by a Board of Commissioners for the Annexed Estates. The Board's mission was cultural as well as economic and political in nature. It had the responsibility for introducing new methods of agriculture and encouraging industry and fisheries, the construction of a new network of communications, the eradication of Roman Catholicism and non-juring Episcopacy from its estates, and the crushing of sedition. Its success in this mammoth task was mixed. A great deal of the records and correspondence dealing with the management of the estates has survived, known collectively as the 'Forfeited Estates Papers (1745)'. The writings of the Board's factors, surveyors, and other officials were not meant for public consumption, and as a result are candid in their comments.

The factor on the annexed estates of Lovat and Cromartie from 1755 to 1774 was Captain John Forbes. Responding to a questionnaire sent by the Commissioners in 1755 to the factors inquiring into the state of the estates under their direction, Forbes offered his opinion on what was needed most to 'improve' the estate. He described Coigach as the most uncivilised and 'Highland' part of the estate, and as the district was far removed from law courts and poorly connected with the rest of the country, greater attention was required to improve it and 'civilize' the inhabitants:

> ... a new erection of a Church is necessary, or at least, ... an Itinerant Preacher, well chosen, and with suitable encouragements, should be settled in the Aird, or the remotest of Coigach, which lyes at a great distance from the parish Kirk; such an Itinerant might be of great use, for instructing the people & inculcating Loyalty, Industry and Obedience to the Laws. And as the English Language is of the greatest Consequence, there should be two English Schools erected here, because the Country is very extensive; as also two spinning Schools.[2]

Forbes's belief in the 'civilizing' power of Presbyterianism and the English language is manifest. He did not feel the need to explain this position; Improvers took it for granted. The Gaelic language was the epitome of the Highlanders' distinctiveness, and no attempt at 'civilizing' them would succeed, it was thought, unless it was replaced by English.

Forbes made the same suggestions for Stratherrick, on the Lovat estate. He believed that the construction of schools was an urgent matter, and that the schoolmasters selected should be well-paid and should not be able to speak Gaelic:

> In order therefore to improve & civilize this part of the highlands, I humbly apprehend that a particular attention to introduce the English Language is of the greatest consequence; And for that purpose schools should be erected, on the different Baronys . . .[3]

Francis Grant was the Board's general riding officer and inspector. In 1756 he made a tour of the Annexed Estates to prepare a report for the Commissioners. Copied into Grant's report was an address delivered to the 'King's tenants' on each estate, which makes apparent the Board's attitude towards them. They were to be held accountable for their own actions; the Commissioners, their new masters, would encourage religion, industry and obedience, but resistance would be punished. Its tone is one that a parent might adopt in admonishing a child:

> As it has been a great Misfortune to the former Proprietor and family much to be regretted that they gave Cause to it, yet it may be to you and all the Tenants not only no loss but a benefit for it will depend on yourselves entirely to be easie and happy. As the Law and your present Masters appointed for the Execution thereof has nothing more in view than that good purpose to make you Prosperous in every respect by Encouraging Religion, Industry and dutifull Obedience to your Superiors. On the other hand the Contrary will be Discouraged & punished as Law Directs.[4]

The Board of Trustees for Manufactures and Fisheries was set up in 1727 and was principally concerned with the encouragement of linen manufacture in Scotland. In January 1763, when its remit for the Highlands was passed to the Commissioners for the Annexed Estates, the Board's trustees wrote to the Lords Commissioners of the Treasury, stating that the term of their mission of encouraging and improving the manufacture of linen in the Highlands, on which they had spent an annual sum of £3000 for nine years, had expired. They wrote that they had accomplished this by raising and maintaining linen stations; paid salaries to teachers for raising and dressing flax; paid salaries to mistresses of spinning schools, and paid the expenses of these schools; paid salaries to master weavers and wheelwrights and maintained apprentices and scholars for instruction in these crafts; paid salaries for inspectors and surveyors of wheel reels and other utensils; and paid premiums to encourage the improvement of lintseed and its cultivation.[5] This was by way of reminding the Treasury of the things the

Trustees had accomplished; what followed was a warning of what might happen if manufacturing in the Highlands ceased to be encouraged:

> ... the Linen manufacture hath been introduced into & is spreading itself through the Highlands, the whole Country is thereby greatly civilised & if the same means be continued is likely to become a very useful part of the United Kingdom but if discontinued, which must be the case if the said annual payment cease your Memorialists apprehend & think it their duty to acquaint Your Lordships that it will soon relapse into its former Sloth & Barbarity.[6]

Before the Highlands and Islands could become an integrated part of Britain, the problem of poor communications had to be resolved. The Annexed Estates Board had made only tentative steps in the wake of General Wade's road network, and a great deal of work remained to be done to make the area more accessible by land and sea. The engineer James Watt (1736–1819) was commissioned in 1785 to make a survey and report on the proposed canal between Fort William and Inverness for the British Fisheries Society, the leading interventionist body in the Highlands after the Annexed Estates Board ceased its activities in 1784. Watt believed that the success of the fisheries depended upon the building of the canal; if a quick route from the east coast to the west ensured a supply of cheaper grain to the West Highlands and Hebrides, the population there might increase. He wrote that the West Highlands were primarily 'grazing countries' and that it was 'naturally impossible to extend their Agriculture.' He felt that the Gaels' crops were 'so defective' that they would be better off using all their land for cattle and importing the grain they needed:

> Were the Improvements in the fishery to take place, the Importation of Grain would very much encrease, because their own Lands would probably produce no more than they do at present, and all that would be necessary for the additional Inhabitants must be imported; and it is probable that industrious hard-working People would consume more in Proportion than the present Inhabitants do.[7]

Roads, bridges and canals were seen as civilising tools no less important than the spread of English or the improvement of agricultural practices. One writer argued in 1792 that the proposed Caledonian Canal would play a crucial part in the elimination of the distinction between Highland and Lowland:

> The first step towards ... civilization, and improvement, proceeded from the several roads of these countries: this having, in some degree, opened an easy intercourse betwixt the inhabitants thereof, and those of the southern and eastern parts of Scotland and of England, had

removed the prejudices which formerly narrowed their minds, and fascinated them to clannish predilection and subordination.[8]

Colonel Robert Anstruther, an inspector of military roads, wrote a memorial in similar vein in 1792: the new roads had exposed the Gaels to their industrious neighbours to the south, and had 'weaned them from their former slavish dependence on their chiefs, removed old Prejudices, and encouraged Industry':

Hitherto the Chief Object of Government by making Roads, was to March Troops into a Country formerly inaccessible; but after the happy suppression of the Rebellion, the Plan was extended with a view to Civilize and improve the Country, to make the Highlanders independent of their Chiefs, and Industrious useful subjects, for which purpose many Salutary Laws were enacted, and several Lines of New Roads were made, connected by Cross Roads, to open the Communication to every Glen and District in the Highlands.[9]

The civil engineer Thomas Telford (1757–1834) had an ambitious plan which involved a degree of social engineering. It required the construction of roads, bridges, and canals, and particularly the proposed Caledonian Canal; such a scheme would provide the short-term benefit of employment with the long-term benefit of an infrastructure upon which further improvements could be made. But if such improvements were to reduce the level of emigration, he wrote, 'it is advisable these Works should be undertaken at the present Time'. Other commentators, such as the Earl of Selkirk (see below), were arguing that emigration was necessary for the economic development of the Highlands. Telford's perspective was not shared by the Government, which was to opt for a communications network which acted mainly to lower the costs of transporting wool and mutton to the Lowlands and which later in the nineteenth century made the new sporting estates accessible to southerners. In contrast, Telford's scheme sought to

... furnish Employment for the industrious and valuable Part of the People in their own country ... they would acquire some capital, and the Foundations would be laid for future Employments. If, as I have been credibly Informed, the Inhabitants are strongly attached to their native Country, they would greedily embrace this Opportunity of being enabled to remain in it, with the Prospect of bettering their Condition, because, before the Works were completed, it must be evident to everyone that the whole Face of the Country would be changed.[10]

Improving the Highlands and Islands

The chiefs held immense power over their clans. When clanship was still the dominant force in Gaeldom, this power held the clans together and gave each clan a focus for its energies. Under the concept of *Dùthchas*, (hereditary right of land tenure), a chief was the trustee of his clan and its assets, and was bound by duty and tradition to pursue the interests of the clan and not just his own interests. But as the clan system crumbled under political and economic pressure from the 1730s onward, chiefs used the prerogative of *Oighreachd* (hereditary right of possession), a legalistic concept which gave them the absolute right of property, to 'improve' their lands and 'civilize' their people. When Archibald Campbell, 3rd Duke of Argyll, set about the reorganisation of his estates, he was determined not to be bound by tradition. In 1756 he wrote to Donald Campbell, his chamberlain (steward) in Tiree, 'I'm resolved to keep no tenants but such as will be peaceable and apply to industry. You'll have cause to intimate this some sabbath after sermon'.[11] James Hogg visited Little Loch Broom in 1803 and found George MacKenzie of Dundonnell agonising over whether to keep the people on the land or let it to Lowland shepherds. Hogg noted that 'he hath, however, the pleasure of absolute sway. He is even more so in his domains than Bonaparte is in France'.[12]

In his *Observations on the Present State of the Highlands of Scotland* (1806), Thomas Douglas, 5th Earl of Selkirk, criticised those chiefs hesitant to 'improve' their estates. There were, he wrote, some chiefs who felt the 'antient feudal notions' to such an extent that they were unwilling to evict their 'old adherents', and as a result submitted to a considerable loss. Whereas some had embraced new methods of estate management,

> there are many others who, from vanity, are desirous of counting a numerous tenantry, and would willingly preserve the population of their estates, if it could be reconciled to their pecuniary interest. These motives, though now wearing fast away, have however had great effect till of late; so that, not withstanding the length of time that has elapsed since the year 1745, a very considerable proportion of the Highlands remains under circumstances directly arising out of the feudal state, or is at this moment in the crisis of change. But the causes which have hitherto retarded the change are so much enfeebled, that they cannot long continue to have a perceptible effect; and, as an unavoidable consequence, the Highlands in general must fall into that state of occupancy and cultivation which is most conducive to the pecuniary interest of its individual proprietors . . .[13]

These sentiments already characterised most Highland chiefs. In a purely economic analysis, wrote Selkirk, the 'antient possessors' of clan lands could not compete against the rewards offered by Improvement; the Gaels 'have had a very unequal struggle to maintain. It would be difficult, perhaps, to quote an instance where they have been able to offer a rent fully equal to that which the graziers would have given; and the competition against them has been continually increasing'.[14] While some Improvers hoped to remedy the problems that caused emigration, the earl was an active advocate of emigration and organised several groups of Highlanders to go to Canada, most notably to the Red River area between 1812 and 1815.[15] He believed that 'emigration was an unavoidable result of the general state of the country, arising from causes above all control, and is itself of essential consequence to the tranquillity and permanent welfare to the kingdom'.[16] His active role in emigration was not without its detractors, and an anonymous writer poured scorn on the earl's seemingly selfless enterprise:

> Does he not turn to the peasant and say, 'Leave your country; leave a land which has no longer use for you; a land where you may have bread indeed, but where you can only earn bread by the dereliction of every habit which could sweeten the morsel. Emigrate therefore; and if you will but turn towards the colony which I protect, and clear a few acres of its forests, you will become affluent and happy beyond the condition of your fathers.'
>
> And does he not look towards the Legislature and plead – 'Encourage emigration – drain off your superfluous people – depopulate your mountains, and send your hardiest sons to foreign climes, there to seek that happiness and protection which the land of their fathers denied them; there to become the sure and steady friends of the country which turned them from her bosom.' – Such, I contend, is the true import of the Noble Earl's advice.[17]

In the minds of Improvers, one thing was obvious: the 'improvement' of the Highlands and Islands and the existence of the clan system were mutually incompatible. Clanship was widely considered to be a strictly military, and not an agricultural, system. Indeed, its aim was not a 'market' efficiency that sought to optimise production, but rather *beathachadh bóideach*, or 'comfortable sufficiency', by which a large population and the clan hierarchy could be supported and the various obligations of the chief could be met. Among the supposed evils of the clan system was the fostering and even the encouragement of idleness, and the Earl of Selkirk sought to explain this alleged trait as a direct result of clanship. He believed that the military orientation of clanship attached supreme importance to the ability of a clansman to fight. What he and others failed to realise was that the Gaels, in common with others living in an agrarian society, did not see agricultural labour as an end in itself but rather as a means of subsistence:

> The greatest part of the country was fit only for pasturage, and the small portions of the arable land which fell to the share of any family, could occupy but little of their time. On two or three occasions in the course of the year, the labours of the field required a momentary exertion, to prepare the soil, or to secure the crop; but no regular and continued industry was requisite for providing the simple necessaries of life, to which their forefathers had been accustomed, and beyond which their desires did not extend. Their periods of labour were short; and they could devote the intermediate time to indolence, or to amusement, unless when they were called upon by the chief to unite for the common defence, or for an attack on some hostile clan. The merit of every individual was estimated by his powers on these occasions; warlike achievements were ever the favourite theme among them; and the amusements of their leisure hours generally consisted of active exercises, or displays of strength and agility, calculated to enhance their character as warriors.[18]

Selkirk's assertion that the Gaels were indolent by nature, and that this condition would be changed by their emigration, was ridiculed by Robert Brown, then sheriff-substitute of the western district of Inverness-shire, and as an opponent of large-scale emigration, he questioned his logic in assuming that 'lazy' people could be made industrious by being forced to face the harsh reality of life in North America:

> His Lordship's mode of correcting this indolence is sudden and violent in its operation. He says, the people are doing no good to themselves at home, and are a burden on their landlords. He therefore proposes to transfer them to a situation, where they cannot obtain a particle of subsistence, except what they extract from the land by the most severe and unremitting labour. How men of such confirmed habits of indolence may be able to endure this violent regimen, remains to be explained. But his Lordship's specific against Highland indolence, reminds me of the mode by which I have been told idle fellows were wont to be punished in Holland, and other places. They were locked in a cellar, into which water was introduced though a pipe, and the culprit was obliged, either to pump it out, or drown.[19]

Of all the villains of Highland folklore, few are detested as much as Elizabeth Gordon, Countess of Sutherland, her husband the Marquis of Stafford, and their henchmen, James Loch and Patrick Sellar. Their ambitious plan involved the removal of the inhabitants of the interior of Sutherland to the coasts where they were to take up fishing, followed by the introduction of sheep farms to the emptied straths. Great hardships were suffered by the estimated 8,000 people forced to move.[20] Whether the plan was well-intentioned or not, it was certainly true that these Improvers believed in their plan.

The Countess of Sutherland 'spoke no Gaelic and had inherited her family's contempt for the tongue, manners and customs of the Highland people'.[21] Nevertheless, she believed that 'improvement' on a massive scale need not disturb her tenants. She wrote to Sir Walter Scott in October 1811, informing him of her confidence 'of considerable improvements being effected in Sutherland and without routing and destroying the old inhabitants, which contrary to the Theories respecting these matters, I am convinced is very possible'.[22]

In his *General View of the Agriculture of the County of Sutherland* (1812), Captain John Henderson put a number of questions to William Young, 'the intelligent gentleman who has the management of the Sutherland estate, and the superintendence and direction of all its recent improvements' (he was the estate's factor from 1811 to 1816). Young's response to a question about sheep farming encapsulated not only the plan for the 'improvement' of Sutherland and the ideology inspiring it, but also the sentiments of those carrying out the plan towards the people under their power. Henderson asked:

> How are the sheep-farms doing on the Sutherland estate? How many Cheviot sheep are on it? Are the sheep-farms to be extended? How are the people to be provided for?

To which Young replied:

> Sheep-farms are paying well on the Sutherland estate. The number of Cheviots are now about 15,000. More ground will be laid off for the same mode of husbandry, without decreasing the population. Situations in various ways will be fixed on for the people. Fishing stations, in which mechanics will be settled; inland villages, with carding machines; moor and detached spots calculated for the purpose, will be found; but the people must work. The industrious will be encouraged and protected, but the slothful must remove or starve, as man was not born to be idle, but to gain his bread by the sweat of his brow.[23]

The person most commonly associated with the Sutherland clearances is Patrick Sellar (1780–1851), a man who pursued so vigorously his duty of evicting tenants that he was brought to trial for his cruelty. Not surprisingly, Sellar, who hailed from lowland Moray, had contempt for Highland ways and often expressed his views at length. In a note to Lord Advocate Archibald Campbell-Colquhoun in May 1815, he justified his employer's plan for the estates and defended his part in them:

Lord and Lady Stafford were pleased humanely, to order a new arrangement of this Country. That the interior should be possessed by Cheviot Shepherds and the people brought down to the coast and placed there in lotts under the size of three arable acres, sufficient for the maintenance of an industrious family, but pinched enough to cause them turn their attention to the fishing. I presume to say that the proprietors humanely ordered this arrangement, because, it was surely a most benevolent action, to put these barbarous hordes into a position, where they could better Associate together, apply to industry, educate their children, and advance in civilization; and I hope I shall be excused for thinking with the greatest deference, that this good motive may be safely applied to a family who have for the last four years to my knowledge, divided, yearly, among the tenantry beyond the total rental of the Estate.[24]

Sellar was merely an agent for James Loch (1780–1855), the estate commissioner of the Marquis of Stafford who is widely credited with having masterminded the reorganisation of the Sutherland estate. Loch wrote that 'it seemed as if it had been pointed out by Nature, that the system for this remote district, in order that it might bear its suitable importance in contributing its share to the general stock of the country, was, to convert the mountains districts into sheep-walks, and to remove the inhabitants to the coast, or to the valleys near the sea'. For Loch, it was a simple matter of political economy to determine the plan for Sutherland:

As there was every reason for concluding, that the mountainous parts of the estate, and indeed, of the county of SUTHERLAND, were as much calculated for the maintenance of stock as they were unfit for the habitation of man, there could be no doubt as to the propriety of converting them into sheep walks, *provided* the people could be, at the same time, settled in situations, where, by the exercise of their honest industry, they should not be exposed to the recurrence of those privations, which so frequently and so terrible afflicted them, when situated among the mountains.[25]

It may be too cynical to suggest that it was in the interests of good public relations alone that the people of Sutherland were to be accommodated on the coasts, instead of being forced to emigrate *en masse*; but the Countess of Sutherland was keen not to be labelled a greedy Highland proprietor. It was inevitable that Improvement was to change Sutherland forever. As Loch pointed out,

It had stood still in the midst of that career of improvement which had so remarkably and so splendidly distinguished the rest of the kingdom;

and remained separated by its habits, prejudices, and language, from all around . . .[26]

In a purely economic analysis, the common Gaels could not compete in the new system that required a maximum return on investment. If they were unable to adjust to the new priorities, some argued, their emigration was inevitable and not wholly undesirable. For those who advocated Improvement at the price of emigration, it was an obvious solution to the problem of overcrowding and scarcity. For Dr John MacCulloch, who wrote a commentary on the Highlands in 1824, it was a matter of efficiency:

It had been seen, that as these people are maintained chiefly as cultivators, and on lands in a state of extreme division, the population of any given tract must thus be greater than under a more extended system, and that the conversion of many small farms into one, must diminish it. But in this case, the agricultural machine is more perfect; the same produce is obtained by fewer hands, or at a less expense; as in manufactures, that is the state of perfection where the greatest return is obtained on the lowest terms. This is the fundamental argument in favour of large farms, as it is against the crowded population of the Highlands . . .[27]

By the 1820s, the Clearances had become a point of contention throughout Britain. Some saw the forced evictions as unavoidable, while others argued strenuously for a more humane approach to the Gaels. Dr MacCulloch had an answer for those who accused Highland proprietors of greed and oppression. 'The proprietors', he wrote, 'have been so long accustomed to hear themselves censured and abused, that they almost begin to imagine they deserve it', while the Gaels 'never think they have so warm a friend as he who assures them that they ought to be unhappy'.[28] He wrote of complaints about proprietors who prevented their tenants' emigration in order to ensure a large pool of cheap labour for kelp manufacture:

It is asserted that the proprietors attempt to crowd the population on these estates, for the purpose of lowering the wages of labour, and thus of keeping both a cheap and ready supply of it at hand for this manufacture, from which they alone derive all the profits. This exquisite remark comes from the same politicians who, in some other place, accuse the same proprietors of depopulating their estates by sheep farming, and of thus causing a ruinous emigration. So difficult it is to ride and drive the ass at the same time.[29]

Improvement had proved to be a two-edged sword by the 1820s. The economic slump which followed the end of the Napoleonic Wars exposed both the vulnerability of the newly-formed crofting communities and the folly of estate managers throughout the Highlands and Islands. As prices for kelp and black cattle collapsed, the Gaels faced privation and emigration while the accumulation of rent arrears led to the bankruptcies of a number of Highland proprietors – a situation with few winners. The humanitarian motives of the early Improvers seemed far removed from the priorities of the newer breed who saw the land as a commodity and the inhabitants as an impediment to progress. James Browne, in his *Critical Examination of Dr MacCulloch's Work* (1825), attacked MacCulloch for his defence of Highland 'improvement':

> The Highland proprietors as a body have no doubt a monopoly of the soil of the country; but they are not equally fortunate either in regard to knowledge or the press; and though they may eject, burn out, impoverish, and expatriate the poor defenceless people, public opinion is beyond their controul. To this tribunal they must submit their conduct; and it is to its candid decision that we appeal respecting the falsehood of the charges which have been so industriously circulated against those who had every possible claim to their countenance and protection.[30]

Arguing the case for Improvement

The case for Improvement in the Highlands and Islands had to be argued. Those proposing the development of the region to Government and private investors had to surmount or circumvent the prevailing belief that the place would forever be a wasteland inhabited by poor and unsophisticated people. They asserted that with proper funding and attention, the Highlands and Islands would become a prosperous part of the United Kingdom, with a booming economy and a population of peaceful and loyal subjects. Schools and churches would be built to civilise and educate, to root out any remaining vestiges of superstition and Roman Catholicism, manufactures and fisheries would be encouraged, and, finally, agriculture would be put on a firm economic basis: it was hoped these changes would preclude any disaffection of the kind that the Whig establishment believed had made the 1745 Rebellion possible.

The Rev. Dr John Walker (1731–1803) was a minister and former Moderator of the General Assembly of the Church of Scotland who toured the Hebrides in 1764 to prepare a report for the Commissioners of the Annexed Estates.[31] His mission was to inquire into not only the physical characteristics of the islands but also the state of the people living there, and the possibilities for improvement. In a letter to Lord Kames, Walker wrote that the Gaels were 'most acute and sagacious',[32] but in his report of 1764 he described a place where people lived like beasts and where no innovation or advancement ever took place. He admitted as much, but believed the Hebrides' potential might be realised if some encouragement were offered. In the preface to his report, Walker argued that the islands, while backward, were not without hope:

> Their Soil remains, as it was left at the Creation: The Inhabitants, when compared to their fellow Subjects, with Respect to Arts, are in almost the same Situation as in the Days of Oscian, yet they are Countries capable of being greatly advanced by Agriculture; capable of many of the most important Species of Manufacture: possessed of the most valuable Fisheries in Europe: and inhabited by a sensible, hardy, and laborious Race of People.[33]

Walker was aware of the Gaels' reputation for laziness and an unwillingness to improve themselves. But as the success of Improvement required a motivated labour force, he attempted to answer such prejudices:

> I call them laborious, contrary indeed to a received Opinion. But it is only from a superficial View, that they are represented as unconquerably averse to Industry and every kind of Innovation. The Culture of their Fields, carried on by the Spade, with the Strength of their Arms, instead of that of Cattle, and many other Operations, in their rude System of Husbandry, exhibits powerfull though indeed ill directed Efforts of Industry. Their extensive Cultivation of Potatoes, by Hand Labour; their hardships and Assiduity in the Manufacture of Kelp: the Success of the Linen Manufacture, wherever it has been introduced and the amazing Progress of Inoculation: show, that the Highlanders are as capable to judge of, are as ready to embrace and can as vigorously pursue any innovation that is advantageous or Salutary as any other People whatever.[34]

Walker contended that the Gaels lacked only the means to improve themselves; he realised that they belonged to an agrarian society with different attitudes towards work and did not suffer from some hereditary antipathy to labour of any kind. This was an important distinction to make; Walker was arguing the case for assistance and encouragement and sought to reassure his readers, by highlighting instances of the Gaels' determined if inefficient efforts, that in the Highland character there was no insurmountable barrier to Improvement:

> Unassisted Exertions of Industry are not to be expected from a People still in the Pastoral Stage of Society; nor from unenlightened Minds are we any where to expect the sudden Discontinuance of Bad Customs. But, whatever the Highlands are defective in industry, it will be found, upon fair Enquiry, to be rather their Misfortune than their Fault: and

owing to their want of Knowledge, rather than to any want of the Spirit of Labour. Their Disposition to Industry, is greater than is usually imagined, and if judiciously directed is capable to rise to the greatest Heights.[35]

By 1784 the forfeited Jacobite estates had been returned to their former proprietors or their heirs. The experiment had met with little success, and many parts of the Highlands and Islands had yet to experience the effects of Improvement.[36] As a result, the case for improving the region still had to be argued, and by this time, such arguments were chiefly directed at private sources of capital. The American War of Independence had caused some British men of wealth to think twice before investing in colonial enterprises, but they needed to be convinced that profits could be made by investing closer to home. Doubts about putting money into Highland development certainly remained, and these had to be allayed.

The year 1784 also saw the formation of the Highland Society, known formally as 'The Highland and Agricultural Improvement Society', and its agenda was the integration of the Highlands and Islands with the rest of Britain through new methods in agriculture. The Highland Society had cultural interests which were to include an inquiry into the Ossian controversy, but its main thrust was the promotion of Improvement principles through the sponsorship of prize essays. These essays acted as a powerful forum for the exchange of ideas; they represented the state of current thinking on Improvement, and as they carried the Society's stamp of approval were of considerable influence. Owing to the prominence of some of its members, the Highland Society was also a political lobby of importance. Its first president was the 5th Duke of Argyll, and its officers included the Earl of Moray, Islay Campbell, the Lord Advocate and John MacDonald of Clanranald.[37] The objectives of the Highland Society were stated in its regulations:

1. An inquiry into the present state of the Highlands and Islands of Scotland, and the condition of their Inhabitants.
2. An inquiry into the MEANS OF THEIR IMPROVEMENT, by establishing Towns and Villages —by facilitating Communication through different parts of the Highlands of Scotland, by Roads and Bridges —advancing Agriculture, and extending Fisheries —introducing useful Trades and Manufactures —and, by exertion to unite the efforts of Proprietors, and call the attention of Government, towards the encouragement and prosecution of these beneficial purposes.
3. The Society shall also pay a proper attention to the preservation of the Language, Poetry, and Music of the Highlands.[38]

One of the first prize essayists of the Highland Society was Dr James Anderson (1739–1808), an economist and agriculturalist who managed farms in Lothian and Aberdeenshire.[39] In his *Account of the Present State of the Hebrides and Western Coasts of Scotland* (1785), Anderson acknowledged the attitudes held towards the Highlands and Islands, but stated that times had changed (after all, the Highland regiments had acquitted themselves well in the American War [see Chapter 6]), and the region now had 'a well-founded claim to national attention'. The Gaels had been neglected long enough, and why explore the globe in search of new opportunities for wealth, he argued, while opportunities existed at home? The English, he wrote, had believed the Gaels to be 'a set of men disaffected to Government, averse to labour, and impatient of all lawful subordination', and that they were 'little better than a lawless banditti'. They believed the Highlands were 'an inhospitable desart, incapable of cultivation, or ever becoming the seat of commerce, of industry, or arts', and as a result 'turned from it with aversion'[40] – as did Lowlanders, it must be added. But, Anderson asserted,

> They have not observed the change that has taken place in all these respects; and the natives, discouraged by neglect, and overawed by those severities inflicted on many of their chiefs, have been afraid to put in their well-founded claim to national attention, lest they should be accused of misrepresentation from interested natives, and met with obloquy, instead of support. — They have thus been suffered to remain neglected and unknown; and while the most distant parts of the globe have been attentively explored, with a view to give encouragement for the manufactures of Britain, those territories, which are so peculiarly our own, and which are much better calculated to encrease the trade, to encourage the manufactures, and to augment the revenues of this nation, than any others that have ever been suffered to remain unknown and un-explored, are not.[41]

Most of those interested in encouraging manufactures and fisheries in the Highlands and Islands believed that the erection of new villages was of vital importance. In his description of the parish of Kincardine, Ross-shire for the *Statistical Account* in 1790, the Rev. Andrew Gallie wrote:

> No corner of Scotland ... is better adapted, for a manufacturing village, than Kincardine ... It lies open to several very populous districts, and, were manufactures once established, and shops opened, it would be resorted to by many ... Those who shall first have the spirit to undertake something in the manufacturing line here, will merit the blessings of hundreds, in a corner half depopulated, and in danger of being totally deserted; besides contributing greatly to their own immediate benefit and emolument.[42]

In the same year, the Rev. J. Anderson of the united parish of Kingussie and Inch stressed the need for a centre in which trade could be conducted. Tradesmen had nowhere to carry on business, wool had to be exported in its raw state because there was no means in the district to produce a more finished product, and the flax which might have proved to be 'a source of wealth to both proprietor and tacksman, has been neglected because skilful people are not collected in one close neighbourhood, to carry it through the whole process'. But as the minister pointed out, 'there is no village either in the parish, or in the whole district. This inconvenience is severely felt'.[43] The idea of planned villages was popular well into the nineteenth century.

The creation of fishing villages seemed an attractive proposition. Sir John Sinclair, editor of the *Statistical Account* and an active Improver on his estates at Ulbster in Caithness, believed that 'there is no species of villages, which merits more to be encouraged, than *fishing* establishments. The produce of their industry may be called almost clear gain. By their exertions, a great addition is made to the food of the country, independent of the produce of the soil; while a hardy and useful race of people are reared, well calculated for the naval defence of the country'.[44]

Villages of either sort were regarded at the time as something of a panacea for the under-development of the Highlands and Islands. However, one man had little doubt that it was new fishing villages that would transform the region. John Knox (1720–1790), who was to the promotion of Highland fisheries what his namesake was to the promotion of Reformation, believed the establishment of fishing villages was the key to improving the quality of life for the Gaels; by earning their living from the sea, they would be freed from the hardships that accompanied subsistence agriculture and would no longer be forced to pay the excessive rents being charged by some landlords. According to Knox, fishing villages should be founded where 'the people should be comfortably lodged, and accommodated with provision, firing, stores of salt, materials and utensils for the herring and white fisheries, independent of lairds, stewards, or intermediate jobbers'. He continued:

> They should enjoy, in the most ample manner, and in all possible cases, the freedom and spirit of the British constitution. The idea of feudal aristocracy, and of feudal subordination should be utterly extinguished; and every man, of whatever degree or profession, should be master of his own time in all seasons, whether at the height of the harvest, or the fisheries, without the interference of any superior whatever. This implies the erection of towns at convenient distances, and in the most eligible situations, on those extensive shores; which towns should be imbued with all the privileges of royal boroughs

[*sic*] for the distribution of justice, as well as the conveniency of the inhabitants in whatever relates to trade, navigation, and fisheries.[45]

Knox produced a pamphlet based on a lecture he delivered to the fisheries committee of the Highland Society of London in March 1786[46] in which he described the poor state of the Highland economy, and inferred that no progress was possible without some assistance from the rest of Britain:

> Here is a considerable body of people without capital, and a coast without towns where the natives can be supplied with nets, casks, salt, hooks, lines, and provisions. Here are no places where fishers, women and children from distant parts, can be accompanied with lodgings, whether in health or in sickness. The inhabitants of these shores have but scanty dwellings to themselves, and are equally ill provided in necessaries for the accommodation of persons who flock thither in the fishing seasons.[47]

Knox had a part in the founding of the British Fisheries Society in July 1786. It was formed when 'several Noblemen and Gentlemen, Members of the Legislature and others, applied for and obtained, near the close of the last Session of Parliament, an Act of Incorporation, forming them into a Society, with a view of attempting the Remedy [of] grievous and impolitic Evils' by encouraging the Highland fisheries through the building of fishing villages.[48] The British Fisheries Society's first governor was the 5th Duke of Argyll, who was also president of the Highland Societies of Scotland and London.[49] In the Society's articles of incorporation, the change in attitude towards the Gaels in the forty years since the Battle of Culloden is clear; they were now people who needed looking after:

> It has often been observed with wonder and regret, that a very considerable part of the Coast of Great Britain continues destitute of the blessings of Art, Industry, and Independence, though inhabited by a numerous tribe of British Subjects, not less capable, not less inclined than their Fellow citizens to become useful Members of the Community; and that many of the Inhabitants emigrate from thence, in large bodies, to cultivate, under incredible hardships, the distant wilds of America, while the surface of their native land is exceedingly short of sufficient cultivation, and while the very numerous adjoining Firths and Seas teem with a wonderful and inexhaustible degree an untouched and unprofitable treasure.
> It has excited indignant sorrow, that their Distresses should drive our Fellow Citizens into foreign parts, at a period when the encouragement of Population ought to be peculiar policy of Great Britain, and more

especially that species of Population which may serve to man her future Navies with expert and hardy Seamen.[50]

When reading the papers of the British Fisheries Society from its early days, one detects a confidence and enthusiasm in the officials, along with the belief that with the application of sufficient thought and resources, the Highlands and Islands would be transformed. The 5th Duke of Argyll sent his agent Lachlan Mactavish on a tour of the Hebrides with the Committee of Directors in July and August of 1787. In his journal of the tour, Mactavish wrote that while the Directors were quite sure that the Hebrides and West Highland coast were ideally suited for the fisheries,

> ... the rugged and mountainous face of the Country, appeared to be such a formidable barr to the General improvement of the Land, as dampened their hope of success, in that particular, very much.[51]

John Knox was not the only writer to advocate the encouragement of the fisheries. James Fea was a Royal Navy surgeon and native of Orkney who wrote an analysis of the subject in 1787. He believed the fisheries could bring prosperity to people who were hard put to survive by agriculture. He wrote that the Islands (including Orkney as well as the Hebrides) were neglected and oppressed, while containing a 'noble race' and a potentially 'immense trade' which needed only encouragement. The phrases he used, such as 'great success', 'constant treasure', and 'little expense', could not help but attract the attention of prospective investors. Fea wrote that the islanders, 'who are entitled to all the rights and benefits of society, are neglected and oppressed' while 'in those climates, which seem purposely formed by nature, an immense trade may be procured, and carried on with great success':

> ... the Scotch Islands are peopled with a hardy, laborious, faithful, brave, and virtuous race of men, who deserve to be treated with more regard, not only on account of their being our fellow subjects, but because they are useful to the Empire at large, and may become greatly more so if properly encouraged ... It is by encouraging the fisheries, a constant treasure, which is peculiarly our own ... These fisheries, so abundant, so rich, and so extensive, would be an inexhaustible source of wealth, which may be procured with little expense ...[52]

A problem with the fisheries was that the success of this capital-intensive enterprise depended very much upon the co-operation of the fish – this difficulty was to become apparent in the nineteenth century. Another man had a more specific proposition. Thomas Telford was commissioned by the Government in 1802 to survey and report on the Highlands, with a view to improving communications there. Telford was concerned about emigration; he believed that a network of roads, bridges and canals would bring lasting employment and prosperity to the Gaels, and held the Highland landowners responsible for not pursuing a more labour-intensive improvement scheme than sheep-farming. He estimated that 3000 people had emigrated from the west coast and central Highlands in 1801 and that three times that number were preparing to leave in 1802. In Telford's opinion, the chief cause of this emigration was the policy of 'converting large Districts of the Country into extensive Sheepwalks. This not only requires much fewer People to manage the same Track of Country, but in general an entirely new People, who have been accustomed to this Mode of Life, are brought from the southern Parts of Scotland'.[53]

Telford believed the Government needed to assume a role in the prevention of large-scale emigration by regulating the landlords' power to evict their tenants. He noted that while 'in the Improvement of a Country, the Interference of Government should extend only to the removing [of] Obstacles ... so as to promote the general Good of the Empire',[54] the urgent case of Highland emigration warranted an exception to the rule of *laissez faire* although he did admit that while

> ... the Evil at present seems to arise chiefly from the Conduct of the Landowners, in changing the Economy of their Estates, it may be questioned whether Government can with Justice interfere, or whether any Benefits are likely to arise from this Interference.[55]

Telford then contrasted two views of Improvement. The first was the conventional wisdom as held by most landowners, which regarded the 'productivity' of the land as the prime consideration. The Gaels were to be made productive as well, even if in the interests of the Empire this was to mean crofting and fishing with an uncertain future, migration to the Lowlands, or emigration:

> In one point of View it may be stated, that, taking the mountainous Parts of Scotland as a district of the British Empire, it is the Interest of the Empire that this District be made to produce as much human Food as it is capable of doing so at the least Expence; that it is the Interest of the Empire the Food so produced, should not be consumed by Persons residing amongst the Mountains, totally unemployed, but rather in some other Parts of the Country, where their Labour can be made productive either in the Business of Agriculture, Fisheries, or Manufactures; and that by suffering every Person to pursue what appears to them to be their own Interest, that although some temporary Inconvenience may arise, yet, upon the Whole, that Matters will in the End adjust themselves into the forms most suitable for the Place.[56]

Essentially, this view was that the people on the land could no longer look to the clan élite for protection as they had in the past. Their continued presence was not indispensable as in earlier times; if they were to be retained on an estate, it was because their labour was needed for making kelp or quarrying slate or manning the fishing boats. The monetary interests of the landlords were all-important in an age of individualism in which large personal fortunes were regarded as beneficial to the country as a whole. Telford, however, took exception to this view of Improvement, believing that the removal of large numbers of people from their native lands was unwise. He predicted, with a fair degree of accuracy, that sheep farming would be over-extended, by which time he thought the depopulation of the Highlands and Islands would be largely complete. Further, he argued, the Gaels had in recent years acquitted themselves well in the army and the navy (a recurring theme) and it would be shortsighted of the Government to allow their emigration and the resulting loss to the recruitment pool. For such reasons, Telford argued for Government intervention to prevent landlords from removing their tenantry:

> In another point of View it may be stated, that it is a great Hardship, if not a great Injustice, that the Inhabitants of an extensive District should all at once be driven from their native country, to make way for Sheep Farming, which is likely to be carried to an imprudent Extent; that, in a few Years, this Excess will be evident; that before it is discovered, the Country will be depopulated, and that Race of People which has of late Years maintained so honourable a share in the Operations of our Armies and Navies will then be no more; that in a Case where such a numerous Body of the People are deeply interested, it is the Duty of Government to consider it as an extraordinary Case, and one of those Occasions which justifies them in departing a little from the Maxims of general Policy; that for this Purpose Regulations should be made to prevent Landowners from lessening the Population upon their estates below a given Proportion, and that some Regulation of this sort would in the End be in favour of the Landowners . . .[57]

Telford's case was not accepted by officialdom, and the living conditions of the Gaels at the turn of the century remained poor as emigration continued on a large scale. While some Improvers such as the Earl of Selkirk openly advocated emigration, others agreed with Telford that another approach should be adopted which would extend the benefits of Improvement to everyone in the Highlands. There was growing awareness of failure by most landlords to take any positive action on behalf of their people; the argument was not that chiefs should retain a large tenantry out of a feeling of feudal obligation, but that greater efforts should be made, with the assistance of the Government, to find a labour-intensive alternative to sheep-farming that would provide a livelihood for the people and benefit the economy of the country as a whole. The landlords were being put on the defensive, and increasingly they were accused of imprudence, or worse, greed. An anonymous essayist writing in 1803 attempted to estimate the changes of population in the Highlands, and in the process named some of the attributes of the people who were emigrating in increasing numbers:

> It would be desirable & a matter of curious speculation, to approximate with any degree of precision, the encrease to which the present number might with care & speedily [sic] be carried; [whilst] considering the productive powers of a moral, uncorrupted people, living peaceably & contentedly in the simplest habits with only natural habits with only natural wants, – religious, a propensity to early marriage, humane, affectionate, sober, frugal, high spirited tho' poor, intuitively sagacious, keenly industrious when labouring for themselves, & above all so patient, capable of fatigue & hardship, with privations in the quantity and quality of food, scarcely to be endured by any other civilized race . . .[58]

What was needed, 'considering at the same time the improvable state of the Soil they cultivate', was, 'a little more attentiveness & encouragement from their Landlords, who on the present footing of things enjoy a moiety of the produce of their labour, without being so rich as other proprietors under different circumstances drawing only a fourth of gross territorial income'; but what was vital was 'the fostering care of a beneficial government, aiding by premiums, freedom from vexatious petty direct taxes, facilitating by the construction of land and water communications or other expensive public works'. If there were indeed a change in landlords' priorities and the dedicated intervention of the Government, especially in the improvement of communications, he estimated 'a threefold population of the present standard; one third to be maintained by agriculture & pasture, an equal number by the fisheries & the rest by other arts manufactures and commerce'.[59]

Improvement and Traditional Values

As the Improvers pressed on with their various schemes for reforming the Highlands and Islands, it was inevitable that there would be a conflict between new and old values: a conflict between opposing cultural imperatives – between one which discounted the past and looked to the future, and one which could not divorce the past from the present. What the Improvers regarded as resistance was often no more than an unenthusiastic response to their plans; however, this lack of willingness to co-operate was usually explained as the Gaels' alleged love of leisure. The Improvers were idealogues or entrepreneurs short on patience, and they reacted bitterly to any recalcitrance or refusal to obey commands. Archibald Menzies, general inspector for the Annexed Estates Board, toured the estates of Perth, Struan and Strathyre in 1767 and was displeased by the tenants' apathy towards the Board's schemes. It was his opinion that the sons of tenants should be sent to the Lowlands (or a 'civilized' part of the Highlands) for training: these boys, after seven years, would have a sense of industry about them and would help to convert their neighbours to the tenets of Improvement. There existed a vague belief that if Highlanders went to live amongst Lowlanders, they would somehow acquire better manners and habits. Menzies put it thus:

> As it will be found too difficult to carry on the best concerted Plan of Improvement with the present Ignorant awkward, lazy Inhabitants; I should humbly Propose, to push with vigor the Scheme formerly adopted by the Board, by causing the Farmers send their sons to be bound apprentices to Farming in such countries as the Board would chuse to Introduce the Culture of, into their own Farmers, to be sent young and to be bound for 7 years; by which means they would be fully instructed in their Trade, and would know how to Execute whatever they should be ordered. I am afraid until that is brought to a bearing nothing of great Consequence will be done . . .[60]

Thirty years later, this strategy still found favour. John Blackadder surveyed Lord Macdonald's estates in Skye and North Uist in 1799 and held to the hope that the planned importation of 'South Country overseers' into North Uist would inspire the people there to change their farming practices:

> . . . it is to be hoped that the Farms proposed to be carried on under the direction of South Country overseers on Lord Macdonald's account, will exhibit such a degree of Profitableness as will in time excite the Tenantry of the Country to follow a different course of Management from what they have done hitherto. If this be not the case, the Country must remain long stationary in point of improvements.[61]

The apparent lack of interest in Improvement on the part of the people must have been frustrating for Blackadder. He wrote that the people of North Uist were 'acute in understanding, seemingly polite, and very tractable', and he found 'many of them possessed of a considerable degree of local Knowledge in rural affairs, some of them possessed of much greater and extended Knowledge of the world'. There was no intellectual barrier to the people's understanding, but he was at a loss to understand their indifference towards new agricultural practices. Blackadder had in fact encountered at first hand the conflict between Improvement and traditional values. Attitudes towards the Gaels had become slightly more sophisiticated over the years, and simple accusations of idleness would no longer suffice, as they had done for Archibald Menzies thirty years earlier. Yet Blackadder thought he discovered among the people he met

> ... a spirit for rejecting new modes of improvement, and an independent cast of mind which will not be bound down (as the Farmers in other countries generally are) by Covenants in Leases to do what other people think right for them to do, if they do not think the thing proposed right themselves. The Reporter found that the Common Farmers discovered no desire to ask questions, and less to answer any relative to Agricultural affairs.[62]

Improvers had difficulty in convincing the Gaels that changes made were in their best interests. Lachlan Mactavish lamented the plight of Captain MacLeod, proprietor of Rodel in Harris; apparently the man was unable to inspire his tenants to take up fishing:

> I was Sorry to learn that altho' He has been uncommonly Zealous in directing the attention of the natives to the fisheries, by very Consistent encouragement such as boat-lines, hooks & ca which he furnishes gratis, yet still they go but unwilling to work; and notwithstanding, that he gives them the highest praise for their fish, over and above the encouragement already mentioned, few or none of them can be got to attend to the business but when he agrees to give them stated wages. But as he hopes that time and Experience will get the better of their prejudices, He means to persevere; being satisfied in his own mind, that when they get a right view of their Interest, no people upon earth can see it more Clearly or pursue it more Steadily than the Generallity of Highlanders.[63]

No one was more bitter than Patrick Sellar. The reorganisation of the Sutherland estates had not passed without incident, and in their haste to carry out 'improvements', the proprietors and their agents failed to consider the fierce attachments all peasants have to their ancestral lands. Sellar understood the nature of the conflict between new and old, but for him it had become a battle of wills. Writing in 1816 about the decidedly unenthusiastic response from the people of Sutherland to the estate's plans, Sellar apportioned part of the blame for the tenants' resistance to the plan to local teachers and ministers. Had these people been recruited from outside the Highlands, things would have gone more smoothly:

I venture to say that what we have seen among the people during the last four years could not have happened had the Teachers of Youth, and the Ministers of the several Parishes been men brought from an industrious Country the sons of industrious Parents, and with a passion for industry in them, had they not been completely the reverse of all this bred in a country of sloth and idleness the sons of highland tenants and whisky smugglers, and with a tone imbibed from the earliest infancy of detestation to every introduction to industry or innovation of the ancient language and manners of the Gael.[64]

Sellar exhumed the idea of a plantation of Lowlanders to instill the notion of hard work into the local populace: those areas of Sutherland where the use of Gaelic was on the decline were by nature more progress-ive than others; Gaelic culture was synonymous with backwardness and squalor. These attitudes were not quite as evident as they had once been, due in part to the popularity of Ossian and Sir Walter Scott, and the growing reputation of the Highland regiments. In Sellar's case, however, the struggle between Improvement and old values had become a battle between his career ambitions and the obstinacy of the Gaels:

I think if Lord and Lady Stafford were pleased to fill up a few of the first vacancies with persons to be searched for in Aberdeenshire or Kincardineshire districts, where the people are extremely industrious it might have the happiest effect. The sure road to the head is by the heart and while the heart is kept subject to ignorance and prejudice, little genuine cooperation can be expected. The want of the Gaelic language will at first be quibbled on by the Clergy, but without much reason, for during the whole line of coast betwixt the Meikle Ferry and the Ord, there are very old people who do not understand the English language, and except the Golspie Fishers very few young ones who cannot speak it fluently.[65]

In defending their reorganisation of estates, Improvers such as Patrick Sellar often compared the allegedly backward agricultural practices of the Gaels with advanced commercial enterprises elsewhere and concluded that the people themselves were the greatest obstacle to economic improvement, while conveniently forgetting the poor soil and harsh climate in much of the Highlands and Islands, not to mention the effects of market and other impersonal forces. According to one commentator, 'the more discerning of contemporaneous commentators, notwithstanding their vested interests in questioning the Whig concept of progress, considered that the commercialization of agriculture within Scottish Gaeldom should take account of existing landed and human resources as well as market demands and that the fashionable pursuit of improvement must offset projected financial benefits against immediate social costs'.[66] The views of the Improvers ruled the day, however, and in general they came to see the retention of a tenantry on the land as beneficial to estate proprietors only insofar as it provided labour for the manufacture of kelp (in coastal areas) and, of course, men for the British army, recruitment to which, although not always profitable, was beneficial to the proprietors' social standing. As a group, the Improvers remained largely impervious to the effects of the 'cultural rehabilitation' of the Gaels brought about by Ossian, Scott, the emergent cult surrounding the Forty-Five, and so on.

NOTES

1. The Annexing Act or 1752 (25 George II c.41). Quoted in Annette M. Smith, *Jacobite Estates of the Forty-Five* (Edinburgh, 1982), p. 23.
2. Scottish Record Office (hereafter SRO), E.729/1/12. Forfeited Estates Papers (1745): Factors' reports c. 1755. Report of Captain John Forbes, factor upon the annexed estates of Lovat and Cromarty (In answer to the Commissioners' orders and instruction of 30 July 1755).
3. Ibid., pp. 26–27.
4. SRO E.729/7/3–4. Forfeited Estates Papers (1745): The report of Mr Francis Grant General Riding Officer and Inspector, 1756.
5. SRO NG.1/1/17/76. Board of Trustees for Manufactures and Fisheries Papers: From a representation to the Lords Commissioners of His Majesty's Treasury, from the Trustees of the Board, in Edinburgh (21 January 1763).
6. Ibid. The Board of Trustees' linen stations in the Highlands were later administered by the Annexed Estates Board, but this method of encouraging manufacturing industry in the region was eventually discarded. The transfer of the linen stations to the Annexed Estates Board was facilitated by the fact that a number of the Trustees were also members of the Board. (Virginia Wills, 'The Gentleman Farmer and the Annexed Estates', in T.M. Devine, ed., *Lairds and Improvement in the Scotland of the Enlightenment, Ninth Scottish Historical Conference, Edinburgh University*, [1978], p. 41.)
7. *House of Commons Sessional Papers of the Eighteenth Century – Reports and Papers*, vol. 53 (fisheries), appendix. no. 27: 'Mr Watt's Survey, Report, and Estimate (1785)', pp. 280, 287–8.
8. 'A Letter from a Freeholder of Inverness-shire, to Lord Adam Gordon', 15 March 1792, from *Prize Essays and Transactions of the Highland Society of Scotland* (Edinburgh, 1799), 1st series, I, p. 344.
9. National Library of Scotland (hereafter NLS), Adv.Ms.33.4.19, pp. 1–2. Col. Robert Anstruther, 'Memorial in relation to the Roads of Communication made at the Public Expence through the Highlands of Scotland' (Edinburgh, 25 March 1799).
10. Parliamentary Papers 1803, IV, p. 17. 'Survey and Report on the Coasts and Central Highlands of Scotland. Made by the Command of the Right Honourable the Lords Commissioners of His Majesty's Treasury, in the Autumn of 1802: by Thomas Telford, Civil Engineer, Edin. FRS.'
11. *Argyll Estate Instructions: Mull, Morvern, Tiree, 1771–1805*, Eric Cregeen, ed. (Scottish History Society, Edinburgh, 1986), pp. xviii-xix.
12. James Hogg, *A Tour in the Highlands in 1803* (Edinburgh, 1986), p. 92.

13. Thomas Douglas, 3rd Earl of Selkirk, *Observations on the Present State of the Highlands of Scotland*, with a view of the causes and Probable Consequences of Emigration (London, 2nd edn., 1806), pp. 25–6.
14. *Ibid.*, p. 32.
15. *A Dictionary of Scottish History*, Gordon Donaldson and Robert S. Morpeth, eds. (Edinburgh, 1977), p. 197.
16. Earl of Selkirk, p. 2. The Earl of Selkirk's Red River settlement was established in 1811 on land granted by the Hudson's Bay Company. The settlement was destroyed by the Northwest Company in 1815, and was restored only to be destroyed again the next year. The colonists persevered and re-established the settlement in 1817.
17. NLS BCL.D5583(4). 'Eight Letters on the Subject of the Earl of Selkirk's Pamphlet on Highland Emigration', Anonymous, 2nd edn. (Edinburgh, 1806), letter II, p. 14.
18. Ibid., pp. 18–19.
19. NLS BCL.D5583–(4). Robert Brown, *Strictures and remarks on the Earl of Selkirk's Observations of the Present State of the Highlands* (Edinburgh, 1806), pp. 106–7.
20. This figure comes from Ian Grimble, 'Clearances', in *The Companion to Gaelic Scotland*, D.S. Thomson, ed. (Oxford, 1983), p. 46.
21. John Prebble, *The Highland Clearances* (Harmondsworth, Middlesex, 1963), pp. 51–2.
22. NLS MS 3881, f. 89. Letters to Sir Walter Scott. This comment referred to the Earl of Selkirk's advocacy of emigration.
23. Capt. John Henderson, *General View of the Agriculture of the County of Sutherland* (London, 1812), p. 135.
24. *Papers on Sutherland Estate Management*, 1802–1816, R.J. Adam, ed. (Scottish History Society, Edinburgh, 1972), 4th series, VIII, p. 156.
25. James Loch, *An Account of the Improvements on the Estates of the Marquess of Stafford* (London, 1820), pp. 70–2.
26. *Ibid.*
27. Dr John MacCulloch, *The Highlands and Western Islands of Scotland* (London, 1824), IV, pp. 138–9.
28. *Ibid.*, III, p. 157.
29. *Ibid.*, III, pp. 157–8.
30. James Browne, *A Critical Examination of Dr MacCulloch's Work* (London, 1825), p. 167.
31. Dr Walker's *Report on the Hebrides of 1764 and 1771*, Margaret McKay, ed. (Edinburgh, 1980), pp. 1–5.
32. *Ibid.*, p. 33.
33. *Ibid.*, p. 33.
34. *Ibid.*, p. 35.
35. *Ibid.*
36. For a full account of the successes and failures of the Annexed Estates Board, see Annette M. Smith, *Jacobite Estates of the Forty-Five* (Edinburgh, 1982).
37. *Prize Essays and Transactions of the Highland Society of Scotland*, 1st series, I, p. vi: Account of the Institution and Principal Proceedings of the Highland Society of Scotland.
38. *Ibid.* p. iii.
39. *The Concise Dictionary of National Biography*, George Smith, ed. (Oxford, 2nd edn. 1906, reprinted 1979), I, p. 21.
40. Dr James Anderson, *An Account of the Present State of the Hebrides and Western Coasts of Scotland* (Edinburgh, 1785), pp. xi–xii.

41. *Ibid.*, pp. xii–xiii.
42. *The Statistical Account of Scotland, 1791–99, edited by Sir John Sinclair*, D.J. Withrington and I.R. Grant, eds. (reprinted Wakefield, 1973–1983), 20 vols., IV, pp. 512–13 (parish of Kincardine).
43. *Ibid.*, XVII, p. 200 (united parish of Kingussie and Inch).
44. Sir John Sinclair, *Analysis of the Statistical Account of Scotland* (Edinburgh, 1825, reprinted 1970), pt. 2, pp. 183–4.
45. John Knox, *A View of the British Empire, more especially Scotland; with some proposals for the Improvement of that Country, Extension of the Fisheries, and the Relief of the People* (London, 3rd edn., 1785), II, pp. 433–4.
46. Jean Dunlop, *The British Fisheries Society 1786–1893* (Edinburgh, 1978), p. 24.
47. SRO GD.9/1/16–17. British Fisheries Society Papers: John Knox, 'A Discourse of the Expediency of Establishing Fishing Stations, or Small Towns, in the Highlands of Scotland and the Hebride Islands' (London, 1786). An Englishman named John Smith proposed an alternative plan to the Highland Society which involved the building of a smaller number of large towns; he predicted that if this were done, a series of cities the size of Liverpool would evolve on the west coast. Smith wrote that his plan would produce 'a hive of labourers and not a cluster of pensioners.' He believed that 'the more the working class are brought by close neighbourhood to be witnesses of each other, the more they will be excited not to consume their hours in lazy basking or vain tattle'. (John Gray, ed., *Some reflections intended to promote the success of the Scotch Fishing Company*, [London, 1789], p. 60.) The Highland Society preferred Knox's more realistic scheme.
48. SRO GD.9/1/199. British Fisheries Society Papers: 'Incorporation of the British Society' (1786).
49. Dunlop, p. 25. The other founding members of the Society were influential as well. The Deputy Governor was the Earl of Breadalbane, and of the thirteen directors, eight were MPs. Prominent members from the Highlands were Francis Humberstone Mackenzie of Seaforth, Lord Gower (also known as the Marquis of Stafford), and the Earl of Moray; from the Lowland establishment were the Marquis of Graham, Adam Fergusson, and George Dempster.
50. SRO GD.9/1/296–9.
51. SRO GD.9/1/25–26. British Fisheries Society Papers: 'To His Grace the Duke of Argyll: a journal of the tour of the Hebrides by the Committee of Directors of the Society by Lachlan Mactavish', July-August 1787.
52. James Fea, *Considerations on the Fisheries in the Scotch Isle ... A General Account Elucidating the History, Soil, Productions, Curiosities, etc. of the Same, the Manners of the Inhabitants, etc.*, printed privately (London, 1787), section 2, pp. 4–5
53. Telford, pp. 14–15.
54. *Ibid.*, p. 14.
55. *Ibid.*, p. 16.
56. *Ibid.*
57. *Ibid.*, pp. 16–17. Telford cited as examples of a better kind of Improvement the new farming practices carried on in Breadalbane and the fishing villages operated 'on the Principle laid down and practised so successfully by Mr Hugh Stevenson of Oban, at Arnisdale on Loch Hourn'.
58. NLS Adv.Ms.35.6.18, pp. 3–4. Anonymous, 'State of the Emigration from the Highlands of Scotland, its extent, causes, and proposed remedy' (London, 21 March 1803).
59. Ibid., pp. 4–5. The well-intentioned plan for the improvement of the system of

communications in the Highlands had an ironic twist. Whereas this writer as well as Telford and others believed that improved communications would in the end obviate the need for emigration, the new network of roads, bridges and canals actually facilitated the advance of sheep-farming by making it cheaper (and therefore more profitable) to transport wool and mutton to Lowland markets. Later in the nineteenth century, as the commercial attractions of sheep-farming became less attractive, this communications system was augmented by the railways which allowed easy access from the Lowlands and England to the 'deer forests'. These were estates, some formerly under sheep and some newly cleared of tenants, which were opened to sportsmen for hunting purposes. Contrary to its original intention, the improvement of Highland communications had the effect of accelerating emigration.

60. SRO E.729/8/17/18. Forfeited Estates Papers (1745): 'Journal of Archibald Menzies, General Inspector, concerning estates of Perth, Struan, and Strathyre (Arnprior), with commissioners' instructions to him, 1767.' The Board's scheme that Menzies referred to was formulated in 1761 and involved the apprenticeship of young men, chiefly the sons of tenants, to Lowland farmers. According to Annette Smith, the idea was reasonable as a means of promoting good farming practices, but as in so many other areas of the Board's work it was unsuccessful and was completely abandoned in 1775. (Smith, *Jacobite Estates of the Forty-Five*, p. 97.)

61. SRO RH.2.8.24.139–140. Macdonald Papers: John Blackadder, 'Survey, description, and valuation of Lord Macdonald's estates of Skye and North Uist' (1799). In making his survey of Assynt in the 1770s, John Home encountered a similar reluctance on the part of tenants to discuss their holdings. At the farm of Bellachlattach he incurred the expense of 'necessarie provisions and Drink to myself and the Lads and Tenants for showing their Marches as they could not be prevailed with to do so without it 15/- in all'. (*John Home's Survey of Assynt*, R. J. Adam, ed. [Scottish History Society, Edinburgh, 1960], p. 57.)

62. *Ibid.*

63. SRO GD.9/1/9. British Fisheries Society Papers: Journal of Lachlan Mactavish (entry 16 July 1787).

64. Patrick Sellar, from 'Note concerning Sutherland' (May 1816), from *Papers on Sutherland Estate Management, 1802–1816*, XIII, p. 184. (For a vivid portrait of Sellar, see Iain Crichton Smith's novel *Consider the Lilies* [Oxford, 1968].)

65. *Ibid.*

66. A.I. Macinnes, 'Scottish Gaeldom: The First Phase of Clearance', in *People and Society in Scotland I, 1760–1830*, T.M. Devine and Rosalind Mitchison, eds. (Edinburgh, 1988), pp. 74–5.

3

Civilisers, Educators, and Evangelisers

IT WAS NOT until the defeat of the Jacobites in 1746 that any real interest was shown in the subject of religion in the Highlands and Islands. To ensure that the region no longer posed a threat to the Hanoverian establishment, outside agencies began to involve themselves in the moral, educational, and spiritual rehabilitation of the Gaels. Their first aim was to see that the established Church of Scotland had no further competition from the rebellious non-juring Episcopalians and Roman Catholics. As attitudes towards these denominations became more liberal in the late eighteenth century, especially as they proved their loyalty to the British constitution, more attention was given to providing the Gaels with a basic education that would focus upon spreading literacy in English to encourage the use of the Bible while at the same time teaching 'civilizing' values such as hard work and the superiority of southern culture and the English language. The task of providing an education for everyone in the Highlands and Islands was beyond the resources of the outside agencies, but the process if anything assisted emigration by raising expectations. The rise of an indigenous evangelical movement which was driven by the work of local lay preachers and spiritual Gaelic poetry not only won the Highlands and Islands for Presbyterianism in the early nineteenth century but acted to transform the Gael from the traitorous barbarian and pagan of popular image to an evangelical who viewed the world as 'a glen of tears' and whose only prospect of happiness lay in an afterlife.

Religion and disaffection after the rebellion

Despite the result of the Battle of Culloden and the 'pacification' that followed, the belief persisted that Jacobitism in the Highlands and Islands still posed a dangerous threat to the establishment. While the estates of attainted Jacobites were annexed to the Crown and the outward symbols of Gaelic culture banned, the presumed dangers of non-juring Episcopacy and Roman Catholicism, closely identified with the Forty-Five, were more difficult to root out. Clergymen of these denominations were considered by Government supporters to be the active agents of the exiled Stuarts and the 'popish' powers of the Continent who sought to revive Jacobite aspirations. As a result, the religious persuasion of the Gaels was believed to be directly relevant to British national security.

In c. 1747 a 'loyal subject' reported to the Duke of Newcastle that several Jacobites in the French service were recruiting men in the Highlands, and 'with the Assistance of Popish Priests, and other equally dangerous Emissaries raised the Rebellion Spirits of the common Highlanders, to such a pitch, that they Seem more inclined to a Rebellion, than ever'.[1] The informant reported that the Jacobite agents were spreading rumours to the effect that Charles Edward Stuart had become a Protestant and that the French, Spaniards, and Prussians would arm and support them in an impending rebellion:

> They represent to these poor deluded and infatuated people That they are enslaved, and entirely Governed by a Military power, And they further Suggest to them, that the only way they can fall on, [is] to rise unanimously, in Arms for the Pretender, on whom they bestow great encomiums, And whose Title to the Crown they make them believe is beyond all dispute.[2]

It was a widely held belief among the Presbyterian establishment in the Lowlands that the 'poor deluded and infatuated' Highlanders were not capable of responsible decisions in either politics or religion. In later years, as it became obvious that Jacobitism as a political force had been eliminated at Culloden, the moral and spiritual state of the Gaels was left to religious and charitable organisations; but in the years immediately following 1746, the activities of Catholic priests in particular were seen to be subversive. The informant wrote that 'popish Priests' throughout Gaeldom 'doe instill Such Religious & politicall principles into the minds of the Gentlemen and common people' in areas where 'nothing is professed but the Roman Catholick Religion' and that their message consisted of the 'indefeasible and Jure Divino Hereditary Right of the Stewart Family'.[3] He wrote that notwithstanding the 'unwearied endeavours' of the Society in Scotland for Propagating Christian Knowledge (established in 1709) and the Royal Bounty (established in 1724 and providing for itinerant missionaries and catechists), 'Popery is prevailing dayly' in the Highlands and Islands, 'where the number of Priests is considerable'.[4]

Young Gaels were 'early byassed & tainted in their principles with the Popish Books, Rebellious pamphlets, declarations, Manifestos, and songs' supplied by the priests, which acted to 'create a dislike in them to the present Royal Family, and constitution as by Law Established'.[5]

In the opinion of another anonymous informant, Roman Catholic priests were not the only agents of disaffection. *The Highlands of Scotland in 1750* is a dossier believed to have been written by Edmund Bruce, a Government official who surveyed the forfeited and other estates in the Highlands and Islands.[6] It is supremely Whiggish in that it is Unionist, Presbyterian, and virulently anti-Jacobite. According to the author, parts of the Highlands were under the sway of non-juring Episcopalian clergymen who were resolutely opposed to the Government and George II. He wrote that Morvern was 'mostly inhabited by Camerons who profess themselves Protestant', but that they along with the people of Ardnamurchan and the Stewarts of Appin 'are the most deeply poisoned with Disaffection to our Happy Constitution in Church and State of any People I ever knew'.[8]

> They Idolize the Nonjuring Clergy and can scarcely keep their temper when speaking of Presbyterians. The Reason of this I take to be that one Mr John McLachlan a Nonjurant of the Highest Kind lived Chiefly among them. This man who was at least half a Papist and a most Active Zealous Cunning Fellow with a pretty good Share of Learning did more harm among the Campbells, McDougals, Stuarts, McLeans, and Camerons, than any Six Priests that ever were in Scotland.[9]

John McLachlan, he wrote, 'often travelled through these and the Adjacent parts of the Country Administering the Sacrament of the Supper, admitting People only on this express Condition that they would not hear any Minister who prayed for King GEORGE'.[10] The Camerons 'boast of their firm adherence to the Protestant Religion in all the Periods of Time since the Reformation', but 'they shewed so little regard to any Religion in their practise that their adherence to Protestancy seems to have been a part of the Pretender's Political Scheme', for 'it wou'd have appeared too glaring to have none but Popish Clans appear zealous for his Interest'.[11] The author must have been unaware of the loyalties of the Rev. John Cameron, a Church of Scotland chaplain at Fort William. Cameron was an ardent Jacobite, perhaps an early nationalist; he was present at the Battle of Culloden and met Charles Edward Stuart the day he left Scotland in 1746.[12]

The Campbells of Argyll received more sympathetic treatment, however. For Whiggish political and religious reformers, the clan was a model for others to follow. Their anti-Stuart credentials extended back to Covenanting times; they had fought for the Government at Culloden; and the leading clan gentry were important members of the Scottish political elite. The reputation of the Campbells 'since the Reformation and their Hearty Disposition to promote and support the Cause of Religion and Liberty is so well known that I need only Remark of this Country in General'. He found that 'the Common People are generally Honest and Religious, Love the Established Clergy, and give no Encouragement to the Nonjurants, and are more Sensible of the blessings of a British subject than most of the other Clans in the Highlands are . . .'[13]

Prelacy and Popery

The Campbells were exceptional: most Gaels *did* give encouragement to the 'seditious' Episcopalians and Catholics. Non-jurors had refused to take oaths of allegiance to the Hanoverian sovereigns after the Revolution, and with the 1712 Toleration Act the split between themselves and their non-Jacobite associates became formal; which made them a political as well as a religious threat in Whig and Presbyterian eyes. That non-jurors had been intimately involved in the rebellion was without question. One of the illustrious 'Seven Men of Moidart' who had landed with Charles Edward Stuart in 1745 was George Kelly, a non-juring clergyman; and clans such as the Camerons and the Stewarts of Appin which were served by non-juring clergy fought in the campaigns of the rebellion, to their ruin. The Forty-Five was and still is considered by some to have been a Roman Catholic enterprise, but give or take the odd Presbyterian, non-jurors taking part in the rebellion outnumbered Catholics by something like two to one. John McLachlan joined the Jacobites, and an excerpt from a letter written in 1748 to Robert Forbes testifies to the losses suffered by the Episcopalians, and to the considerable ignominy McLachlan suffered as a result of living in the midst of the victorious Campbells:

> Now I live for the most part like a Hermite, because all my late charges almost were kill'd in battle, scattered abroad, or cow'd at home; and the people of this country are generally so bigot in Whiggism and so insolent on their late success, that it is vastly mortifying for me to live among them.[14]

Where once the Episcopalians had been dominant in the Highlands, they now came under pressure. They shared with the Presbyterians the problem of poor communications and the difficulty of recruiting qualified Gaelic-speaking ministers and catechists, but were banned and short of funds as well. One of the most faithful supporters of the cause was Robert Forbes (1708–1775), an Episcopalian clergyman who was captured on his way to join the rebellion in September 1745. His most enduring legacy is *The Lyon in Mourning*, a collection of Jacobite material compiled from 1747 to his death which remains an important source of information about the Forty-Five.

Forbes became Bishop of Ross and Caithness in 1762, and wrote a journal of his first episcopal visit there. Forbes's acceptance of the need for bilingual worship was reinforced by his experience of the language barrier when he visited Muir of Ord near the Black Isle. He was reluctant to give a sermon as he spoke no Gaelic, but upon hearing the catechist's warning that 'honest souls would take it highly amiss if they did not see me perform both Prayers and Sermon', he did so, his words being translated by two assistants. He commented that 'indeed the external Devotion of the people was admirable, and past all Description, as all the Highlanders have a remarkable serious Turn of mind'.[15]

Forbes was similarly impressed with the devoutness of the Gaels during his visit to Argyll in 1770. During a stay with the Episcopalian congregation at Ballachulish he noted in his journal that in all parts of the Highlands 'the devotion of the people was extremely remarkable, and very affecting, insomuch that it drew Tears from mine Eyes. With eager Countenance they kept their Eye fix'd on the clergyman from first to last'.[16] During his visit to Callander in the same year he received an indication that at least in one place the thievery that was thought to be endemic in the Highlands was not a problem:

> At Calendar, within a Stone-Cast of the Highway, we saw a fine Field of Shirts, Bed and Table-Linen, which Mrs Forbes supposed to be watched all night; but the Landlady told us they knew no such custom there, though in a Highland-Country, where there are several persons who can speak nothing but Galic, an Experiment, this, which We durst not try about Edinburgh or Leith, or any part of the South Country.[17]

Non-juring Episcopalians in the Highlands were regarded as outlaws of a sort until the death of Charles Edward Stuart in 1788. Their difficulties were not merely political, however. They were financially hard-pressed as the Presbyterians controlled all teinds (the one-tenth share rendered by parishioners for the support of churches and ministers); the problem of finding clergymen willing to work under such conditions, particularly those with Gaelic, proved to be a chronic one. A letter written by Stewart of Invernahyle and others to Forbes's successor Bishop Petrie in 1782 asked for more regular visits by clergymen to Appin, 'and that such of them as are deficient in the Galic language bring a sufficient person along with them, for the benefit of the common People, who are now fully resolved to break off unless they are more regularly supplied for the future than they have been for some time past'.[18] They noted that 'as we have had the Rev. Mr Taylor, from Perthshire, twice of late, who does not speak the Galic language, we hope, in the first place, your Reverence will send us one who is acquainted with that language, in hopes it will have the desired effect as to the Common People'.[19]

The Episcopalians were clearly worried that unless the provision of

Gaelic-speaking ministers improved, their flock might be lost to the dreaded Presbyterians or to the Roman Catholics, who would have been known through the Jacobite connection and had the advantage of external funding. But the problems of the Scottish Episcopal Church in the Highlands were to continue well into the nineteenth century. The report of the Gaelic Episcopal Society in 1830 noted that in Morvern 'there are many persons who are members of the Episcopal Church who are visited twice a year by Mr MacLennan, at Fort William. A catechist for this district would be invaluable'.[20] MacLennan himself wrote:

> In the classic country of Morvern, and in Sunart, they require a chapel and a clergyman, or a catechist, being at different distance of from twenty to fifty miles from our chapel, which obliges me to go over that immense tract of country twice a year. They also require a gratuitous supply of prayer books.[21]

In common with the non-juring Episcopalians, Roman Catholics were on the defensive following the Forty-Five. Religion aside, they were identified with treason and sedition, and many Government supporters seriously considered the Catholic Highlanders to be a standing army for the Jacobite cause. In passing the death sentence on Simon Fraser, Lord Lovat, Lord Hardwicke said the defeat of the Jacobites had prevented 'this Kingdom from becoming a province to some of the great Popish Powers, who have so long watched for the destruction of our liberties'.[22] Roman Catholics played an important role in the conflict from the outset, regardless of 'popish' manoeuvres. It was a Roman Catholic bishop, Hugh MacDonald, who blessed the standard of Charles Edward Stuart at Glenfinnan in August 1745, and the Catholics of Moidart, Arisaig, Knoydart, Morar, Glengarry and Lochaber joined the cause under their respective chiefs.[23]

The brutal campaign that followed Culloden sought to root out Catholic priests and their followers in the Highlands and Islands. In the spring of 1746, Government warships arrived at Barra and landed troops. The people there were told that the island would be devastated unless the Catholic priest living among them were surrendered: a missionary gave himself up.[24] The Duke of Cumberland issued orders to demolish all Catholic chapels in the Highlands and arrest any priests who were found,[25] and in Glenlivet, Braemar, Strathaven, and throughout the West Highlands and Hebrides, frequent searches were made by Government forces to capture Catholic priests and missionaries.[26]

In the aftermath of Culloden, the second most wanted man in Scotland was probably Hugh MacDonald, the son of MacDonald of Morar and Gaeldom's first Roman Catholic bishop, who was hunted incessantly for years after the Forty-Five. In a report of 1753 to Propaganda, the

Vatican-based body which directed foreign missions, MacDonald gave this account of Government persecution:

> For some years past we have been suffering more than ordinary persecution. Sometimes it happens by the mercy of God that the virulence of our enemies is somewhat relaxed, but then, under the instigation of malevolent persons, it suddenly breaks out with new violence. The soldiers too, in hopes of gaining as much money as they know has already been paid to their comrades for captured priests, are constantly endeavouring to lay hands on the clergy.[27]

MacDonald was finally apprehended by Government agents in November 1755. At his trial at the High Court in Edinburgh in February 1756 he was charged with being 'held and repute a Jesuit, priest, or trafficking Papist', and was sentenced to be 'banished forth of this realm, with certification, that if he ever return thereto, being still Papist, he shall be punished with the pain of death'.[28] MacDonald changed his name and carried out his duties more covertly. Presbyterian commentators such as the Rev. John Walker and the Drs Hyndman and Dick credited the Roman Catholic clergy with considerable feats of conversion, but their claims were probably exaggerated to attract Government funding for missionary schemes. While the priests did receive outside funding, they endured the same difficulties as their Protestant counterparts, such as poor communications and a lack of qualified clergymen. In a report of the Highland vicariate of 1764, MacDonald described South Morar as being 'extremely rough country, so that in some parts it is difficult to travel even on foot', but that it was 'all Catholic, and contains 318 souls'.[29] He wrote that even if each of the districts of Moidart, Arisaig, and South Morar were provided with a missionary, they would have more than enough work to do, 'but alas', he observed, 'through all these areas there is no-one to serve the faithful people except Mr William Harrison, who had to attend as best he can to the islands of Canna and Eigg also'.[30] Harrison was a man 'of burning zeal for the salvation of souls, in whose service he has endured, and continues to endure, incredible hardships', and because of the large area he had to cover, 'he scarcely ever spends two considerable nights in one place, but must go travelling though worn out with toil'.[31] Indeed, after the Forty-Five many districts of the Highlands and Islands did not have a single Roman Catholic priest or lay worker, some for thirty years, due to the dangerous political situation and the physical difficulty of the task.[32]

Colin MacDonald of Boisdale made strenuous efforts to convert his Catholic tenants of South Uist to Protestantism, and his use of strong-arm tactics was dubbed by Catholic Gaels *Creideamh a' bhata bhuidhe*, or the 'yellow-stick belief'. MacDonald, who was raised a

Catholic but converted to the Church of Scotland, sought to convert the people initially by procuring the attendance of Catholic children at schools on the island established by his father. A Catholic historian of the late nineteenth century reported with horror 'scurrilous and even immoral sentences were set to the poor children to copy; and in the Lent of 1770 attempts were made to force flesh-meat into their mouths'.[33] The parents withdrew their children from the schools in protest, and MacDonald responded by assembling his tenants and ordering them to sign a declaration renouncing Catholicism or face eviction. The islanders refused, stating their readiness to beg from door to door rather than embrace the Church of Scotland. MacDonald responded with the proposal that if the children were brought up in the 'reformed' manner, the tenants could retain their holdings without further molestation. The tenants answered that they valued the souls of their children as much as their own.[34]

MacDonald reported to the Commissioners of the Annexed Estates in February 1771 that, excepting the island's gentry and their dependents, all the people of South Uist were Roman Catholics.[35] He 'had done all in his power to encourage the Protestant Religion, by keeping a Schoolmaster at his own house for his own children and Brethren, and such of his Tenants & Servants as he could prevail upon to resort thereto,' and in doing so he had 'incurred the Displeasure of most of the Roman Catholicks'.[36] He further reported that his father had mortified £5 'to be applied to make up a Salary for a Schoolmaster to be kept on his own lands for the Encouragement of the Protestant Religion' with the hope that 'some other charitable person or Society would contribute to the Salary of such a Schoolmaster'.[37]

The Annexed Estates Board preferred to leave educational and religious missions beyond their estates to other agencies, but MacDonald hoped they would make an exception in his case. If the Commissioners would augment the £5, he would 'give all the encouragement in his power to accommodate such a Schoolmaster, by giving him a house Garden ground for planting potatoes grasing for milk cows &c to the value of £5 ster. more, or the £5 in Cash, if preferred to these it is impossible to get a proper Teacher to go to so remote, and so disagreeable a part of the Country – among Strangers & Roman Catholicks without a suitable Salary'.[38] His plea was of no avail, but the islanders for their part had come to realise that they would have to choose between their homes and their religion, and they chose the latter: they appealed to Bishop Hay, Vicar apostolic of the Lowlands, for assistance in emigrating to America. Subscriptions were raised from Catholics throughout Scotland, and a large number of the South Uist Catholics left.[39] This episode is one case of emigration resulting from causes other than economic, although

MacDonald of Boisdale was an 'enterprising' landlord who was probably glad to be free of such obstinate tenants. The Catholic hierarchy did not view the outcome in an entirely negative light. In a letter addressed to Propaganda and dated 10 July 1772, the three Scottish bishops expressed the hope that this exodus might have a good result: the spread of the 'true faith' in distant lands.[40]

By the end of the eighteenth century, however, official attitudes to Scottish Catholics had relaxed to the extent of the Government giving a grant towards the training of Scots boys for the priesthood, and priests throughout Scotland were praying for King George.[41] The fanciful idea that Catholics in Scotland consituted a standing army for France or Spain had been consigned to the dustbin. But while the Roman Catholic Church was no longer officially discouraged in the Highlands and Islands, and indeed in 1799 the proposed Highland College (a seminary) received £300 from the Government,[42] its position in Gaeldom was nevertheless unpromising for other reasons. Abbé Paul MacPherson, one-time rector of the Scots College at Rome, wrote that a high proportion of Catholic Gaels had emigrated to America or had 'changed the barren hills of the Highlands for the fruitful plains of the Lowlands'.[43] MacPherson commented that the few Catholics remaining there lived on the margins of existence but 'they also find greedy Chieftains and Lairds ready to catch at their miserable superfluities', so that nothing remained 'for the poor clergy'.[44]

Civilising Gaeldom

Captain John Forbes, factor on the annexed estates of Lovat and Cromartie, believed that the civilising effects of education and religion were vital to the success of the Annexed Estates Board's schemes. 'Education' meant the teaching of the English language, and 'religion' meant the presence of the Church of Scotland to the exclusion of others. For the improvement and civilisation of the people of Beauly on the estate of Lovat he recommended in 1755 the erection of a new church in Glenstrathfarrar, 'where the people are grossly ignorant, & among whom there are a great many Papists and scarce a person can be found who can speak one word of English', and two schools which would cure the Gaels of their ignorance of that language.[45] Forbes went on to describe a 'pernicious' habit among the Gaels that was subsequently denounced alike by Patrick Sellar and the evangelicals (often hypocritically) of a later era: the distillation of *uisge-beatha*. In later years, the Gaels were forced to distill and sell whisky to pay their rents, but in 1755 distilling was for local consumption. However, Forbes thought the practice

... has contributed, among other things, to render the people so poor & idle as they are at present, for it makes them neglect their Farms, habituates them to drinking, & of consequence debauches their Morals, breeds quarrels, & subjects them to many fines and penaltys for Concealments and Nonentrys.[46]

Another Government representative involved in the economic improvement of the Highlands who was equally concerned with the moral and religious state of the Gaels was Alexander Schaw, the principal undertaker of the Board of Manufactures' linen station at Glenmoriston. In a report of 1755 to the directors of the Society in Scotland for Propagating Christian Knowledge, he wrote of how the men of Glenmoriston were 'engaged in the Rebellions of 1715 and 1745 and this owing to the craft[y] subtility of the Popish Missionaries'.[47]

They know no more than by heresay, that there is a God ... were they to be asked anything further they would be found to be as ignorant as the wild americans and any of them that profess religion are gross papists and it can hardly be otherways as they are deprived of the means of knowledge and education having no schools among them no minister to instruct them nor publick worship and being thus neglected. The Popish priests, who are indefatigable in making Proselytes corrupt the minds and moralls of the people and Instill into them Rebellious principles destructive to our happy constitution & Revolution principles.[48]

Five years later, the General Assembly of the Church of Scotland (in conjunction with the SSPCK, see below) sent Drs Hyndman and Dick on a fact-finding mission to inquire into the religious state of the Highlands and Islands. Their subsequent report described the inadequate provision of ministers, churches, and schools in many parts. Hyndman and Dick wrote of the difficulties faced by Kirk ministers at a time when travel in the region was still something of an adventure. Many of the parishes there were too large for even the most energetic of ministers, they wrote, and several of the parishes more closely resembled 'rather a Province requiring the Labors of a Body of Clergy Men than a district fit for the Inspection of a single Pastor'; and when the difficulties in communication were taken into account, 'it is easy to Conceive that during the great part of the year, many of the Inhabitants must be deprived of all Correspondence with their Pastors, [and] be destitute of the public means of Religion'.[49]

They reported that 'many parts of the Highlands and Islands, have no School for Teaching the Children to Read, and making them acquainted with the principles of Religion',[50] and that this would be exploited by the Catholic priests to subvert the impressionable Gaels. By this time, Jacobitism was a spent force, and Charles Edward Stuart was a middle-aged alcoholic quite incapable of causing further trouble; nevertheless, the fact that many Gaels were not firm Presbyterians (and therefore 'loyal') worried Hyndman and Dick:

> The Youth being destitute of the means of proper Instruction at home, and hindered by poverty from going to seek them Abroad, continue in a state of Ignorance, Inherit the prejudices and Errors of their ancestors, and become an easy Prey to those who wish every opportunity of infusing Opinions contrary to true Religion, and to the Just Principles of Civil Government. While large tracts possess no means of Educating their Youth, it is easy to foresee the continuance if not the Increase of all these evils under which the Inhabitants have so long laboured.[51]

The connection between the presence of Catholic priests and the possible re-emergence of Jacobitism was not as arguable in 1760 as it had been in the years immediately following 1746. But the belief that the Roman Catholic faith and the British constitution were incompatible still persisted. 'The priests of this Communion', Hyndman and Dick reported, 'are numerous and active, and altogether their sallarys be small, yet the advantage of a foreign Education, which they receive from a publick fund, and the influence of their politick Religion gives them over the minds of the people, have Contributed to Cheque the progress of the Reformation, and at some periods, to gain proselites to their own Church.'[52] In an area so inadequately supplied with Presbyterian churches and schools as the Highlands and Islands, 'where so little good seed of any kind is sown, it is not to be wondered that the Enemy should Sow his Fares, and that these should bring furth a plentifull increase'.[53]

While the Catholics had established several strongholds, namely in Banffshire and parts of the West Highlands and Hebrides, their numbers hardly threatened the position of the Church of Scotland. Alexander Webster's census of 1755,[54] supported by the General Assembly and the SSPCK, counted in Argyll 61,957 Protestants and 4,329 Catholics, these mostly found in Ardnamurchan;[55] in Inverness-shire, 53,899 Protestants and 5,664 Catholics;[56] and in Ross-shire, 42,901 Protestants and only 20 Catholics.[57] The most marked religious divide revealed by Webster's census was to be found in the Uists and Barra: in North Uist Webster counted 1,909 Protestants and no Catholics; in South Uist and Benbecula, 2,040 Catholics and 169 Protestants;[58] and in Barra, 1,100 Catholics and only 50 Protestants.[59] On the Catholic side, the Highland vicariate reported to Propaganda in c. 1762 that there were some 12,900 Catholic *communicants* within its area.[60]

The difficulties posed by the lack of good communications in the 'reformation' of the Gaels were equalled by the language barrier. The Church of Scotland did not have enough Gaelic-speaking ministers to meet the challenge (although the commonly-held opinion was that rather than provide a Gaelic-speaking clergy, it was up to the Gaels to learn English), and in 1755 the synods of Argyll and Glenelg had complained to the General Assembly of 'the distressed Situation of their Bounds by the want of Preachers having the Irish Language'.[61] Hyndman and Dick wrote that the Gaels' ignorance of English 'lays them under great disadvantages, both with regard to Religion, and to Civil life'.[62] They observed, 'the knowledge of the Gaelic language becomes a necessary Qualification in every Minister who is to serve in these countrys and the difficulty of supplying vacant Parishes is greatly increased.'[63] But the language barrier extended beyond the provision of ministers: the 'common people' of the Highlands and Islands were unable to transact business 'with the more Southern parts of great Britain without the intervention of their superiors who know the English language, and are thereby kept in that undue dependence and unacquaintance with the arts of life which have long been the Misery of these Countrys'.[64] They failed to mention that seasonal migration to the Lowlands had undoubtedly contributed to a growing bilingualism. They concluded, 'till the partition arising from different languages be removed, & the Common language of great Britain be defused over the Highlands, the Inhabitants will never Enjoy in their full extent the benefits of Religion and Civil Government'.[65]

In summary, Hyndman and Dick recommended to the General Assembly the erection of new parishes and the building of new churches, these to be supplied with qualified ministers.[66] 'Should this plan take place,' they wrote, 'the popish missionarys could not avail themselves of the necessary absence of Pastors from the remote parts of their Care, In order to poison their flocks with principles of Superstition, and Disloyalty.'[67]

The Rev. Dr John Walker was sent by the General Assembly in 1765 to inquire into the religious state of the Highlands and Islands, and he shared many of Hyndman and Dick's attitudes. His mission was 'to gain such intelligence, and to make such Observations, as might be conducive, to promote the laudable designs of the Church, in Instructing the Inhabitants of those Remote Parts, in the Right Principles of Religion and Government'.[68] Walker described the 'great disadvantages' of a region that was 'far remov'd by [its] distant Situation from the more enlightened parts of the Kingdom',[69] and the inability of the Gaels to understand English, which prevented them from reading the Bible (there being no Gaelic version at this time). According to Walker, they also suffered from 'the mistaken Principles of their ancestors' and the 'prejudices of an uncivilized state', which combined to prevent them from 'acquiring proper notions of Religious and civil Liberty'; and as these handicaps were aggravated by 'the Activity and success of the Emissaries of the Romish Church, the difficulties are but too evident, to which the poor Inhabitants are subjected'.[70] However, Walker was eager to point out that the Gaels were not pagans, or what Presbyterians believed was the same thing, 'papists'. 'I constantly observed,' he wrote, 'that wherever they have access to Schools, to publick worship, and to the ordinances of Religion, there, they are more regular in their morals, more civilized in their manners, and in their way of Life, more active and Industrious, than their countrymen, who are Strangers to these advantages.'[71] He wished to reassure sceptics and/or Lowland bigots that the Gaels would take full advantage of any opportunity to become 'civilized'. He acknowledged the efforts of the Government and the Church of Scotland to promote Christianity among the Gaels, but observed with regret, 'the Popish Religion is visibly on the increase' due to the extent of the parishes, the spiritual ignorance of the people, and the hard work of the priests. 'In some parts of the Highlands, the inhabitants have quitted the Protestant Religion . . . merely by being left destitute of the ministry and assistance of the Protestant Clergy.'[72]

Although Walker wanted to help rehabilitate the Gaels, he did not accord them much sophistication in choosing their faith. The conversion of the people to Roman Catholicism was 'a more easy business, than it would be in any other Country'[73] because of their ignorance of religion and their veneration for the past and their ancestors. These characteristics, he argued, 'are powerful Arguments, of which, the Priests never fail to make proper use, and are very successful ones, in persuading them to return to the Superstitions of the Church of Rome'.[74] Walker feared that the continued presence of Roman Catholicism in the Highlands and Islands would corrupt the Gaels 'not only in the Principles of Religion, but in those of Government'.[75] Presbyterian churchmen such as Walker believed that Roman Catholicism and progress of any kind were mutually incompatible because of the alleged superstition and aversion to change inherent in that faith. If the Gaels were 'lost' to the priests, every attempt to reform them would fail; in the Catholic districts of the Highlands and Islands, 'not only the morals and manners of the People, but the very soil, is more rude and uncultivated. The Popish inhabitants are as tenacious of the old customs, as they are of the old Religion'.[76] The way to oppose the spread of Roman Catholicism among the Gaels was to improve the provision of Presbyterian ministers and churches, and the spread of education. Without better provision of schools, he argued, 'it is scarce to be expected, that the state of the Country is ever to be much altered for the better, or that Religion, Industry, and civilized manners, are ever to make considerable Progress'.[77]

The provision of schools – the SSPCK

The monumental task of providing schools for the people of the Highlands and Islands was in the eighteenth century left for the most part to the Society in Scotland for Propagating Christian Knowledge (hereafter SSPCK). Founded in 1709 and always an Edinburgh-based organisation, it reflected the contemporary state of Lowland attitudes towards the Gaels, from the nadir of 1745 to the rehabilitation that took place from the late eighteenth century onwards. The Society never intended its school system to be an alternative to the parish schools; rather, it stipulated that its schools could only be instituted in those parishes that already had them. The Education Act of 1696 obliged each parish to have a schoolhouse and a master paid for by the landowners, but this provision (where it was observed) was little better than useless in the large and sparsely-populated parishes of the West Highlands and the Hebrides. In recognition of this, the SSPCK schools were ambulatory, enabling them to provide instruction in a community and then to move on.

In an anonymous account of the SSPCK written in 1809, in reality a fund-raising pamphlet, the inquiries made by the society's founders 100 years earlier were said to have 'soon furnished them with melancholy proofs of the profound ignorance, and gross barbarism of the neglected inhabitants'.[78] They had found the Gaels to be 'destitute of almost all means of knowledge and improvement', and although each parish was supplied with 'Protestant' ministers (the term Presbyterian was avoided so as not to put off any potential contributions from England), the parishes were too large to be served by a single clergyman.[79] 'From these causes,' the writer continued, 'it is certain and not to be wondered at, that intellectual darkness, the grossest and most profound, brooded over this unhappy country, that its inhabitants were ignorant of the first principles of the Christian system, and that what notions they had of a religious nature, were only a mixture of popish and pagan superstition.'[80] The Gaels' shortcomings were not merely intellectual or theological, however: 'their minds were fierce ... their manners barbarous ... they were plunderers of the loyal and peaceful inhabitants of the lowlands of Scotland; and in general, hostile to the happy constitution of Government established at the Revolution'.[81] On the face of it, the SSPCK was founded out of motives of patriotism and Christian love. 'It was impossible for cultivated and benevolent minds to comprehend without commiseration, a people, and those their own countrymen, in so unhappy a condition. The generous Founders of this Society pitied them, and formed a noble plan for their relief.'[82] But education then as now had a socialising function which can be described as indoctrination, and in the eighteenth century, education for the 'lower orders' sought to teach the people to know their place, both socially and politically:

> By establishing Schools for the instruction of youth, [the founders] wished to rescue their uncorrupted minds from the ignorance and barbarism of their fathers, to establish in them the first principles of science and religion, and to open to them the channels of further improvement, by teaching them to speak and to read the English language.[83]

The SSPCK's desire to spread literacy through the Highlands and Islands was not based on the modern notion that it is essential for good citizenship; rather, the Society's stated aim was to enable the Gaels to achieve salvation. The Society declared in 1796: 'The grand and important end which the Society do always and have always proposed to themselves by their appointment is the Salvation of Souls',[84] and in the same document it stated, 'the great object of the Society from the beginning has been and still is to send the Scripture to the Highlanders and to teach them to read them'.[85] As English was the official language of Scottish Presbyterianism, and as the SSPCK directors were for the most part Lowlanders who believed in the superiority of English over Gaelic, it followed that English was the medium of instruction in the Society's schools. A problem that came to the directors' attention in 1751 was that while the Scriptures were taught in English in their schools, the students understood nothing but Gaelic. The directors, 'considering the Hurt and Prejudice to the Design of the Society by the Schoolmasters teaching the Children to read English Books in the remote parts of the Highlands without understanding that Language', resolved that any students speaking Gaelic either in the schoolhouse or when playing outside would do so 'in pain of being chastised' and that the schoolmasters were to appoint censors to make note of such transgressions. Further, the schoolmasters were instructed to explain the meaning and interpretation of the English words (presumably in Gaelic) so that the children would understand what they read.[86]

Gaelic (as well as Latin, which was an important key to advancement in mainstream Scottish education) was banned in the schools from the time of the Society's incorporation, although it commissioned a Gaelic-English dictionary which was compiled by the poet Alexander MacDonald in 1741. Until 1767, it was an offence to teach Gaelic to pupils. With the publication of the first Gaelic New Testament in that year under SSPCK auspices, however, the schools became bilingual. This change of policy was not made because the Society's directors dropped their policy of spreading the knowledge of English, but because they believed that the use of Gaelic would further their evangelical ambitions. Curiously, James Boswell gave the credit for the Society's about-turn to Samuel Johnson. Boswell wrote:

> It seems some political members of the Society in Scotland for Propagating Christian knowledge had opposed the pious undertaking, as tending to preserve the distinction between the Highlanders and Lowlanders. Dr Johnson wrote a long letter to a friend, which, being shown to them, made them ashamed, and afraid of being publicly exposed; so they were forced to a compliance. It is now in my possession and is, perhaps, one of the best productions of his masterly pen.[87]

Gaelic culture may well have received a boost from this most unexpected quarter! At any rate, by the 1770s the SSPCK could claim to have made considerable progress in the 'civilization' of the Gaels, which involved education, evangelization, the instilling of 'loyalty', and not least, the continuing attack on Roman Catholicism. According to a pamphlet published in 1774, the schools had 'wrought change in many places: ignorance hath been in a great measure dispelled; the English language hath made considerable progress; the arts of civilization have been in some degree introduced; and thousands have been educated in the principles of loyalty and the Protestant religion, who lately fought the battles and extended to distant parts of the world the glory of Britain'.[88] The SSPCK considered itself to be in the vanguard of opposition to Roman Catholicism (as well as non-juring Episcopacy) in the Highlands and Islands. Almost thirty years after Culloden, the Catholic Church in Scotland had lost any rebellious intentions it may have had; but in the Society's fund-raising pamphlets it played upon anti-Catholic sentiments to elicit support. Sectarian hatred remained strong enough for anti-Catholic riots to break out in the towns of the Lowlands in the 1770s. 'When Popery, the foe of liberty, which enslaves the mind, and corrupts the heart, is making daily and too successful attempts on our fellow-subjects; shall Protestant brethren, and countrymen, not use every effort to diffuse the principles of a religion which alone makes loyal subjects, useful citizens, and good men?'[89] It was as if the minds of Gaels were empty vessels into which loyalty and patriotism, good habits and religious beliefs could be 'infused'. The SSPCK argued that it was the means of such a reformation, for its 'invariable objects' had been

> . . . to spread the knowledge of the English language among the natives of the Highlands and Islands; to infuse into their minds sentiments of loyalty to their Sovereign, and of love to their country; to train up their children in the principles of the true Protestant Reformed religion, and to make them useful members of the community, by early forming them to habits of industry and virtue . . .[90]

The state of 'civilization' and religion in the 1790s

The *Statistical Account*, edited by Sir John Sinclair and published from 1791 to 1799, is useful in determining the extent to which the various efforts at 'civilizing' the Gaels were successful. Compiled about fifty years after the Forty-Five, if anything it pointed to the fact that the process of reforming the Highlands and Islands after the Lowland fashion was an uneven one. As was to be expected, the areas more accessible by land and sea to the Lowlands changed more quickly. The Rev. David Dunoon, who provided the return for Killearnan in the Black Isle in 1794, reported that during the previous forty years the 'manners' of the people had 'undergone a very pleasing alteration'.[91] Before that time, 'the generality of the inhabitants were . . . ignorant in the extreme, and much disaffected towards our civil and ecclesiastical establishments'; but since the change, the churches were attended 'with regularity and devotion', and the people had learned 'not indeed the chearless refinements of modern Philosophy, but in the perusal of the gospel of peace, to find a healing balm to soothe and to comfort them under the pressure of all the calamities of life'.[92] According to the parish return of 1791 the people of Inverness had undergone a similar transformation. They were reportedly decent, regular in church attendance, well affected to the Government, neighbourly, and industrious, and among them 'instances of dissipation and profligacy' were rare.[93] Their customs and habits had undergone during the previous thirty years 'an alteration greatly to the better. Even the lower farmers and cottagers are by far more industrious than they were formerly, more cleanly in their persons and houses, and improved considerably in their apparel. They make a pleasing appearance on Sunday'.[94]

In a community such as Harris, it was a different story. According to the parish return provided by the Rev. John MacLeod in 1792, the remoteness of the place from the Lowlands was compounded by the scattered nature of the population. 'Unfortunately the people of this country are so detached from each other,' MacLeod wrote, 'that there is really no fixing on a station in which any one public institution can be of universal benefit. This circumstance in their local situation, is one great cause of the low state both of knowledge and industry in which we find them.'[95] The chronic shortage of qualified clergymen meant that for most people in Harris, public worship was a rare occasion. MacLeod admitted that the resulting religious state of the people was due to poor provision by the Church rather than their own shortcomings, arguing that the people were virtuous in a number of ways and capable of becoming good Christians once given the chance:

> Their vices are such as must be supposed, among a people professing Christianity, to proceed from difficulty of access to gospel ordinances, and from a total want of police. We would therefore spread a veil over them. They are more than counterbalanced by their virtues, almost the pure fruits of nature. They are sober, docile, sagacious, and capable of industry, were a channel opened to them in which industry might be profitably exerted. They are kind and courteous to strangers, hospitable and charitable even to excess. They have the strongest attachment to their native country, and entertain the most ardent gratitude to benefactors.[96]

North-west Sutherland was as remote from the Lowlands as Harris, but like the Campbells, the MacKays were 'loyal' (and staunchly Presbyterian since the reign of James VI) and therefore did not need to be 'civilized'. According to the Rev. Alexander Falconer's return of 1791–2, the people of Eddrachillis 'are all Presbyterians, and have been so, for so long a time back, that the present generation have no remembrance of seeing in the country any residenter of another persuasion'.[97] Despite their distance from the south, Falconer found the people to be 'remarkable for their attendance upon divine ordinances and public worship, for the sobriety and regularity of their manners and lives, without being addicted to any particular vice in any remarkable degree'.[98]

> Their character for peaceableness, and their harmony among them- selves, is uncommon. For the last 20 years and more, scarce one instance had happened of any of them receiving any bodily hurt from another . . . They love also to appear as decent and clean as possible; so that the fishers, who frequent this place, have declared they make the most decent and cleanly appearance of any Highlanders on the whole coast.[99]

In his return for the parish of Kintail in 1792, Roderick Morison reported that there were 654 Protestants but, alarmingly to him, 186 Roman Catholics as well.[100] The presbytery of Lochcarron had passed an act in 1778 which made the keeping of accurate baptismal registers mandatory, and to pay for this, all parents who wanted their children baptised were to pay one shilling. The result of this change, explained Morison, was that 'many of the most ignorant in Glenelchaig hearing of the new act, considered it as a heavy grievance; and, to avoid its consequence, applied to Roman Catholic priests for baptism, and in the heat of passion dragged whole families after them'.[101] Morison failed to consider, or refused to admit to, the possibility of Episcopalians choosing to become Catholic rather than Presbyterian. Another explanation was that the number of Catholics had increased as a result of intermarriage. 'When a Protestant man marries a Roman Catholic woman he has very little domestic peace or happiness till he profess that religion, in which, he is often told by the wife, salvation can only be expected. This is a web which catches many a silly fly.'[102] A third reason offered by Morison was a curious effect of the West Highland climate which he alleged the Catholic priests exploited in order to gain converts:

> It is to be regretted that the people are subject to low and melancholy fits, which (as is conjectured) arises from too much hazy and damp weather; on these occasions a priest, with whom the art of exorcism is supposed to be found, attends for relief to the distressed. If it happens that a kind providence thereafter removes the malady, the glory of the cure redounds to human frailty, and the pretended miracle becomes the ground and ostensible reason of conversion.[103]

The last reason given by Morison for the growing numbers of Catholics in his parish was simple ignorance, but he hoped that a school established by the SSPCK would remedy the situation. 'The people in the district of Glenelchaig,' he wrote, 'where Popery prevails most, are extremely ignorant, and easily become the dupes of trafficking priests.'[104] Morison expressed the hope that the SSPCK 'will soon appoint a school, whereby the blessings of knowledge may be more liberally diffused through this valley, which is in the near neighbourhood of a Popish district'.[105]

Evangelical religion and Gaeldom

The battle for the hearts and minds of the Gaels in the years after the Forty-Five was inconclusive. With the death of Charles Edward Stuart in 1788, Episcopalian non-jurancy was a dead issue. Likewise, Roman Catholicism was fast losing its rebellious tag, and its reputation for 'loyalty' was further enhanced with the raising of the predominantly Catholic Glengarry Fencible Regiment in 1794. Episcopalian and Catholic clergy were thus enabled to consolidate their positions in north Argyll, and South Uist, Benbecula, and Barra. The Lowland-based interventionist bodies found the task of instructing the Gaels according to the tenets of the established church difficult, and while the Church of Scotland was dominant in the Highlands and Islands by the late eighteenth century as never before (largely due to the problems of the other churches), it was far from secure.

The Presbyterian establishment in the Highlands and Islands was largely unaffected by the first Secession of 1733 in which the Associate Presbytery was formed, or the second Secession of 1761 from which emerged the Relief Presbytery. The religious scene in the region was to be transformed not through the efforts of outside agencies but by a largely indigenous evangelical movement which in a relatively short time was joined by the majority of people in the Highlands and Islands. When the split between the Evangelical and Moderate factions became irreconcilable on a national scale with the Disruption of 1843, Gaels joined the Free Church in large numbers: the deepening split between the Evangelical and Moderate factions had come to represent the widening social divisions in Gaeldom as a whole.

The rise of evangelicalism can be traced largely to the work of local lay preachers and the educational schemes of the Gaelic school societies, combined with the growing popular dismay at some Kirk ministers' lack of interest in (or even connivance at) the injustices of eviction, clearance, poverty, and emigration.[106] The Moderate faction of the established church resented the threat posed by evangelicals to the religious *status quo* in Gaeldom; a modern corollary could be the Catholic church's reaction to the spread of 'liberation theology' in Central America, and in the 1980s, to the success of US-based 'televangelists' in gaining converts there. Evangelical religion acts to turn the attention of its adherents away from the injustices of worldly life and towards an afterlife, an effect which has its attractions for oppressed people.

Evangelicalism in the Highlands and Islands had both a spiritual and a social mission. In religion it stressed the reorganisation of ecclesiastical structures, strict observance of the Sabbath, the importance of catechism and family worship in the Gaelic language, and placed great emphasis upon the provision of Bibles, even if the Lowland-dominated General Assembly preferred the English-language version. In the social sphere, evangelicals sought to encourage piety and set out to reform Gaelic social customs such as the 'immoral' music, dancing, drunkenness and fighting that often surrounded baptisms, marriages and funerals, supposedly solemn occasions; evangelicals also attacked a lax sexual morality which permitted adultery and fornication to go unchecked. True to the Calvinist tradition, Highland evangelicals worked to suppress the remnants of paganism such as the telling of unchristian Fingalian stories.[107] While they may have been 'killjoys', the zeal with which they sought converts brought them success in a region where the more conventional approach of the established church had been characterised by more than a degree of complacency. The evangelical message offered the Gaels a sense of spiritual dignity at a time when their way of life was being torn apart by impersonal forces.

Two men who had considerable influence on the evangelical movement in the Highlands and Islands were the Haldane brothers, James and Robert. They were staunchly Calvinist lay preachers of the Baptist and Congregationalist tendency who organised Sunday schools, published evangelical tracts, conducted preaching tours throughout Scotland, and in 1805 claimed to have trained 200 lay preachers.[108] James Haldane, a former seaman, made a preaching tour of parts of the Highlands and Orkney in 1797. He raised the ire of Moderates there for his Antinomian views and his lack of formal credentials, but his outdoor revival meetings were well attended. He told the people that what they heard in the sermons in their local church was not the Gospel; rather, the Gospel was a message of election, assurance and salvation, and the Bible was the literal Word of God.[109] It is not surprising that James Haldane's appraisal of the religious state of the people of Inverness was less glowing than that of the Kirk ministers in the *Statistical Account*. Haldane wished for 'the revival of real religion in this place, if it shall please God to send zealous ministers among them, of which many of the people are truly desirous'.[110] While he was quick to criticise the lack of zeal of the Moderate-dominated established church, he commented favourably on the Gaels' thirst for 'real religion'. 'It is remarkable,' he wrote of the popularity of *Na Daoine* (or The Men, see below), 'to observe the number which flock to hear any of the neighbouring gospel ministers . . . It is not at all uncommon on such occasions to see three or four thousand people assemble in the open air to hear the word of life.'[111]

Niel Douglas made a similar tour in 1797. A Gaelic-speaking lay preacher, he was appointed by the Relief Synod (most of the original Relief Presbytery of the second Secession rejoined the established church in 1779 but the rest remained as the Relief Church or Synod) to inquire into the religious state of the Gaels. The Relief Synod was opposed to the lay patronage system and the links between Church and state.[112] It had devised a scheme to send Gaelic-speaking ministers to the Highlands 'to preach the Gospel', not in opposition to the SSPCK, it said, but 'to be fellow-labourers with them in the good cause of enlightening men in the knowledge of Christ'.[113] Douglas shared James Haldane's view of the inadequacy of the established church ministers: 'no sooner do you enter a company in the Highlands, than they begin to entertain you with the conduct of their clergy, they seem so full of the subject, and so disgusted in general at their manners'.[114] He found that this was the case 'not only with the common people, but even among the higher ranks, some of whom professed themselves ashamed and grieved at the inconsistencies, which they so often saw in persons of that sacred profession'.[115] The Seceders favoured the revival meeting to spread the Gospel, and Douglas used his ability to speak Gaelic to advantage at a rain-soaked open air assembly in Argyllshire in July 1797:

> The tears of many visibly flowed, notwithstanding their efforts to conceal them, and their deep sighs and moans might easily be heard. At the close numbers were overheard to say, The Lord, pity us; We have been all our days in ignorance. The very recollection of these circumstances deeply affects in transcribing them, and makes my bowels yearn afresh towards the poor people.[116]

Douglas wrote of Argyllshire, 'I had found a number of intelligent people here, some of them, I hope, real Christians',[117] and when he saw the people gathering for the meetings he was 'quite overcome with compassion for them'.[118] But his enthusiasm was not shared by his colleagues in Edinburgh. 'But it is so, that the mission to the Highlands seemed to excite very little public attention among them.'[119] He reflected that 'this surely could not arise from a sordid besotted spirit, because it was undertaken by Dissenters', nor was it due to 'disregard to our countrymen, as if their souls were less precious than the soul of an African, or an Otaheitan', or from 'a spirit of vain ambition, and the desire of human applause, as if a home-mission was not so much calculated to gratify this and its kindred passions, as a foreign one'.[120] Wherever the fault lay, Douglas was sure that the souls of many Gaels were in mortal danger; the Gaels deserved at least the same attention as was given to the 'heathens', but as things stood, 'publicans, harlots, and Heathens, are more easily prevailed on to come into the Kingdom of Heaven than they'.[121]

The activism and enthusiasm displayed by evangelicals both within the Church of Scotland and outside caused concern to the Moderates, who sought to maintain the *status quo* in all things religious and political. Moderatism gave unswerving support to the established order to the extent that many Moderate clergymen saw evangelicalism as a manifestation of the radicalism inspired by the French Revolution. As the Gaels were considered to be unsophisticated, it was feared that revival preachers might spread disaffection as the Roman Catholic priests were thought to have done years earlier.

Alexander Carlyle, minister of Inveresk, a Scottish Enlightenment worthy, and a leader of the Moderate faction, refused to allow an evangelical missionary to preach in Gaelic to the Highland soldiers stationed in his parish in 1795: 'these times of sedition and mutiny . . . require that every person in office should be left to do his own duty, and ... strangers should be cautious of intermeddling with the religious tenets or principles of any set of people, especially those of the army'.[122] If such a contemptuous attitude towards the Gaels existed among Moderates, it is understandable that support for the evangelicals should spread in the Highlands and Islands, not only among the adherents of the lay preachers but a growing number of Kirk ministers also. A pattern began to emerge in the early years of the nineteenth century of Evangelicals within the Church of Scotland pressing for a more active role in spreading the Gospel through Gaeldom, while the Moderates insisted that religious provision to the area was quite adequate.

An anonymous article in *Blackwood's Edinburgh Magazine* in May 1819 argued that the Gaels did not need the services of Secessionist missionaries because 'religion is among them and around them'.[123] Political or other causes might have caused a decline in knowledge, faith or observance among them, and they no doubt needed some assistance in spiritual matters, but it was unfair of some to accuse the established church of neglecting the Gaels; the prospect of relieving their 'state of ... ignorance' in comparison with the Lowlands was 'no very distant prospect'.[124] The moral and religious state of the Highlands and Islands was better than might be expected, and 'for ourselves, we cannot agree with those many pious persons who describe, in such dark and mysterious language, the utter oblivion into which true Christianity is there said to have sunk'.[125]

The writer went on to warn of the dangers of an uninformed opinion. 'We see them half-clothed, shrivelled, poor, speechless, and a-gaze; and we pursue our journey in pity of their abject state. But in doing so, it is possible that we may be the objects of pity far more than they.'[126] The Gaels did not need to be evangelised; though poor, ignorant and simple, they were Christians. The writer expressed the prevailing Moderate view of religious activism out-with the established church as dangerous. Seceders were not only spreading unsound doctrine and practices but could cause turmoil and even another split within the Kirk itself. Organisations with evangelical credentials but which were recognized by the Church of Scotland, such as the SSPCK or the Gaelic school societies, were more respectable and safer vehicles for civilising the Highlands and Islands.

In rejecting the charge often made by the Seceders that the religious provision of the established church was as poor as in a 'heathen' country, the writer correctly pointed out that the Gaels maintained their Christian beliefs through the oral tradition, and while it was 'indeed melancholy' that the Scriptures were handed down through the generations in this way, it was 'indeed the word of God' nevertheless. 'Is every Highlander who cannot read the Scriptures, therefore ignorant of what they contain? Assuredly not.' They were known for their astonishing feats of memory in poetry and genealogy, and while there might have been glens without a Bible, 'there are none without many of its holiest contents engraven on the hearts of some of its inhabitants'.[127]

The *Blackwood's Edinburgh Magazine* article included excerpts from a speech delivered by Dr Alexander Irvine, a leading Moderate who worked on the SSPCK's Gaelic Bible, to the General Assembly committee for the state of religion in the Highlands and Islands in 1818. Dr Irvine said that at a time when Britain and Europe were ignorant and barbarous, Gaeldom was the seat of religious knowledge. This was due to Columba's mission in Iona, 'whose light was never totally extinguished in the Highlands and Isles'.[128] He too attested to the oral tradition of religion amongst the Gaels. While Roman Catholicism was overthrown in the region, he said, and the vacuum was inadequately filled by the Church of Scotland, 'many of the people, from a sense of religious duty, retained and acquired knowledge, both to refute error, and defend truth. Their memory is wonderfully tenacious, and the more so, that they cannot always trust to art'; and perhaps referring to the oral tradition of *Na Daoine*, Dr Irvine reported that he had met people who could neither read nor write but 'who give an account of sermon almost verbatim; who could tell the contents of a chapter of the gospel they heard once read; who could repeat many of the Psalms and their own sacred songs, and many passages of the Bible, with wonderful propriety and accuracy'.[129] He admitted that while the Roman Catholic priests 'taught errors not yet altogether eradicated from among Protestants, they propagated most diligently the fundamental truths of the gospel, as I had often an opportunity of observing'.[130]

Dr Irvine was less complimentary about the missionary efforts of the Seceders whom he belittled for their lack of proper – i.e. established church – credentials. Their 'unstudied, incoherent, unguarded, and often fantastic' sermons had no other aim but 'to make them proselytes of terror'.[131] He informed the General Assembly that the effect of the missionaries on the people under their sway was anything but 'tranquil'. 'Many of the converts,' he said, 'became emaciated and unsocial. The duties of life were abandoned.'[132] They had become 'sullen, morose, and discontented', and 'some of them began to talk of their high privileges, and their right, as the elect few, to possess the earth, that is, to dispossess every one but their faction'.[133]

It was certainly lamentable to see poor children starving and roaring for bread, when their parents were perhaps twenty miles off attending a conventicle. The business of the farm was neglected; the rent fell behind. The landlord was pronounced unchristian, because he insisted on his dues, and because, upon their refusing to pay them, he declined having such tenants.[134]

Dr Irvine implied that at least some of the Clearances were due to the meddling of the evangelical 'interlopers' – the Seceders caused only chaos. He had more horror stories to relate. 'And to add to the mischief, families became scenes of discord and disorder, which none but an eye-witness can comprehend. All this was termed religion.' And hinting that the entire social order in the Highlands and Islands was under threat, he said: 'Unless parents became converts to the Missionary or Independent scheme' (which could include Baptists and Congregationalists as well as the more orthodox Seceders), 'their authority ceased; the children were taught to disobey them as a duty; so were servants their masters'.[135] Irvine and other Moderates valued church unity above all else and did not object to religious missions to the Gaels provided that they were led by the Kirk or some other 'official' body. The Moderates believed that if a problem did exist, it could be solved simply by the improved provision of churches and ministers. They did not give much thought to the actual wants of the people; and they held the prevailing Lowland attitude shared by interventionist bodies such as the Annexed Estates Board, the SSPCK, and others, that the Gaels were incapable of 'civilizing' themselves. Yet, in the end it was not by the efforts of these bodies that religious life in the Highlands was transformed, but rather as the result of an indigenous evangelical movement which inspired the Gaelic school societies and most importantly the lay preachers known as *Na Daoine*.

The provision of schools: the Gaelic school societies and others

A powerful tool of Highland evangelicalism was created with the founding of the Edinburgh Society for the Support of Gaelic Schools in 1811. It had the objective of rescuing the Gaels 'from a depth of ignorance, which exposed to the most imminent peril multitudes of their immortal souls'.[136]

It sought to address a problem that had plagued previous attempts by the SSPCK and others to educate the Gaels – the language barrier. In common with the SSPCK, its chief aim was to spread the Gospel through the operation of ambulatory schools but, together with a non-denominational approach, it departed from the norm with a policy of teaching the people to read the Bible in Gaelic. The founders of the Society were careful to acknowledge that the efforts of the SSPCK had been 'highly beneficial, as a means of promoting civilization and Christian knowledge in the Highlands and Islands',[137] but although the SSPCK was maintaining 290 schools at which nearly 16,000 young people were taught, they observed, 'it is a melancholy fact that many parts of the Highlands and Islands continue in a state of great ignorance, and that only a small proportion of the inhabitants can read in any language'.[138] The founders resolved that the people of the 'more highly favoured' parts of Scotland were bound 'both by consideration of patriotism and of religion, to exert themselves for ameliorating the temporal and spiritual condition of these highly interesting, but hitherto neglected parts of their native country'.[139]

To accomplish this aim, the Society resolved that 'the most expeditious, cheapest, and most effectual method of promoting the instruction of the inhabitants of the Highlands and Islands, is the erection of Circulating Schools, for the express purpose of instructing them in the Gaelic language', and that the only objective 'shall be to teach the inhabitants to read the Holy Scriptures in their native language'.[140] The Society further resolved to confine its attention 'to those parts of the Highlands and Islands which are more destitute of education'.[141] To emphasise that the Society was to be composed of lay people, and perhaps also to ensure that no religious schism would divide its ranks, the founders resolved that their teachers 'shall neither be Preachers nor Public Exhorters, stated or occasional, of any denomination whatever'.[142] It was to gain the popular title *Na Sgoilean Chriosd* (the Schools of Christ).[143]

The Edinburgh Gaelic School Society's ambitious plan was greeted enthusiastically by evangelicals, and auxiliaries were soon formed in Inverness and Glasgow, which in contrast to the parent body adopted a bilingual policy. The Sixth Annual Report of the Edinburgh Society included a testimonial from the Rev. John Shaw, minister of Bracadale on Skye, who believed that its plan was the best yet devised for extending religious knowledge to the Gaels and that it would bring them not only salvation but would tend 'greatly to promote civilization in the uncultivated tracts to which it is directed'.[144] He had no doubt that the name of the Society would be 'long cherished among the hills of the North, after it has ceased from its labours, as the best benefactor of the inhabitants; yea, and with respect to many souls, its memorial shall be held in everlasting remembrance'.[145] In another testimonial to the Edinburgh Society, the Rev. Shaw wrote: 'The blessing of the present generation that was ready to perish, is coming upon you, and it is impossible to calculate how many, in future ages, will arise and glorify God in your behalf'.[146] None of the Gaelic school societies was primarily concerned with spreading literacy or preserving the Gaelic language or even promoting educational advancement: they were in the business of saving souls. Shaw believed that the endeavour was contributing in its own way to rehabilitating the Gaels: 'It brings to bear upon them, that mighty engine of civilization, comfort, and holiness – the Scriptures, pure and unadulterated. Go on, then, and prosper; and may the Lord stir up many, that shall be able and willing to help you in these labours of love'.[147]

The Edinburgh body received a further testimonial from the Rev. Alexander Stewart, minister of Dingwall and translator of the Old Testament into Gaelic. He reported that through their children, parents were becoming evangelised, and 'thus the walls of the cottage were illuminated by the taper which was lighted in the School'.

> Prayer has been introduced into families, where no form of devotion existed before: Swearers, liars, and drunkards, have appeared to stand in awe of their own children, knowing how they had been taught at School, to abhor these vices as sins which provoke the wrath of God, and drown the soul in perdition.[148]

In its desire to spread the Gospel through the Highlands and Islands by the most efficient means, the Edinburgh Gaelic School Society taught its students to read and write Gaelic using only religious texts. Subjects were excluded which other educators would have considered essential, such as English or arithmetic, and perhaps we need look no further to discover the reason why Gaelic did not develop into a commercial or technical language. While teaching Gaels to read and write in the language was (and remains) important, an opportunity to expand Gaelic into the new fields of knowledge that came with the Industrial Revolution was not seized. As one writer has put it, 'these schools seem to us now not so much an educational achievement as an educational opportunity lost'.[149] However, the Glasgow and Inverness auxiliaries, although smaller and less influential that their Edinburgh parent, decided to include English and arithmetic in their curricula. The Glasgow Society instructed its teachers to establish whether a prospective student could read the Gaelic Bible; if not, then this deficiency was to be corrected before advancing onto other subjects: no student was to be taught anything 'without being able, first, to read the Scriptures in the vernacular tongue'.[150]

Regardless of their shortcomings, the strength of the Gaelic school societies lay in their extention of the benefits of education to girls and illiterate adults, their ability to reach even the remotest areas, and their non-denominational approach to education which sought inclusion of all persuasions, including Roman Catholics. In time the Catholic clergy co-operated with the various schemes – perhaps they supported the change towards morality and piety that the schools engendered. The Rev. Anthony McDonald, a priest on the Isle of Eigg, wrote a letter in 1821 commending the work of the Edinburgh Society:

> In this very Island, I can testify that a wonderful change has been produced on the habits of the people; their improvement in morals is more visible and striking; formerly they devoted the Sabbath entirely to idle conversation or frivolous amusements, as they had nothing of serious nature to engage their attention, but now they regularly attend Divine worship, and read the Scriptures in their private families. In many instances the parents are instructed by their children, by hearing them read the Word of God, in their native language.[151]

The Education Act of 1803 sought to cope with the changing distribution of the Scottish population but it was as ineffectual in the Highlands and Islands as in the growing industrial centres of the Lowlands. In order to assess the shortcomings of the existing system, a parliamentary select committee on the education of 'the poor' published in 1818 the replies to a questionnaire sent to parish ministers throughout Britain. These revealed that the provision of education varied widely, and generally the areas more accessible to the Lowlands were better provided. The Rev. H. Fraser, minister of the consolidated parishes of Ardchattan and Muckairn, wrote that in his area 'the poorer classes have even more ample means of education than most of the parishes in the county; a desire for which is common to the whole of the Highlands, who generally labour under a disadvantage of distance'.[152] Similarly, the Rev. Hugh McDougall, minister of Killin on Lochtayside, reported that 'the poorer classes have the best opportunities of educating their children, as they are not only taught free, but generally have their books supplied gratis'.[153] The situation in more outlying areas was altogether different. The Rev. Donald McLean of the Small Isles parish wrote of the situation on Rum, Canna, Eigg, and Muck: 'The poor are miserably deficient in the means of education; the parish consists of four islands very much separated, it is impossible for all children to attend, although earnestly desirous of doing so'.[154] According to the Rev. Alex Bethune of Harris, 'the poorer classes are without the means of education, and most of them are very desirous of possessing them'.[155]

It is evident from the returns to the select committee inquiry that there was an increasing demand for better educational provision in Gaeldom, but poverty and poor communications remained formidable barriers. The Rev. William McRae, minister of Barvas (Lewis), reported that due to the size of the parish, one-fifth of the children could not attend the school, and those who could 'are scarcely able to pay any fees'. However, he found that parents were 'very desirous of having their children educated', which McRae believed was evidenced by the popularity of the Gaelic society schools.[156] The Rev. James Russell, minister of Gairloch in Wester Ross, wrote that the means of education in his parish were insufficient due to the scattered nature of the population, but wrote that prior to the introduction of the schools 'a great apathy prevailed among the lower classes to the advantages of instruction', but as the benefits of education became known 'their sentiments have undergone a complete change, and they are now as zealous as they were formerly indifferent about the education of their children'.[157]

The chronically poor provision of education in the Highlands and Islands was confirmed by a survey conducted in 1826 by the Inverness Society for Educating the Poor in the Highlands, the Inverness auxiliary Gaelic school society. It revealed that despite the existence of 171 parish schools, 134 SSPCK schools, 77 Edinburgh Gaelic School Society schools, 48 schools of the Glasgow auxiliary and 65 Inverness auxiliary schools, only half of the estimated demand for education was being met.[158] After their initial period of growth, the Gaelic school societies began to experience funding problems as a result of the post-1815 recession; in the 1820s, the General Assembly of the Church of Scotland was spurred on by its Evangelical faction to join the list of organisations operating schools in the Highlands and Islands and in 1824 appointed a committee to inquire into the existing means of education and religious instruction in the region. The inquiry demonstrated 'a deplorable want of schools and catechists in many parts of the Highlands and Islands' and spoke of securing 'the sympathy and liberality of the benevolent, for the remedy of this evil'.[159] After studying the committee's report, the General Assembly released a statement that echoed the words of the parish ministers taking part in the parliamentary inquiry in 1818: '*Many* children, it is stated in the returns of the clergy, are prevented from attending a school by their distance from it, and by the poverty disqualifying parents for paying the school fees, or purchasing school books; but *few* or *none* are prevented by indifference'.[160]

The General Assembly acted upon the committee's findings by setting up another committee dedicated to increasing the provision of education and religious instruction. By 1829 this new committee could boast in a report to the General Assembly of an establishment of 85 schools with over 6000 pupils. Of these, '2512 were learning to read Gaelic; 5491 English; 3057 Writing and Arithmetic; 63 Book-keeping; 114 Latin;

57 Geography, and 76 Practical Mathematics or Mensuration'.[161] The committee had also wished to extend its efforts 'for the purpose of instructing the female youth in the branches proper to their sex', but was unable to do so because of financial constraints. However, it expressed the wish that 'both sexes should be instructed in the branches that were common to both, than one in the branches peculiar to itself'.[162]

The committee had also sought to extend the benefits of education to another neglected group: Roman Catholics. According to the committee, a considerable proportion of its pupils were Catholic children who were not forced to learn anything that was against the wishes of their parents and their priests. They attended the schools 'without jealousy, or reluctance, and receive every branch of literary instruction in the same classes with the Protestants, from the same school-books, and without any sort of distinction betwixt the two denominations', but the committee resolved that the schools' religious instruction was to adhere exclusively to the tenets of the established church, adding that 'the Catholic children are invited to participate so far as their advisers may think proper to direct them'.[163] The participation of Catholics in the General Assembly schools, as well as in the Gaelic society schools, would never have been possible without the assent and co-operation of priests.

The grinding poverty of the Gaels proved to be a serious barrier to the committee's efforts. A letter to the committee by Kingussie schoolmaster William McPhail stated that while the price of the required schoolbooks was beyond the means of many pupils, the parents were willing to do without the necessities of life in order to have their children educated. McPhail elaborated further:

> The very richest here, if there are any more so than others, are so far from being able to pay fees, that it is no uncommon thing for their children to shun school because their parents cannot purchase the necessary school books; and the parents, in this situation, offer me part of their subsistence in barter for the book, though that subsistence is often far too scanty for themselves. They will offer me a daily part of their small, and in winter their rare, pittance of milk and potatoes, which are their only food, – sometimes dearly imported by them from a distance. Though equally necessitous myself, I cannot always be prevailed on to accept of those contributions.[164]

By the 1820s the SSPCK had expanded its activities to include the publishing of Gaelic books and had also established Raining's School, a teacher-training college at Inverness. Patrick Butter, an inspector of schools for the Society, complained in 1824 than in many cases schoolmasters could not speak Gaelic despite the fact that their pupils understood nothing else. 'The plain consequence,' he wrote, 'is that in the great majority of instances the education of the poor highlander comes in the result actually to nothing.'[165] Butter discovered a preference among parents not only for the teaching of the English language but also for its use as the medium of instruction. He explained this as arising from a desire to become bilingual; the Gaelic school societies of Inverness and Glasgow had a bilingual policy, and certainly the Gaels increasingly saw English as the language of economic improvement and advancement in general. (One wonders if they could have been convinced of the unsuitability or inferiority of their own language by the non-Gaelic speaking schoolmasters themselves.) Butter suggested that this attitude might have arisen from the people's 'sensible perception of a want in this particular whenever they come into contact with any person from the South or when they happen to go southward on business', which produced a resolve to be taught English 'if they are to attend school at all'.[166]

The well-named John Tawse, another SSPCK schools inspector, visited the school at Helmsdale in 1827. Of the pupils, he wrote: 'I was very much pleased with their appearance and with the manner in which they went through their exercises,' and the children 'read and repeated with great accuracy, and several of them seemed to have a considerable knowledge of grammar and they answered the questions in the shorter catechism very readily ...'[167] Tawse found, however, that the people of Helmsdale 'seem to be very indifferent about religion, more so than even in most fishing villages', and reported that the parents laughed at the teacher when he asked them to send their children to the Society's Sabbath school.[168] Tawse threatened the parish minister with the removal of the SSPCK school unless the Sabbath school were better attended, and wrote a letter on the subject 'with the view of its being shewn to the Marchioness of Stafford'.[169]

Three years later, Tawse inspected the school at Stornoway and was well pleased with what he found. He had 'every reason to be satisfied with the appearance and proficiency of the Scholars', and reported that they could read and write well in English and Gaelic. They performed well in the shorter catechism and Scripture history and understood 'the principles and leading doctrines of Christianity'; on the whole the schools had made 'as respectable an appearance as I could have wished, and much better than I expected'.[170] By 1830, the people of Lewis had been thoroughly evangelised, and their preference for the more vigorous forms of Presbyterianism has shown no sign of abating since. By way of explaining how a formerly 'uncivilized' people had become so accomplished, Tawse wrote:

> It is well known that a few years ago, a great awakening took place among the people in the Lewis, and so much alive are they to the necessity of religion and personal piety, that a person who does not possess not only personal piety but great devotion of character will not be esteemed as a Teacher in the Island, and his weight influence and example would be much lost.[171]

Tawse was far less impressed with the school at Kilmaluag, in the parish of Kilmuir in Trotternish, Skye, which he inspected the same year. Education suffered from the inaccessibility of the school in a rugged area, a problem compounded by a 'very great indifference on the part of the people to the education of their children, and to the religious instruction of themselves and their families'.[172] He hinted that too little effort was being made to remedy this indifference 'by those whose more immediate duty it is'.[173] Meanwhile, the SSPCK pressed on with its plans for educating girls. Patrick Butter had found that parents considered the role of education to be that of 'enabling the scholar to migrate from his native country', and as females were not thought capable of holding office or acquiring a fortune, 'their attendance on school is deemed an unnecessary waste of time'.[174] But in 1830 John Tawse visited an itinerant sewing school at Balmacara, Lochalsh and found the girls there 'variously employed in all different kinds of needle work, some of it very fine, while one was generally employed reading some edifying book aloud'.[175] The schoolmistress had made 'a most remarkable change in the neatness order and habits of the people',[176] and the establishment of more schools such as the one at Balmacara 'would do more for improving the habits and manners of the females in the Highlands than any other local institution I have yet seen'.[177] As the skills taught by the school had no other application than in the factories of the Lowlands or beyond, the education offered acted as an intended spur to migration. Tawse's belief that the 'habits and manners' of Highland girls and women needed special attention indicates that their rehabilitation had yet to occur.

The state of 'civilization' and religion in the 1820s

By the 1820s the Gaels were indeed becoming 'civilized'. Where people in the Highlands and Islands had been illiterate and ignorant before, they were now renowned for their enthusiasm for education; and where people had been for the most part only nominally Protestant, they were now on the way to becoming the most vehement Calvinists in Scotland.

This change was increasingly reflected in the attitudes of Lowlanders towards Highlanders – adjectives such as 'barbarian' and 'pagan' were rarely used, and comparisons between the Gaels and the 'savages' of North America and elsewhere were made less frequently.

There were some Lowlanders, however, who continued to view the state of the Highlands and Islands with some alarm. In 1820 the Associate Synod, the remnant of the Associate Presbytery of the first Secession, devised a plan to provide 'a more abundant and regular supply of the means of religious and moral improvement to the destitute inhabitants of the Highlands and Islands'.[178] The Synod seemed to dismiss all but its own previous efforts in explaining the necessity of the plan. It remarked upon

> the disproportion of the instructors to the population, especially when the geographical situation of the country is considered, – the deficiencies (to use the softest term) of many of the existing instructors, – the prevalence of Roman Catholic superstition, the ignorance and immorality which generally prevails among the inhabitants, – the anxious desire which many of the inhabitants are discovering for instruction, and the important advantages which have already resulted from occasional itinerant exertions.[179]

In the view of the Associate Synod, the spiritual condition of the Highlands and Islands was still poor. This opinion was shared by the Rev. John Macdonald when he visited St Kilda, the most remote of the Hebrides, in 1822 and again in 1824. His visits were made under the auspices of the SSPCK, and despite the fact that the Society had established a school there as early as 1711, the Rev. Macdonald found that the St Kildans 'cannot read, and how to pray they know not . . .'[180] His attitude toward the people of St Kilda was similar to that of other churchmen-explorers of the nineteenth century when encountering 'barbaric' people. He discovered that the St Kildans

> . . . are fond of receiving and relating news. [I] endeavoured to gratify them as much as I could; and they, in return, entertained me with all the little tales of their island. I found that this gave me readier access to their minds, and enabled me with better effect to introduce, now and then, something about religion; for as yet we were not yet sufficiently prepared for entering fully on that subject . . .[181]

When the Rev. Macdonald did gain access to the minds of the people with regard to religion, he found that 'their views respecting it are rather defective, and in many important points extremely inaccurate'.[182] He was 'agreeably surprised at finding that they could repeat many of the questions of the shorter catechism', although he believed 'they under-stood little of the meaning of them'.[183] In addition to the St Kildans' spiritual shortcomings, the Rev. Macdonald wrote: 'I fear they cannot be exempted from the charge of almost habitual *indolence*'.[184] However, he believed that familiarity with the Scriptures would cure both evils. 'How desirable on this, as well as on many other accounts, that they might become savingly acquainted with that Gospel, which teaches its true subjects, to be Diligent in Business, Fervent in Spirit, Serving the Lord! In this as in many other respects, they admit of much improvement.'[185]

A more objective attempt to assess the progress of 'civilization' among the Gaels was made in 1826 with the publication of *Moral Statistics of the Highlands and Islands of Scotland*, a survey conducted by the Inverness Society for the Education of the Poor in the Highlands. The survey indicated that only one-half of all Gaels were literate. In the Hebrides and western parts of Inverness-shire and Ross-shire, 70 per cent were illiterate; in the remaining parts of those counties, and in Sutherland, Cromarty, and the Highland parts of Moray, Nairn, and Caithness, 35 per cent were illiterate; and in Argyll and Highland Perthshire, 30 per cent of the people were illiterate. The survey further discovered that in the western parts of Inverness-shire and Ross-shire, there was one copy of the Bible for every person over eight years of age, while in other parts of the Highlands and Islands, there was an average of only one Bible for every three people.[186] While it highlighted the extent of illiteracy in Gaeldom, by revealing the fact that the supply of Bibles had outstripped literacy, the survey illustrated the increasing desire for education among the Gaels: people were procuring Bibles in anticipation of learning to read them.

The evangelical emphasis upon morality was not being forgotten. *An Account of the Present State of Religion throughout the Highlands of Scotland*, an anonymous essay written by an evangelical layman of the established church in 1827, contrasted the state of morals and religion in Skye before and after the arrival of evangelical religion. Before that time, 'gross ignorance of spiritual matters abounded among the inhabitants, [and] ignorance of this kind is invariably accompanied with debasing superstition: and so it was in Skye'.[187] In addition, the people of Skye were addicted to profane language:

> The first speech uttered by children was mixed with curses and oaths; and how could it be otherwise, when their parents habitually indulged themselves in this vice, and set the example to their offspring? It has been reckoned that upwards of sixty oaths and imprecations were used in the island. The language of the father to the obstinate child was, 'Devil take you.' The wife would curse the husband. The children would curse one another, and their neighbours. When they did not approve of the weather, they would curse the wind, the rain, and the snow. They would *damn to the devil* the shoes and clothes they wore.[188]

Before they were evangelised, the people of Skye were lewd: 'This sin abounded to an extraordinary degree among them. We shall avoid details which here might be given, as they would greatly shock morality'.[189] The people seemed to prefer secular to spiritual pursuits, and even on the Sabbath this was the case: 'Much precious time that might have been profitably spent in acquiring useful and Christian knowledge, was spent by the inhabitants of Skye on the most useless trifles. They were most indolent and negligent in temporal concerns, but much more so in spiritual matters'.[190] People spent much of their time enjoying poetry and Fingalian stories: 'even on the Sabbath evenings they would group together for this purpose, and for other amusements quite unlawful on that day'.[191] Non-observance of the Sabbath was common among them, and 'in going to, and retiring from sermon, the conversation was exclusively of a worldly nature. In Skye, after sermon some would resort to the public house, and not in a few instances would remain there until they became intoxicated, and closed the scene with a battle'.[192]

For most Christians, funerals are solemn events. For the Gaels, they were once occasions of much singing, dancing, drinking, and fighting. According to the nineteenth-century antiquarian Charles Fraser-Mackintosh, funerals were often used as opportunities for settling old scores. He related an episode in December 1814 when a number of Glenelg men, 'from time immemorial ... notorious amongst the rest of the neighbourhood for their savage deeds', seized upon the opportunity provided by the funeral of a local woman to attack a party of Lochalsh men who had also attended the funeral.[193] Such behaviour was to be drastically altered by the evangelicals, who often pointed to such practices when discussing the barbarities of the past. The essayist described the attitudes on Skye concerning funerals before the arrival of evangelical religion:

> Some free enough to acknowledge that they experienced delight at hearing of the death of a man or a woman, because of the prospect it afforded them of getting their full of whisky. The friends of the deceased were particularly anxious to solemnize the funeral with a great feast. This woeful and barbarous practice was so general, and of so long standing, that persons when arrived at old age, manifested a great anxiety to lay by a certain sum of money against their funeral. And upon their death-beds, while indifferent about the state of their souls, they would not forget matters regarding their funeral; often expressing that they could not be happy unless men were drunk and fought at their funerals.[194]

The religious and moral situation on Skye was to change in 1805, when a Mr Farquharson, a lay missionary of the evangelical Society for Propagating the Gospel at Home, visited the island. According to the essayist, 'Mr Farquharson's sermons were very pointed and justly severe against the sins that overspread the island'.[195] The parish minister of Kilmuir became an evangelical in response to the preacher's sermon; monthly meetings were instituted; and the demand for Bibles increased to the point where the minister procured a supply from the Bibles Society in London.[196] Not all of the lay preacher's efforts were beneficial, however: 'In the year 1812, by means of these meetings, an uncommon awakening [was] attended with distress and trembling, and some were so affected as to cry out'.[197] The essayist pointed to the extreme reactions of the more acutely affected people:

> During the space of six months a considerable number of persons who before were ignorant and careless were awakened. Yet offences ensued because of two reasons; first, because many of those who were awakened apostatized and went back to their former ways; second because there were some among those who were awakened, particularly females, who became fanatical in the proper sense of the term.
>
> They pretended to have dreams and visions, and to have received a spirit of penetration, which enabled them to foretell who should be saved, and who not. A few of these were at this time so positive in their own conceit, of the certainty of what they affirmed, that they neither could be advised nor reasoned out of it by the most intelligent Christians around them.[198]

Evangelical religion was to have an impact on Skye, but in 1827 the essayist was moved to write that 'the great mass of the population ... still remain ignorant and unconcerned about their everlasting interests', and despite the years of work by the SSPCK, Gaelic school societies, lay preachers and others in the most 'unenlightened' parts of the islands, the state of morality had not improved since 1805 in proportion to the improvement in literacy and the supply of Bibles.[199] But then, evangelicals are not easily satisfied. The writer blamed the failure on the scarcity of evangelical ministers and teachers and the poor support given by parish ministers to the Gaelic schools. He also reported that the revelry surrounding funerals, complete with drinking, fighting and piping, had persisted: 'If true religion had made any considerable progress among them, these heathenish practices would have been banished from these parishes'.[200]

In the end, it was an indigenous movement that won the Highlands and Islands for evangelicalism. It could be argued that an evangelical tradition had existed in the Highlands and Islands since the days of Columba, but the modern emergence of evangelical religion in Skye, the northern Highlands and the Western Isles can be traced to *Na Daoine*, or The Men, a group which gained importance in the early years of the nineteenth century, and in Argyll and Highland Perthshire to a number of evangelical Gaelic poets who gained a considerable following. *Na Daoine* have been described as 'spiritual tacksmen': a class of lay leaders whose extensive knowledge of the Scriptures and aura of spirituality together with an ability to preach to large numbers in Gaelic won many converts for the cause of evangelical Presbyterian religion. Ever fearful of schism, the established church wished to discourage such 'unofficial' preachers. In 1749, the Presbytery of Tongue wrote of the fellowship meetings held by *Na Daoine*: 'There are in the several parishes some who take it upon themselves to read the Scriptures and other books in the Irish language, and to solve doubts of conscience at these meetings'. The presbytery, fearing that the lay preachers' lack of training might cause harm, and mindful of its monopoly on religious matters, prohibited 'any to convene the people to reading and conference' unless the parish minister's permission were obtained.[201] *Na Daoine* were not loved by estate proprietors or the Moderate clergy, and for their part, their antipathy towards Moderatism and lay patronage earned them few friends in the establishment; one of their number, Murdo Macdonald of Bayble, gained notoriety when he prayed to God for the removal of the Moderate ministers of Lewis and two of them died within the year.[202] *Na Daoine* wore flowing cloaks and long hair, and were fond of mystical expressions; some of them reputedly possessed the Second Sight.[203] Undoubtedly powerful in prayer and strict in their piety,[204] they told of having great encounters with Satan in which, naturally, they triumphed.[205]

A number of *Na Daoine* were teachers for the Edinburgh Gaelic Schools Society and its auxiliaries,[206] and together with the evangelical poets of the eighteenth and nineteenth centuries they helped to develop the Gaelic language as a medium for evangelicalism.

Gaelic poetry and Highland identity

Gaels have always expressed their thoughts in poetry, and their ideas about themselves can often be found there. In the past, religious Gaels complained of the earthy nature of their literature which praised the heroic, violent and overtly sexual aspects of life. John Carswell, the first Protestant bishop of Argyll and translator of the Book of Common Order (*Foirm na n-Urrnuidheadh*) in 1567, the first book printed in Scottish Gaelic, decried what he saw as

> . . . the blindness and darkness of sin and ignorance and of understanding among composers and writers and supporters of the Gaelic, in that

they prefer and practise the framing of vain, hurting, lying, earthly stories about Tuath de Dhanond, and about the sons of Milesius, and about the heroes of Fionn Mac Cumhail with his giants ... rather than to write and to compose and to support the faithful words of God and the perfect way of truth.[207]

The conflict between the religious and the secular in Gaelic poetry was to intensify in the eighteenth century, a time when Gaeldom as a whole underwent traumatic change. The Rev. Alexander Pope, minister of Reay in Strathnaver, was a collector of Ossianic ballads, and wrote in 1763 of the attempts by the Presbyterian clergy to suppress them: 'Many of them indeed are lost, partly owing to our clergy, who were declared enemies to these poems; so that the rising generation scarcely know anything material about them'.[208] Pope was a friend and admirer of the Gaelic poet Rob Donn (1714–1778), also of Strathnaver. Like Pope, Rob Donn was a Presbyterian, but that did not prevent him from writing poetry of a decidedly secular nature. This work found a censor in the Rev. Dr Mackintosh Mackay, an evangelical who edited an 1829 collection of Rob Donn's poetry. In his introduction to the collection, Mackay wrote unashamedly:

We have to acknowledge the blame or merit of having suppressed a few of the bard's humorous sallies, which seemed to us of immoral tendency, or at least unworthy of record. To those who feel disposed to censure this suppression, we tender no apology whatever.[209]

With the coming of evangelical religion to the Highlands and Islands, changes in the Gaelic character were reflected in poetry. A poetic example of the old Gaelic order can be found in the work of Alexander MacDonald, also known as *Alasdair Mac Mhaighstir Alasdair* (c. 1700–1770). The best-known of the eighteenth-century Gaelic poets, MacDonald was a teacher and catechist for the SSPCK (for whom he compiled a Gaelic dictionary) until he deserted his post to rally to the Jacobite cause. His Jacobite poetry was the eighteenth-century equivalent of a military recruiting advertisement. One poem, 'A New Song' (or *Oran Nuadh*), is a call to arms which praises the qualities of the Highland warrior – recklessness, courage, loyalty, and even bloodthirstiness:

> A warrior stout, of sturdy build,
> White-handed, vigorous, active,
> With bagpipes thrust beneath his arm
> Awakes our warlike passions,
> With tunes both sweet and spirit-rousing
> Urging us to slaughter,
> The music of his stirring airs,
> Would fire our reckless spirits.[210]

A contemporary of Alexander MacDonald was John MacCodrum, or *Iain Mhic Fhearchair* (1693–1779). MacCodrum was a *seanchaidh* (oral historian and genealogist) in the old Gaelic tradition, and in something of an antiquarian exercise was appointed bard to Sir James MacDonald of Sleat in 1763. The chief died three years later, and his successor, the Eton-educated Sir Alexander (later Lord) Macdonald was of the new breed of Highland chief who had little time for the trappings of clanship.[211] MacCodrum was a Jacobite as well as a Presbyterian; he belonged to the old order but was 'civilized'. He was a survivor of an age that was at least symbolically destroyed at Culloden, and in the later years of his life he witnessed the emigration of many people from his native North Uist;[212] he was well-placed to comment upon the most uncertain time that had ever faced his people.

In his poetry can be found what has come to be the accepted response of the Gaels to the injustices of the Clearances, and in keeping with tradition, MacCodrum managed to avoid blaming the chiefs themselves directly. For their part, the common people were free from blame, in contrast to the belief promulgated by evangelical poets that such suffering was a form of divine punishment. In what is believed to be his last song, 'Song to the Fugitives' (*Oran do Na Fogarraich*),[213] the poet mourned the destruction of the traditional order but did not admit that 'the nobility without pity' was the Gaelic ruling elite itself:

> 'Tis a sad matter to consider, the land is being made dearer, our people have swiftly left and sheep have come in their place . . .

> . . . The warrior chiefs are gone who had a yearning for the truth, who had regard for their faithful followers and had a yoke of their foe; they were mindful of the tenantry, (and) not in order to fleece them; widows and orphans were liberally provided for; without want was every poor man around those heroes, who would not look low – their minds were too stately (for that).

> Look around you and see the nobility without pity for poor folk, without kindness to friend; they are of the opinion that you do not belong to the soil, and though they have left you destitute they cannot see it as a loss; they have lost sight of every law and promise that was observed by the men who took this land from the foe: but let them tell me whether they will not lose their right to it, without means of saving it, when you go into exile.[214]

If Alexander MacDonald and John MacCodrum represented the old Gaelic order, then Dugald Buchanan, or *Dughall Bochanan* (1716–1768), may be taken to represent the new. The evangelical poets were open to outside influences, and Buchanan is said to have been particularly influenced by the English evangelical preacher George Whitefield's second Scottish visit of 1742.[215] Buchanan is considered to be the outstanding Gaelic poet of the evangelical movement, and his poetry provides a counterpoint to MacDonald's warlike sentiments. As a twentieth-century editor of his poems explained, 'Buchanan knew well the weakness of his countrymen – their admiration for martial glory, their proneness to quick enthusiasm rather than steady self-control, their emotionalism, and their worship of personal prowess'.[216] Buchanan's poem 'The Hero' (*An Gaisgeach*) is the portrayal of a warrior, a Christian warrior, with many of the same virtues that Alexander MacDonald praised in his Jacobite poetry, but here they are spiritual not militaristic. As his editor put it, 'it was a courageous assault upon the inveterate paganism of a gallant race'.[217]

> It is not bravery to mangle men;
> It is not fame to be in combat oft;
> Barbaric pride is not nobility of soul;
> True valour is not fierceness without ruth.
>
> But hero true is he who wins,
> O'er Fears of life and dread of death;
> Who meets with an undaunted breast
> The share that Destiny upon him thrusts.[218]

As a Highland church historian of the old school once wrote, 'Buchanan and his fellow Evangelicals won the battle for the soul of the Highland people. In the generations that followed, the Christian warrior rather than the pagan hero became the accepted ideal'.[219] When Buchanan turned his attention to temporal affairs the results were rather less convincing. His poem 'The Skull' (*An Claigeann*) of c. 1764 has been cited by modern writers as an example of the evangelical response to the injustices experienced by the Gaels. It is a meditation on a skull thrown up by a gravedigger's spade and includes a reference to Gaeldom's erstwhile chiefs, who had now become greedy landlords, and to worldly and indifferent ministers, presumably those of the Moderate faction:

> Or a lord of the land
> Do I hold in my hand,
>   Whose acres were fertile and wide,
> Who was generous and good,
> And clothing and food
> To the naked and needy supplied?
>
> Or wert thou wont to flay
> Those under thy sway,

Ever grinding the peasants with rent,
And pressing them sore,
Arresting their store,
Though their need should have made thee relent?

Was thine office to preach?
Didst thou warmly beseech
    Thy people in God's great name?
Didst thou turn back again
Those who hurried amain
Blindfold into hell's fierce flame?

Or, alas! did they share
But a stepmother's care?
    Was God's heritage nothing to thee?
Didst thou leave the poor flocks
To the care of the fox,
If their fleeces secured could be?[220]

Despite the social comment of 'The Skull', Dugald Buchanan was no thorn in the side of the British establishment. He was paid £20 per annum for acting as teacher and catechist for the Annexed Estates Board on its estate at Kinloch Rannoch:[221] his job in effect was to 'civilize' his fellow Gaels. His poetry more generally expressed the Evangelical belief that worldly suffering is God's punishment for sin, and only in the afterlife can happiness be found. Its message was one of withdrawal from temporal affairs to an almost fatalistic acceptance of divine will. Buchanan's response to the Clearances holds the landlords to be inhumane (and by implication unchristian) but does not advocate challenging the *status quo*. According to Donald Matheson (1719–1782), an evangelical poet from Sutherland and a contemporary of Buchanan, the turbulent changes being suffered by the Gaels were divine retribution for centuries of paganism and barbarity:

Our ancestors marred
At the very beginning,
Their strength and their case
    In old ways of sinning;
The corruption widespread has left me,
Like a poor withered tree –
    Of all bloom it bereft me.[222]

As evangelicalism gained ground in the early nineteenth century, the Gaels began to see the world and themselves in a new light. The clans had been eager to become involved in political causes on an international scale (Jacobitism), but as evangelical religion replaced clanship as the driving force of Gaelic society there was a general retreat from temporal affairs and a rejection of old ways.

The outside agencies that intervened in the Highlands and Islands after the 'Forty-Five to bring order and economic prosperity to the region believed their success to be dependent upon the concurrent spiritual and moral rehabilitation of the Gaels. In their eyes, the transformation of the Gaels from rebellious and indolent barbarians to loyal and industrious Presbyterians required the supplanting of Gaelic by English and the elimination of the non-juring Episcopalian and Roman Catholic clergy whose influence prevented the instilling of 'proper' beliefs, morals and habits. The task of educating the Gaels was left for the most part to the SSPCK, an evangelical society which saw the promotion of literacy as a means of saving souls rather than as aiding the development of a skilled and well-informed citizenry, and which operated on the premise that 'civilization' was something the Lowlands could pass on to the Highlands.

The evangelical movement which was to spread throughout Gaeldom came not as a result of the efforts of Lowland-based bodies but rather through the efforts of the Gaelic school societies, which fostered strong local links, the lay preaching of Na Daoine, and evangelical Gaelic poetry. Their message preached a withdrawal from worldly affairs and an acceptance of divine will in the face of adversity; this provided the Gaels with an alternative to the cultural disorientation that attended the disintegration of clanship and was undoubtedly more attractive than the message of the Moderate-dominated Church of Scotland whose ministers were often perceived to benefit materially from the 'improvements' that left the people destitute and without hope. By the 1820s the Gaels were generally thought to be sober and religious – a drastic change indeed from the 1740s.

NOTES

1. NATIONAL LIBRARY OF SCOTLAND (HEREAFTER NLS): MS 98, ff. 39–40. Excerpts from 'Informations' regarding the Highlands, c. 1747, anonymous, Un to his Grace the Duke of New Castle one of His Majesty's Principall Secretarys of State.
2. Ibid.
3. Ibid.
4. Ibid.
5. Ibid.
6. Andrew Lang, ed., The Highlands of Scotland in 1750 (Edinburgh, 1898), p. vii.
7. Ibid., p. 70.
8. Ibid., pp. 70–71.
9. Ibid., p. 71.

With the Hanoverians on the British throne, the exiled Stuarts fomented rebellion in the Highlands, culminating in the '45. General Wade (left) made the area accessible to Government forces by building roads and bridges. The Duke of Cumberland (right), the victor of Culloden, unleashed bloody repression.

As 'peace' returned, curiosity succeeded hatred and fear. Dr Johnson, seen here on tour in the Highlands, was a major influence in changing lowland attitudes.

No longer a threat, the Highlands could be visited for their picturesque qualities. This is a view of Skye from Raasay, in 1820, by William Daniell.

James Macpherson published *Fragments of Ancient Poetry* in 1760, based on authentic bits of verse. But fake or not, his 'translations' of Ossian, a legendary Gaelic bard, took Europe by storm (Napoleon was an admirer) and fed the Romantic appetite. The 'noble' Highlander was born.

Not all Highlanders had been
Jacobite 'rebels'. The 2nd Duke of
Argyll was an efficient political manager
on behalf of the government in London,
with considerable powers of patronage
and a desire to change traditional
Highland ways.
(PAINTING, BY WILLIAM AIKMAN, COURTESY OF
NATIONAL GALLERIES OF SCOTLAND).

The 'useful' Highlander: a tartan-clad John Murray, 4th Earl of Dunmore,
by Sir Joshua Reynolds (1765). Tartan is no longer forbidden; again the
'picturesque' asserts itself. Dunmore became Governor of New York,
Virginia and the Bahamas. (NATIONAL GALLERIES OF SCOTLAND).

Hostile depictions of Highlanders from earlier in the century. (Above:) lazy fishermen are carried to the boats from their hovels by their ugly wives (from Burt's *Letters from the North of Scotland* (1754). (Right:) a caricature of 'Bonnie Prince Charlie' when he could still frighten the life out of the government in London. He wears something more like a mini-skirt than a kilt.

The visit of King George IV to Scotland in 1822 was the first by a British monarch in nearly 200 years. After the commotions of the Jacobite risings, it was time to draw England and Scotland together. Stage-managed by Sir Walter Scott, it was a great success. Scott is shown here in a bust carved in Rome by the Danish sculptor Thorwaldsen. Scott's writings had popularised Highland themes.

Assisting Scott was Major-General David Stewart of Garth, formerly of the Black Watch (always a 'loyal' regiment), a Highland landowner and author of *Sketches of . . . the Highlanders of Scotland*, a work that went a long way towards rehabilitating the Highland image.

A fanciful depiction by Sir David Wilkie of George IV receiving the
keys of Holyrood Palace, Edinburgh during his visit. Tartan is very evident,
and indeed, to the puzzlement of some Lowland Scots, was beginning to be
taken as representing Scotland as a whole.

Tartan again: a scene, drawn by Wilkie, during George IV's visit.
The seeds of 'Balmorality' and Harry Lauder had been sown. Scottish exports
would have to be tartan-wrapped. The Highlander had had his revenge.

10. *Ibid.*
11. *Ibid.*, pp. 85–86.
12. Henry Paton, ed., *The Lyon in Mourning, or, A Collection of speeches, letters, journals, etc., relative to the affairs of Prince Charles Edward Stuart, by Bishop Robert Forbes*, three vols. (Scottish History Society, Edinburgh 1895–1896), I, p. 99. The Rev. John Cameron is the only Presbyterian churchman mentioned in *The Lyon in Mourning*.
13. Lang, pp. 133–135.
14. J.B. Craven, ed., *Records of the Dioceses of Argyll and the Isles 1560–1860* (Kirkwall, 1907), pp. 196–197.
15. J.B. Craven, ed., *Journals of the Episcopalian Visitations of the Right Rev. Robert Forbes, M.A., of the Dioceses of Ross and Caithness, and of the Dioceses of Ross and Argyll, 1762 & 1770* (London, 1923), pp. 160–161 (entry for 25 July 1762).
16. *Ibid.*, pp. 315–316 (entry for 8 July 1770).
17. *Ibid.*, p. 321 (entry for 10 July 1770).
18. Craven, *Records of the Dioceses of Argyll and the Isles*, p. 260.
19. *Ibid.*
20. *Ibid.*, p. 298.
21. *Ibid.*
22. David Norman Mackay, *Trial of Simon, Lord Lovat of the '45* (Edinburgh, 1911), p. 293.
23. William Forbes-Leith, *Memoirs of Scottish Catholics During the Seventeenth and Eighteenth Centuries*, two vols. (London, 1909), II, p. 334.
24. *Ibid.*, II, p. 342.
25. *Ibid.*, II, p. 328.
26. *Ibid.*, II, p. 347.
27. *Ibid.*, II, pp. 362–364.
28. *Scots Magazine*, Feb. 1756, p. 100.
29. Roderick Macdonald, 'The Highland District in 1764', *Innes Review* (Edinburgh, 1964), p. 148.
30. *Ibid.*
31. *Ibid.*
32. Christine Johnson, *Developments in the Catholic Church in Scotland 1789–1829* (Edinburgh, 1964), p. 148.
33. Alphons Bellesheim, *History of the Catholic Church in Scotland*, translated by D. Oswald Hunter Blair, four vols. (Edinburgh, 1890), IV, p. 219.
34. *Ibid.*
35. SRO E.728/39/2: Memorial by Colin MacDonald of Boisdale, Esq., Feb. 1771, to the Commissioners for the Annexed Estates.
36. Ibid.
37. Ibid.
38. Ibid.
39. Bellesheim, IV, p. 219.
40. *Ibid.*, IV, pp. 219–220.
41. Johnson, p. 1.
42. *Ibid.*, p. 124.
43. *Ibid.*, p. 238.
44. *Ibid.*,
45. SRO E.729/1: Report from Captain John Forbes, factor upon the annexed estates of Lovat and Cromarty (in answer to the Commissioners' order and instructions of 30 July 1755), pp. 17–18.
46. Ibid., p. 7.

47. John Mason, 'Schools on the Forfeited Estates in the Highlands' (unpublished typescript, SRO, 1949), p. 6; from SSPCK minutes of General Meeting, 5 June 1755 (SRO GD.95/1/4).
48. Ibid; from SSPCK minutes of Directors of the Society, 20 March 1755 (SRO GD.95/2/7).
49. SRO CH.8/212/1: Report of Drs Hyndman and Dick, appointed by the General Assembly to visit the Highlands and Islands (1760), pp. 78–79.
50. Ibid., p. 81.
51. Ibid.
52. Ibid., pp. 83–84.
53. Ibid., p. 84.
54. James Gray Kyd, ed., *Scottish Population Statistics (including Webster's Analysis of Population 1755)* (Edinburgh, 1975)
55. *Ibid.*, pp. 33–35.
56. *Ibid.*, p. 60.
57. *Ibid.*, pp. 1–62.
58. *Ibid.*, p. 60.
59. *Ibid.*, p. 59. Webster's estimates are haphazard by late twentieth-century standards. He counted the number of people on the 'roll of examinables', that is, those who could be examined on the catechism (usually from 6–8 years of age). Webster used the following formula to approximate the total number of inhabitants per parish (n being the year of age at which catechism was begun in that parish):

No. of examinables × ([30+n]/31)
(D.J. Withrington, 'The S.P.C.K. and Highlands Schools in the Mid-Eighteenth Century', *Scottish Historical Review* (Edinburgh, 1962), vol. XLI no. 132, pp. 90–91.

60. James Darragh, 'The Catholic Population of Scotland since the year 1680', *Innes Review* (Edinburgh, 1953), IV, p. 54. Darragh estimates there were around 33,000 Catholics in Scotland between 1755 and 1765, considerably more than Webster's total.
61. William Ferguson, 'The Problems of the Established Church in the West Highlands and Islands in the eighteenth century', *Records of the Scottish Church History Society* (Edinburgh, 1972), vol. XVII, p. 28.
62. SRO CH.8/212/1, p. 81.
63. Ibid. Hyndman and Dick failed to mention the effect of seasonal migration to the Lowlands in search of employment on bilingualism.
64. Ibid., pp. 81–82.
65. Ibid., p. 82.
66. Ibid..
67. Ibid..
68. SRO CH.1/1/55: The Rev. John Walker's Report to the General Assembly on the state of the Highlands and Islands, 1765, p. 590.
69. Ibid., pp. 595–596.
70. Ibid., p. 596.
71. Ibid.
72. Ibid., pp. 610–611.
73. Ibid., p. 614.
74. Ibid.
75. Ibid., p. 615.
76. Ibid.
77. Ibid., p. 610.

78. Anonymous, *A Short Account of the Society in Scotland for Propagating Christian Knowledge in the Highlands and Islands* (London, 1809), p. 1.
79. Ibid., pp. 1–2.
80. Ibid., pp. 4–5.
81. Ibid., p. 5.
82. Ibid.
83. Ibid., p. 6.
84. SSPCK Account of Funds, 1796; quoted in John MacInnes, *The Evangelical Movement in the Highlands of Scotland 1688–1800* (Aberdeen, 1951), p. 238.
85. Ibid.
86. SRO GD.95/2/7: SSPCK Minutes of Committee Meetings, 5 March 1751, pp. 30–31.
87. Quoted in J.L. Campbell, *Gaelic in Scottish Education and Life, Past, Present, and Future* (Edinburgh, 1945), p. 55.
88. Anonymous, *An Account of the Society in Scotland for Propagating Christian Knowledge, From its Commencement in 1709. In which is included, The present state of the Highlands and Islands of Scotland with regard to Religion* (Edinburgh, 1774), p. 52.
89. *Ibid.*.
90. *Ibid.*, p. 53.
91. *The Statistical Account of Scotland, 1791–99, edited by Sir John Sinclair*, D.J. Withrington and I.R. Grant, eds., 20 vols. (reprinted Wakefield, 1973–1983), XVII, pp. 432–433 (parish of Killearnan).
92. *Ibid.*.
93. *Ibid.*, XVII, p. 108 (parish of Inverness).
94. *Ibid.*.
95. *Ibid.*, XX, p. 87 (parish of Portree).
96. *Ibid.*, XX, p. 94.
97. *Ibid.*, XVIII, p. 386 (parish of Eddrachillis).
98. *Ibid.*, XVIII, pp. 386–387.
99. *Ibid.*.
100. *Ibid.*, XVII, p. 528 (parish of Kintail).
101. *Ibid.*.
102. *Ibid.*, XVII, pp. 528–9.
103. *Ibid.*, XVII, p. 529.
104. *Ibid.*
105. *Ibid.*
106. See T.M. Murchison, 'The Disruption', in *Companion to Gaelic Scotland*, D.S. Thomson, ed. (Oxford, 1983), p. 63.
107. See John MacInnes, *The Evangelical Movement in the Highlands, 1688–1800* (Aberdeen, 1951), *passim*.
108. A.L. Drummond and James Bulloch, *The Scottish Church, 1688–1843* (Edinburgh, 1973), p. 153.
109. Rosalind Mitchison, *A History of Scotland* (2nd ed., London, 1982), p. 368.
110. J.A. Haldane, *Journal of a Tour through the Northern Counties of Scotland and the Orkney Isles, in Autumn 1797, undertaken with a view to promote the knowledge of the Gospel of Jesus Christ* (Edinburgh, 1798), p. 86. 'Sold for the benefit of the Society for Propagating the Gospel at Home.'
111. *Ibid.*
112. Drummond and Bulloch, p. 62.
113. Niel Douglas, *Journal of a Mission to part of the Highlands of Scotland, in summer and harvest 1797, by appointment of The Relief Synod, in a series*

of letters to a friend, designed to shew The State of Religion in that country, and The claim the inhabitants have on the compassion of fellow Christians, by Niel Douglas, minister of the Gospel (Edinburgh, 1799), p. 173.

114. *Ibid.*, p. 85.
115. *Ibid.*, pp. 85–86.
116. *Ibid.*, p. 57.
117. *Ibid.*, p. 59.
118. *Ibid.*
119. *Ibid.* p. 136.
120. *Ibid.*, pp. 136–137.
121. *Ibid.*
122. Mitchison, p. 369.
123. Anonymous, 'On the State of Religion in the Highlands of Scotland', *Blackwood's Edinburgh Magazine*, May 1819 (No XXVI, vol. v.), p. 138.
124. *Ibid.*
125. *Ibid.*
126. *Ibid.*
127. *Ibid.*, p. 139.
128. Excerpts from a speech by Dr Alexander Irvine of Little Dunkeld delivered to the General Assembly committee for the state of religion in the Highlands and Islands and the necessity of erecting new parishes in 1818, from 'On the State of Religion in the Highlands of Scotland' (see above), p. 139.
129. *Ibid.*
130. *Ibid.*
131. *Ibid.*, p. 142.
132. *Ibid.*
133. *Ibid.*
134. *Ibid.*, pp. 142–143.
135. *Ibid.*, p. 143.
136. *The Sixth Annual Report of the Society for the Support of Gaelic Schools* (Edinburgh, 1817), p. 24.
137. *Ibid.* (Resolutions of the Gaelic School Society [Edinburgh], 16/1/1811).
138. *Ibid.*
139. *Ibid.*
140. *Ibid.*
141. *Ibid.*
142. *Ibid.*
143. V.E. Durkacz, *The Decline of the Celtic Languages* (Edinburgh, 1983), p. 123.
144. *The Sixth Annual Report of the Society for the Support of Gaelic Schools*, p. 2.
145. *Ibid.*
146. *The Third Annual Report of the Calton & Bridgeton Association for Religious Purposes; with A Summary Account of the Societies aided from its funds* (Glasgow, 1818), p. 95.
147. *Ibid.*
148. *Ibid.* pp. 18–19.
149. John A. Smith, 'Gaelic Schools', in *Companion to Gaelic Scotland*, p. 259.
150. Durkacz, p. 113.
151. Inverness Society for the Education of the Poor, *Moral Statistics of the Highlands and Islands of Scotland* (Inverness, 1826), appendix: letter from the Rev. Anthony McDonald, Catholic clergyman on Isle of Eigg (16 March 1821), p. xv.

152. Parliamentary Select Committee on the Education of the Poor: digest of Returns to Circular Letter, &c. (1818), p. 1289.
153. Ibid., p. 1415.
154. Ibid., p. 1370.
155. Ibid., p. 1368.
156. Ibid., p. 1427.
157. Ibid., p. 1428.
158. Inverness Society for the Education of the Poor, 'Report on the Present State of the Highlands and Islands of Scotland', prefixed to *Moral Statistics of the Highlands and Islands of Scotland*, p. 28.
159. *Statement as to the wants of schools and catechists in the Highlands and Islands, by a committee of the General Assembly of the Church of Scotland* (Edinburgh, 1825), p. 3.
160. *Ibid* p. 5.
161. *Report of the Committee of the General Assembly, for increasing the means of Education and Religious instruction in Scotland, particularly the Highlands and Islands. Submitted to the General Assembly, May 1829* (Edinburgh, 1829).
162. *Ibid.*, p. 11.
163. *Ibid.*
164. *Ibid.*, p. 30.
165. SRO GD.95/9/3: Patrick Butter, 'Journal of a Visit to the Schools of the Society in Scotland for Propagating Christian Knowledge' (1824), p. 16.
166. Ibid.
167. SRO GD.95/9/4: SSPCK schools visits by John Tawse (1827–1830), p. 87.
168. Ibid.
169. Ibid., pp. 87–88.
170. Ibid., p. 179.
171. Ibid., pp. 181–2.
172. Ibid., pp. 173–174.
173. Ibid., p. 174.
174. SRO GD. 95/9/3, p. 35.
175. SRO GD.95/14/24: John Tawse, 'Report on a visitation of Schools in Skye, Lewis, and mainland parishes of Inverness-shire' (1830), p. 24.
176. Ibid., p. 25.
177. Ibid.
178. Associate Synod, *Report of the Religious State of the Highlands & Islands of Scotland; with a plan for its amelioration* (Edinburgh, 1820), p. 7.
179. *Ibid.*, p. 7.
180. SRO GD.95/11/12: 'Report on and Journals of two visits (in 1822 and 1824) to the Islands of St Kilda by the Rev. John Macdonald, minister of Urquhart' (1825), p. 14.
181. Ibid., p. 9.
182. Ibid., p. 10.
183. Ibid., p. 12.
184. Ibid., p. 29.
185. Ibid.
186. *Moral Statistics*, pp. 27–28.
187. Anonymous, *An Account of the Present State of Religion throughout the Highlands of Scotland ... by a Lay Member of the Established Church* (Edinburgh, 1827), p. 49.
188. *Ibid.*, pp. 52–53.
189. *Ibid.*, p. 53.

190. *Ibid.*, p. 55.
191. *Ibid.*
192. *Ibid.*, pp. 53–54.
193. Charles Fraser-Mackintosh, *Antiquarian Notes* (Inverness, 1898), p. 234.
194. Anonymous, *An Account of the Present State of Religion*, p. 56.
195. *Ibid.*, pp. 59–60.
196. *Ibid.*, p. 60–61.
197. *Ibid.*, p. 62.
198. *Ibid.*, p. 63.
199. *Ibid.*, p. 68.
200. *Ibid.*
201. John Macinnes, 'The Men', *Records of the Scottish Church History Society* (Glasgow, 1944), vol. VIII, p. 27.
202. Durkacz, p. 127.
203. MacInnes, p. 36.
204. *Ibid.*, pp. 40–41.
205. *Ibid.*, p. 41.
206. Durkacz, p. 141.
207. MacInnes, *The Evangelical Movement in the Highlands of Scotland, 1688–1800*, p. 58.
208. *Ibid.*
209. Ian Grimble, *The World of Rob Donn* (Edinburgh, 1979), pp. 80–81.
210. *Highland Songs of the Forty-Five*, J.L. Campbell, ed., (Scottish Gaelic Texts Society, Edinburgh, 1984), pp. 63–64.
211. *The Songs of John MacCodrum*, William Matheson, ed. (Scottish Gaelic Texts Society) (Edinburgh, 1938), pp. xxviii–xxix.
212. *Ibid.*, p. xxviii.
213. *Ibid.*, p. xxx.
214. *Ibid.*, pp. 199–203.
215. D.S. Thomson, *An Introduction to Gaelic Poetry* (Edinburgh, 1990), p. 205.
216. *Buchanan, the Sacred Bard of the Scottish Highlands* Lachlan MacBean, ed. (London, 1919), p. 101.
217. *Ibid.*
218. John MacInnes, 'Gaelic Religious Poetry, 1650–1850', *Records of the Scottish Church History Society* (Glasgow, 1950), vol. X, p. 44.
219. John MacInnes, *The Evangelical Movement in the Highlands of Scotland, 1688–1800*, p. 2.
220. MacBean, pp. 113–115.
221. Annette M. Smith, *Jacobite Estates of the Forty-Five* (Edinburgh, 1982), p. 34.
222. Nigel Macneill, *The Literature of the Highlanders* (Inverness, 1892), pp. 240–241.

4

Travellers

PRIOR TO THE Forty-Five, few people from the Lowlands, England
or abroad ever ventured beyond the Highland line. Fear, ignorance
and the difficulty of travel kept them away, but the outcome of
the battle of Culloden meant to many that the Gaels were at last
tamed, and the military roads begun by General Wade in 1727 (but
used to advantage by the Jacobites) were at least the beginning of a
modern communications network. For some years after the Forty-Five,
travellers' accounts of the Highlands and Islands were preoccupied
with the conflict, and these were almost invariably written from
a Whig perspective. The Gaels were regarded with contempt for
their support of the Stuart cause, which was explained as resulting from their poverty and their generally backward and barbaric
nature.

With the elimination of the Jacobite threat, interest was awakened
in the race of 'noble savages' first described by Martin Martin in his
Description of the Western Isles of Scotland (1703). Martin's work
directly motivated Samuel Johnson's tour of 1773, in which he sought
an ancient culture unrefined by modern innovation. Johnson discovered
that he was too late, but his account marked the move away from a
bland and uncritical acceptance of the standard Whig pronouncements
on Highland 'improvement'. At the same time, Johnson wanted to find
evidence to disprove the authenticity of James Macpherson's *Ossian*,
which first appeared in 1760. Nevertheless, Ossian lured increasing
numbers of visitors to the Highlands in search of a wild and primitive
place inhabited by people also fitting that description. As Gaeldom
became a favourite subject for Romantic writers such as Walter Scott
in the early nineteenth century, a tourist industry emerged in the region,
and improved communications made travel to the West Highlands and
Hebrides easier if less of an adventure.

There are a number of recurring themes in the accounts of various
travellers' changing attitudes towards Jacobitism and the Gaels' involvement with it: the impact of Ossian and later the Romantic movement
upon perceptions of the Highlands; the abolition of clanship; and last,
the travellers' unflagging fascination with the manners and customs of
the Gaels.

Memories of the Forty-Five

Politics dominated most travellers' thinking towards the Highlands for more than thirty years after the rebellion, and misconceptions such as the assumption that Jacobitism was espoused throughout Gaeldom, and the idea that the clan system would have survived but for the defeat of the Jacobites, were repeated again and again. Those of the Whig persuasion could hardly hide their delight at the outcome, and the carnage that followed it was easily dismissed. This euphoria lasted for some time.

Richard Pococke (1704–1765), an Anglican bishop, made tours of Scotland in 1747, 1750 and 1760, during which he was made burgess of Aberdeen, Glasgow, and other cities.[1] He passed by Culloden in 1760 and saw the mass graves of the Jacobites there. In his journal of the tour, he commented that following the battle, the dead Highlanders 'were all instantly stripped by the women who went loaded with Spoils to Inverness, and the bodies were soon naked all over the field'. However, he pointed out that 'it is said the few that fell of our soldiers were not stripped: those in the field of Battle were killed by Musket Shot and Canon Ball; the others by the broad sword'. He made the obligatory political comment that all visitors of his time made in reference to the battlefield; his being that 16th April 1746 was a day 'of such consequence to the British Dominions, and Crowned the Duke with immortal Lawrels'.[2] Presumably Pococke was unaware that the majority of Jacobites were Episcopalians.

Thomas Pennant (1726–1798), a Welsh traveller and naturalist, visited Culloden during his tour of 1769 and expressed similar sentiments. For both commentators, the Government victory there in 1746 marked a new era not only for Gaeldom but for Scotland as a whole – an assimilation into the British system which they viewed as the desirable replacement of diversity with uniformity. Pennant referred to Culloden as 'the place that North Britain owes its present prosperity to', and his use of that term instead of 'Scotland' was common for thirty years after the battle, which was viewed as a watershed.

Pennant wrote of the nearby Culloden House and its one-time occupant, Duncan Forbes of Culloden, 'a warm and active friend to the house of Hanover, who spent great sums in its service, and by his influence, and by his persuasions, diverted numbers from joining the rebellion', but who nevertheless 'met with a cool return for his attempt to sheath, after victory, the unsatiated sword' – a reference to the Duke of Cumberland's blood-thirsty pacification of the Highlands. But, he went on: '. . . let a veil be flung over a few excesses consequential of a day, productive of so much benefit to the united kingdoms'.[3] The most famous visit to the Highlands and Islands during this period was undoubtedly that of Dr Samuel Johnson (1709–1784), the leading English man of letters of his time. He was a staunch Tory – Carlyle called him the 'last of the tories'[4] – but he was not greatly interested in Highland politics. By the time Johnson visited Scotland in 1773, Jacobitism as a political movement was extinct. The 'Young Pretender' was in his fifties, broken and nearly forgotten (the cult that grew around him had not yet developed) and a threat to no-one:

> The political tenets of the Islanders I was not curious to investigate, and they were not eager to obtrude. Their conversation is decent and inoffensive. They disdain to drink for their principles, and there is no disaffection at their tables. I never heard a health offered by a Highlander that might not have circulated with propriety within the precincts of the King's palace.[5]

However, not all travellers could resist a jab at the defeated clans. Mary Anne Hanway, a young English aristocrat who toured parts of the Highlands in 1775, commented on Charles Edward Stuart's support in the early stages of the rebellion. It was her opinion, based on 'the observations I have been enabled to make of the life and manners of the people', that it should have come as no surprise that the Jacobites so easily gained volunteers and captured towns. Her explanation was that those 'well-affected to government' were greatly outnumbered 'in comparison with that ignorant multitude, which run with the stream, and are one moment ready to join the Pretender's standard, and the next, on sight of our troops to discard their new-acquired friends and throw up their bonnets for KING GEORGE'. She continued: 'is it then a matter of wonder that towns should yield, which had it not in their power to make the least resistance to this rabble of desperadoes? for such, and not an army, it might, with justice, be stiled.'[6]

Ossian and Romanticism

After the 'translations' of ancient Gaelic poetry by James Macpherson in the early 1760s, attitudes towards Gaeldom became less predetermined by politics. Macpherson presented the Gaels not as backward barbarians but as 'noble savages', and later, in the full bloom of Romanticism, the poems and novels of Walter Scott presented an idealised picture of the Highlands in the days of clanship. Reflecting this cultural rehabilitation of Gaeldom, the themes that were discussed by travellers prior to the Romantic movement, such as the poverty, idleness and rebelliousness that were thought to be inherent in the clan system, were supplanted by a new emphasis on Gaeldom as a mysterious and magical place inhabited by a noble race of hardy mountaineers. In general, scenery and the noble savagery of Macpherson's and Scott's fictional heroes became more noteworthy than the actual state of the Gaels. With Romanticism came a new appreciation of the Highlands and Islands as an area of outstanding natural beauty, and places once considered dismal and uninviting now beckoned tourists bent on experiencing the scenic wonders that England and the Lowlands lacked. Loch Lomond and the Trossachs were attractions easily accessible to outsiders and became particular favourites of sightseers, especially following Scott's depiction of the area in his poem 'The Lady of the Lake' (1810).

Robert Heron (1764–1807), a writer on various subjects who was employed by Sir John Sinclair in the preparation of the *Statistical Account*,[7] wrote a guidebook to Scotland in 1799. His enthusiasm for the Trossachs, that safe and picturesque point of entry to the Highlands, predated Scott's: 'every object that can affect the mind with ideas of the rude grandeur and sublimity of Nature, seems here assembled; and no traveller of taste can view this scene without delight and astonishment'.[8] The Englishwoman Sarah Murray (1744–1811), widow of the Earl of Dunmore and author of *A Companion and Useful Guide to the Beauties of Scotland*, also published in 1799, was equally taken with the Trossachs:

> The awfulness, the solemnity, and the sublimity, of the scene at the ford, and by Loch Catherine, is beyond, far beyond description, either of pen or pencil! Nothing but the eye can convey to the mind such scenery: – well may it be called Loc-a-chavry, the lake of the field of devotion.[9]

James Hogg (1770–1835), the Borders shepherd who came to prominence as a writer, visited the Highlands in 1803 and communicated his impressions to Walter Scott, who had included ballads contributed by Hogg's mother in his *Minstrelsy of the Scottish Border*. Hogg too was impressed with the Trossachs; upon entering the area, his initial reaction was that 'Nature hath thrown these together in a rage. But on seeing the spreading bushes overhanging the rocks, and hearing the melody of the birds, I softened the idea into *one of her whims*'. Such scenes were not to be found in the Borders, and 'as I had set out with a mind so intent on viewing the scenery of the Highlands,' he wrote, 'and coming to such an interesting place on the very day that I entered them, I was more than ordinarily delighted.'[10]

Dorothy Wordsworth likewise toured the Highlands in 1803, with her brother William and Samuel Taylor Coleridge, and she also was enthralled with the Trossachs. Her account is apolitical. She considered the Highlands to be less a place where people lived than a subject for poets and artists. She was overcome with the 'excessive beautifulness' of the place:

> We had been through many solitary places since we came into Scotland, but this place differed as much from any we had seen before, as if there had been nothing in common between them; no thought of dreariness or desolation found entrance here; yet nothing was to be seen but water, wood, rocks, heather, and bare mountains above ... A road, which has a very wild appearance, has been cut through the rock; yet even here, among the bold precipice, the feeling of excessive beautifulness overcomes every other ... [11]

When Dorothy and her companions approached Tarbet, at Loch Lomond, they encountered a boy tending a herd of cattle. The sight filled her heart with awe and sent her pen in a characteristically romantic direction. Her tone is condescending in the extreme, and her reference to 'a half-articulate Gaelic hooting' confirms that she belonged to the Samuel Johnson school of Highland scholarship:

> While we were walking forward, the road leading us over the top of a brow, we stopped suddenly at the sound of a half-articulate Gaelic hooting from the field close to us. It came from a little boy, whom we could see on the hill between us and the lake, wrapped up in a grey plaid. He was probably calling home the cattle for the night. His appearance was in the highest degree moving to the imagination; mists were on the hillsides, darkness shutting in upon the huge avenue of mountains, torrents roaring, no house in sight to which the child might belong; his dress, cry, and appearance all different from anything we had been accustomed to. [12]

'It was a text,' she concluded, 'containing in itself the whole history of the Highlander's life – his melancholy, his simplicity, his poverty, his superstition, and above all, that visionariness which results from a communion with the unworldliness of nature.'[13]

The cult surrounding the Forty-Five was gaining adherents. James Hogg was an Episcopalian (and not a Whig), and it was therefore not unnatural for him to identify in some ways with the Jacobite cause. He was moved to indignation over the Duke of Cumberland's campaign of pacification; when he came upon the ruin of the Cameron of Lochiel stronghold at Achnacarry, burned by Government troops in 1746, he saw that 'the marks of the fire were still visible, not only on the remaining walls of the house and offices, but also on a number of huge venerable trees, which the malevolent brutes had kindled'.[14] Hogg confessed:

> While traversing the scenes where the patient sufferings of the one party, and the cruelties of the other, were so affectingly displayed,

I could not help being a bit of a Jacobite in my heart, and blessing myself that, in those days, I did not exist, or I should certainly have been hanged.[15]

A *Voyage Round Great Britain* was compiled by William Daniell in 1813. Daniell (1769–1837) was a professional landscape artist who specialized in northern English and Scottish subjects,[16] and the book, a large, elegantly bound volume featuring his colour engravings, provides ample proof that a market had developed for nearly anything which portrayed the Highlands. In his preface Daniell explained the appeal of Highland scenery:

> The country on which we are about to enter is one of the most picturesque in the whole circuit of the island. It has been repeatedly explored and described; but the curiosity of the public respecting it is still unsatisfied, especially in whatever regards the illustration derived from the pencil. None of the tours in the west of Scotland now extant contain engravings at all worthy of their respective subjects; and it is a matter somewhat surprising, that a tract so inviting to the painter should not have called forth a single series of views.[17]

Robert Southey, the Englishman who became poet laureate in 1813,[18] visited the Highlands in 1819 with Scots engineer Thomas Telford. Surprisingly for a court poet in the Romantic age, Southey was on the whole more interested in agricultural issues than in scenery. But no-one, it seemed, was immune to grand and sublime sights. Southey went to Ballachulish, 'one of the finest spots we have seen, or can expect to see', an area that might have been considered gloomy and forbidding, but not by Southey – he described it in truly poetic style:

> The evening was glorious. To the west the Linnhe Loch lay before us, bounded by the mountains, which are of the finest outline, there is a dip somewhat resembling a pointed arch inverted; and just behind that dip the sun, which had not been visible during the day, sunk in serene beauty, without a cloud; first with a saffron, then with a rosey light, which imbued the mountains, and was reflected upon the still water up to the very shore beneath the window at which we stood, delighted in beholding it. The effect was such that I could almost have wished I were a believer in Ossian.[19]

John Eddowes Bowman was very much caught up by the Romantic ideal, and he knew Scott's novels by heart. For him, Scott provided an ideal vision of the Highlands and Islands, full of beautiful glens and brave people, without the deprivation and emigration that earlier travellers had found distasteful. At the beginning of his journal, Bowman explains his motives for making the visit. It seems that his impressions had already been predetermined

> I had for many years felt a strong desire to visit Scotland: – its wild and romantic scenery; its many monuments of rude and barbarous ages; the marvellous events of its ancient and modern history; and the spirit of liberty which still lingers among its mountains, and breathes in its native poetry, had long operated, as so many talismans, to allure me to its soil . . .[20]

The analytical perspective of eighteenth-century travellers is not to be found. Rather than a place to be feared, detested, or reformed, the Highlands had become a grand backdrop for a brave race doing brave deeds. Even Rob Roy MacGregor, formerly considered a vagabond cut-throat and a menace to civilisation, did not escape the treatment, and was reduced to a character from a historical novel. Indeed, Scott's fiction had become a palatable alternative to an often messy past. Bowman recorded his impressions of Loch Lomond:

> This tract was formerly held by the formidable Clan of the MacGregors, which under the celebrated Rob Roy was the terror of the whole country. We fancied that this must be the spot to which Osbaldistone and the wily Baillie Jarvie were conducted by one of Rob Roy's gillies, when they crossed the lake on their return to Glasgow after their adventurous journey to Aberfoil, as the latter place lies over the mountains in this direction.[21]

Bowman took a boat ride on the loch, and a piper provided a suitable accompaniment. 'Here the views are most sublime, affording every gradation of form and colour necessary for a grand picture,' wrote this connoisseur of scenery, 'and as the vessel alters her course, which she constantly and most judiciously does, the grouping of the scenery is perpetually changing giving the idea of enchantment.' He certainly had a vivid imagination:

> The bagpiper on board our vessel was playing some Jacobite tunes and Gathering pibrochs; and we could not help peopling the neighbouring glens and mountains in our imaginations, with hundreds of kilted highlanders, whose common practice it was, within the memory of old persons still living, at such a summons from their chief, to rush down from their retired dwellings to the appointed place of rendezvous, to pillage and slaughter any hostile clan . . .[22]

The extinction of clanship

The period 1745–1830 saw the demise of the clan system. Clanship had been identified with barbarity and treason in the years after 1745, but by the time George IV visited Scotland in 1822, the chiefs and clan gentry had successfully made the transition to landed proprietors, taking up their places in the polite society of Edinburgh, London and the Continent. This change was made possible through the reorganisation of Highland estates along commercial lines; clansmen were no longer viewed as military assets in the traditional sense but merely as recruits for the Highland regiments of the British army, and together with their families as an obstructive and ultimately disposable supply of labour.

Travellers to the Highlands and Islands noticed and often commented upon these changes, but what they wrote was more often than not based on preconception and hearsay than close observation. At first the chiefs who 'civilised' their clans and 'improved' their lands were roundly applauded, notable exceptions being Johnson and Boswell. But as Romanticism took hold and Scott's poems and novels told the world of the idyllic, albeit violent society, of the clans, the chiefs were just as often condemned for neglecting their duty. Clearance and emigration were denounced, but rarely was an alternative solution suggested.

Johnson and James Boswell (1740–1795) were wistful about the loss of the Gaels' fierce independence that the breakdown of clanship seemed to symbolise: they had hoped to find boldness and defiance, but instead found capitulation. Boswell recorded an exchange that took place with Lord Macdonald during their visit to the chief's estate in Skye. Given Macdonald's Eton education, and his being 'a gentleman of talents', Johnson had been 'very well pleased with him in London'. But unfortunately for Lord Macdonald, Boswell wrote, 'my fellow-traveller and I were now full of the old Highland spirit, and were dissatisfied at hearing of racked rents and emigration'. Unhappy at meeting a chief without a clan, Johnson remarked: 'Sir, the Highland chiefs should not be allowed to go farther south than Aberdeen. A strong-minded man like Sir James Macdonald, may be improved by an English education; but in general, they will be tamed into insignificance'.[23]

Johnson and Boswell attempted to provoke Lord Macdonald by impressing upon him what they believed to be his duties as the chief of a Highland clan, but with little success. Alas, the guests were more imbued with the 'old Highland spirit' than was their host. Johnson is still attacked for his ill-informed remarks on the Gaelic language and the Ossian controversy, but he was more critical (and publicly so) of the chiefs' abandonment of their hereditary responsibilities than a number of revered Gaelic poets. As Boswell relates:

My endeavours to rouse the English-bred Chieftain, in whose house we were, to the feudal and patriarchal feelings, proved ineffectual Dr Johnson this morning tried to bring him to our way of thinking, – Johnson. 'Were I in your place sir, in seven years I would make this an independent island. I would roast oxen whole, and hang out a flag as a signal to the Macdonalds to come and get beef and whisky.' – Sir Alexander was still starting difficulties. – Johnson. 'Nay, sir; if you are born to object, I have done with you. Sir, I would have a magazine of arms.' – Sir Alexander. 'They would rust.' – Johnson. 'Let there be men to keep them clean. Your ancestors did not let their arms rust.'[24]

While he displayed the typical Whig tendency to curse anything that smacked of feudalism, Thomas Pennant was quite content with those chiefs who combined improvement and progress with the enlightened paternalism that he believed was part of the clan system. He was a guest at Dunvegan Castle in 1774 and was greatly impressed by the MacLeod chief, a man who 'feels for the distresses of his people, and [is] insensible of his own', to the extent that he 'has relieved his tenants from their oppressive rents', and in doing so 'has received instead of the trash of gold, the treasure of warm affections, and unfeigned prayer', a situation characteristic 'among those accustomed to a feudal government'.[25]

Essentially, Pennant argued for the replacement of hereditary responsibility with charity; he wrote that 'the highlanders may bless the hand that loosened their bonds, for tyranny more often than protection was the attendance on their vassalage,' but that the 'gleams of kindness that darted every now and then amidst the storms of severity' had produced 'a sort of filial reverence to their chieftain' which he believed to be 'in a great degree retained'.[26]

Pennant wrote that as a result of the changes brought about since the Forty-Five, such as the abolition of heritable jurisdictions (which the Whigs took to be the basis of the chiefs' power), 'the noxious part of the feudal reign is abolished; the delegated rod of power is now no more'. But he stressed that 'the tender relation' and the 'mutual inclination to beneficence' of the old system should be retained; 'the chieftain should not lose, with the power of doing harm, the disposition of doing good'. According to Pennant, these sentiments were shared by the chief, and 'ripen into actions that, if persisted in, will bring lasting comfort into his own bosom, and the most desired of blessings amongst a numerous clan.'[27] Pennant did not mention that it had become common practice for chiefs to retain their tenants somewhere on their estates not out of sentiment but rather to manufacture kelp and to facilitate military recruitment.

Mary Anne Hanway saw the passing of clanship as something eminently desirable, and attributed it to the civilising influence of

England. She was typical of many visitors from south of the border, who believed in the inherent rightness of the English way of doing things. They wanted to spread goodness and light, in the form of progress and industry and the English language, England always serving as the ideal. Gaeldom represented a great challenge to this form of cultural manifest destiny.

Hanway believed that by the time of her tour in 1775, there was no-one in Scotland who objected to the Treaty of Union. In the past, she wrote, 'it very frequently happened, that, a chieftain would involve his slavish subjects in the calamities of public contest, to gratify his private ambition, his envy, or his avarice. Such, in fact, was the general practice all over this country, till the union with England regulated the power, and put an end to the inhospitable bickerings of these petty princes, and chieftains'.[28] Since the Union, however,

> ... many wise acts since passed, have given a proper proportion of liberty to the commonality. Industry, civilization, and plenty, are the natural consequence of such political, public measures: Notwithstanding this, it was a good while before either the higher or lower degrees of the Scots, could be taught to consider the union of the kingdoms as either constitutional or salutary. Time, however, with its reconciling power, hath rubbed off these prejudices; and I dare say there are none of either rank, who do not rejoice at the friendship which subsists between the two countries.[29]

In contrast to Hanway, the travel writer Sarah Murray was well-informed concerning issues that faced the Gaels; her account can be seen as a continuation of Johnson's criticism of Highland 'improvement'. When she wrote her guide in 1799, the numbers emigrating from the Highlands and Islands were on the increase as evictions became commonplace. 'When proprietors lived on their property like patriarchs of old, spending their incomes amongst their tenants, connections and dependents, they were rich in love and money.' 'But now,' she continued, 'almost every laird with his family must in winter reside in London or Edinburgh, where he spends more than he can afford, and gets deeply into debt . . . this is the cause of the alienation of estates as well as the oppression of poor tenants, and the source of emigration:'

> What is the cause of that dire necessity? The first cause is luxury; the second, oppression. The remedy, I am afraid, is scarcely now practicable; because, when proprietors of land have learned how to spend on luxury, more than their property can fairly and justly produce; and they have screwed up their poor tenants to a far higher pitch than they can possibly bear, is it likely that they will relax in their oppression, or retrench in their luxurious mode of living? The

poor Highlander's alternative therefore is, either to starve in, or fly from, his native land.[30]

James Hogg visited the seat of George Mackenzie of Dundonell, on Little Loch Broom, in 1803 and found his sheep-farming expertise consulted by the proprietor. Hogg described a situation that was repeated numerous times throughout the Highlands and Islands, and was the very essence of the crisis that faced Gaeldom. 'His glens are so crammed full of stout, able-bodied men and women,' Hogg wrote, 'that the estate under the present system must have enough to do maintaining them.' He found what arable land there was to be 'impoverished by perpetual cropping', and except for one farm held by newcomers, 'the extensive mountains are all waste; for the small parcels of diminutive sheep which the natives have, are all herded below, nearest the dwellings, and are housed every night;'

> Dundonell asked me what I thought it would bring annually if let off in sheep walks. I said I had only a superficial view of it, but that, exclusive of a reasonable extent near the house, to be occupied by himself, it would bring not below £2,000. He said his people would never pay him the half of that. He was loath to chase them all away to America, but at present they did not pay him above £700.

> He hath however, the pleasure of absolute sway. He is even more so in his domains than Bonaparte is in France. I saw him call two men from their labour a full mile, to carry us through the water. I told him he must not expect to be served thus by the shepherds if once he had given them possession.[31]

By the time Robert Southey toured the Highlands in 1819, the improvement in the image of the Gael had reached an advanced stage. The unattractive aspects of the Forty-Five were forgotten, and the Highland regiments had been warmly praised for their loyalty and fearlessness in wars around the world. The Highlands as portrayed by Walter Scott had seized the popular imagination, although the reality was commercialism and not a picturesque feudalism.

Southey's was one of the dissenting voices. His political stance is difficult to pinpoint – he was often accused of espousing one philosophy, abandoning it for another, and then denouncing the former.[32] He wrote that there was 'a considerable ferment in the country concerning the management of the M[arquis] of Stafford's estates'. He explained that 'a political economist has no hesitation concerning the fitness of the land in view, and little scruple as to the means', and admitted that in the light of the poverty and the overall impression of sterility that the Highlands conveyed, 'the traveller who looks only at the outside of things, might easily assent to this reasoning'. He judged the stone huts inhabited by the Gaels to be the worst housing he had ever seen, and felt they deserved better (even if the Irish Gaels did not!):

> But these men-sties are not inhabited, as in Ireland, by a race of ignorant and ferocious barbarians, who can never be civilized till they are regenerated – till their very nature is changed. Here you have a quiet, thoughtful, contented, religious people, susceptible to improvement.

> To transplant these people from their native mountain glens to the sea coast, and require them to be cultivators, others fishermen, occupations to which they have never been accustomed – to expect a sudden and total change of habits in the existing generation, instead of gradually producing it in their children; to eject them by process of law from their black-house, and if they demur in obeying the ejectment, to oust them by setting fire to these combustible tenements – this surely is as little defensible on the score of policy as of morals.[33]

Highland manners and customs

Visitors to the Highlands and Islands were intrigued by the strange manners and customs of the people they encountered. The terms used by some travellers in describing Gaels are similar to those of some twentieth-century Westerners when describing people of Third World countries: wretched, idle, dirty, ignorant, backward, etc. Lowlanders and those in the south were amazed that people in Britain actually lived as the Gaels lived. They spoke a different language, they wore odd clothes, they lived amongst wild surroundings in primitive conditions; in short, they were as different from themselves as could be possible. While the Gaels were still considered a threat, these differences were not merely curiosities but were threatening in themselves; but as Gaeldom was pacified and economically integrated with the rest of Britain, they became spectacles. Richard Pococke visited Tongue on the northern coast of Sutherland in 1760. He was impressed: 'The people are in general extremely hospitable, charitable, civil, polite, and sensible'.[34] On the other hand, Thomas Pennant was taken aback by the scenes of poverty he witnessed, but what he found even more objectionable was sloth: lazy people would never be able to improve themselves. He wrote of the standard of housing in Upper Deeside: 'the houses of the common people in these parts are shocking to humanity, formed of loose stones, and covered with clods, which they call *devols*, or with heath, broom, or branches or fir: they look, at a distance, like so many mole hills'. He continued:

> The inhabitants live very poorly, on oat meal, barley cakes, and potatoes; their drink whisky, sweetened with honey. The men are thin, but strong; idle and lazy, except when employed in the chace, or any thing that looks like amusement; are content with their hard fare, and will not exert themselves farther than to get what they deem necessaries . . .[35]

Pennant did not refrain from making sweeping generalisations about the 'national character' of the Gaels. His words were influential, as they became accepted as truth by subsequent travellers for decades. 'The manners of the native Highlanders may justly be expressed in these words: indolent to a high degree, unless roused to war, or to any animating amusement', but, he added, 'from experience', that they were always ready 'to lend any disinterested assistance to the distressed traveller, either in directing him on his way, or affording their aid in passing the dangerous torrents of the Highlands'. He also found the Gaels to be 'hospitable to the highest degree, and full of generosity: [they] are much affected with the civility of strangers, and have in themselves a natural politeness and address, which often flows from the meanest when least expected'.[36]

Pennant noted that the Gaels were naturally curious people, being 'excessively inquisitive after your business, your name, and other particulars of little consequence to them: most curious after the politicks of the world; and when they can procure an old newspaper, will listen to it with all the avidity of *Shakespear's* blacksmith'. Of their character, he wrote that they had 'much pride, and consequently are impatient of affronts, and revengefull of injuries', but were 'decent in their general behaviour; inclined to superstition, yet attentive to the duties of religion, and are capable of giving a most distinct account of the principles of their faith'.

Regardless of his many prejudices, Pennant was a keen observer (a fact grudgingly admitted by Johnson) and could detect the disintegration of the Gaels' traditional way of life, which in his view was inevitable but not undesirable:

> In many parts of the Highlands, their character begins to be more faintly marked; they mix more with the world, and become daily less attached to their chiefs: the clans begin to disperse themselves through different parts of the country, finding that their industry and good conduct afford them better protection (since the due expectation of the laws) than any their chieftain can afford; and the chieftain tasting the sweets of advanced rents, and the benefits of industry, dismisses

from his table the crowds of retainers, the former instruments of his oppression and freakish tyranny.[37]

Pennant attributed the lack of adequate food supplies in the Highlands and Islands not only to bad weather and poor soil, but to the evils of whisky distilling. For him, this custom more than any other factor explained the near-constant dearth the Gaels suffered. In fact, the high rents and congestion found on 'improved' Highland estates forced many to distill whisky not for consumption but for sale on the illicit market. On his visit to Islay in 1774 he was moved to write:

> The produce is corn of different kinds; such as bear, which sometimes yields eleven-fold; a ruinous distillation prevales here; insomuch that it is supposed that more of the bear is drank in form of whisky; than eaten in the shape of bannocs.[38]

When he visited the Highlands in 1784, the French traveller Barthélemy Faujas de Saint Fond was a guest of the 5th Duke of Argyll at Inveraray Castle. The Campbell chiefs and clan gentry were Gaels but of an entirely different sort than the poor peasants about whom Pennant complained. The Argyll estate surpassed all others in the Highlands in embracing the tenets of Improvement; the 2nd Duke had begun to cut the ties of clanship as early as 1737 with the selling of tacks to the highest bidder. But the Frenchman was an innocent tourist, more impressed by the urbanity of the company than with the management policies of the House of Argyll. He wrote:

> We were received at the house with every mark of friendship in the midst of a numerous company and an amiable family, who joined to the most polished manners those prepossessing dispositions which are the natural dowry of sensitive and well-born minds. After the first compliments, we placed ourselves at the dinner-table, and as every thing pleased and interested me in this house, which was pervaded, if I may use the expression, with a kindly sympathy, I said to myself, 'The good woman of Tarbet was right. Here is indeed a charming family.' French was spoken at this table with as much purity as in the most polished circles of Paris.[39]

The more unusual aspects of Gaelic culture attracted the attention of travellers. During her visit to the Highlands, Mary Anne Hanway discovered that 'in many houses, they still retain the ancient custom of the piper playing all the time the company are at dinner, on his horrid bagpipes ... this is to me more dreadful, than the grunting of pigs, the screaming of owls, and the squalling of cats. All these creatures in a concert would be to my ears pleasing, compared to that discordant instrument to which I have a natural antipathy'.[40]

Dr Johnson singled out Gaelic and the bardic tradition for abuse. He had a great desire to expose Ossian as fraudulent; having compiled the first comprehensive English dictionary, his preference for that language is perhaps understandable, but he was unwilling to admit the possibility that the Gaels could have their own literary tradition. 'Of the Earse language,' he wrote, 'as I understand nothing, I cannot say more than I have been told.' However, this lack of first-hand knowledge did not prevent him from declaring that Gaelic 'is the rude speech of a barbarous people who had few thoughts to express, and were content, as they conceive grossly, to be grossly understood'. He then proceeded to display a number of misconceptions concerning Gaelic language and literature which could only have come from a Lowland informant:

> After what has been lately talked of Highland Bards, and Highland genius, many will startle when they are told, that the Earse never was a written language; that there is not in the world an Earse manuscript a hundred years old; and that the sounds of the Highlanders were never expressed by letters, till some little books of piety were translated, and a metrical version of the Psalms was made by the Synod of Argyle. Whoever therefore now writes in this language, spells according to his own perception of the sound, and his own idea of the power of the letters. The Welsh and the Irish are cultivated tongues. The Welsh, two hundred years ago, insulted their English neighbours for the instability of their Orthography; while the Earse merely floated in the breath of the people, and could therefore receive little improvement.[41]

Perhaps Johnson's motive in denying the very idea of a Gaelic literary tradition lay in his unwillingness to concede that yet another vibrant culture existed (or might still exist) in the British Isles in addition to that of his native country. His claims that 'Earse' was never a written language, that no extant Gaelic manuscript was over a century old, and that 'the sounds of the Highlanders was never expressed by letters' until 'books of piety' were translated, presumably from English, were certainly made in ignorance of the *Book of the Dean of Lismore*, an anthology of Gaelic material dating from the fifteenth and early sixteenth centuries, the existence of which was known before Johnson made his assertions. Johnson went on to accuse the Gaels of a general intellectual laziness:

> He that goes into the Highlands with a mind naturally acquiescent, and a credulity eager for wonders, may come back with an opinion very different from mine; for the inhabitants knowing the ignorance of all strangers in their language and antiquities, perhaps are not

very scrupulous adherents to truth; yet I do not say that they deliberately speak studied falsehood, or have a settled purpose to deceive. They have inquired and considered little, and do not always feel their own ignorance. They are not so much accustomed to be interrogated by others; and seem never to have thought upon interrogating themselves; so that if they do not know what they tell to be true, they likewise do not distinctly perceive it to be false.[42]

While Johnson focused his attention upon the Ossian controversy, other travellers were moved by less esoteric matters. Something that travellers rarely failed to mention was the distinctiveness of Highland dress. Here was tangible evidence for even the most obtuse that the Gaels were unlike other Britons. Some observers admired it, while others denounced it as the dress of heathens. Along with the bagpipe, tartan, the kilt, belted plaid and anything else that could be considered 'Highland garb' was banned by the Government in 1747 (except for military use) in an attempt to eradicate the symbols of rebellion. But in the early years of the nineteenth century, Highland dress became popular, largely due to the fame of the Highland regiments. The fashion became an institution when Sir Walter Scott decreed that for the purpose of the visit of George IV to Edinburgh in 1822, it was to be considered the national dress of Scotland.

Barthélemy Faujas de Saint Fond held to the dubious but widely held belief that the belted plaid was originally introduced to Scotland by the Roman legions, and he saw a parallel between the failure of Rome to conquer the area beyond the Highland line and more recent attempts to subdue the clans. 'What is quite certain is that the modern descendants of the ancient Caledonians are so attached to this form of dress, which reminds them of their ancient valour and independence, that the English [sic] government, having repeatedly attempted to reduce them to lay it aside, have never been able to succeed.' A less romantic but more plausible explanation would be that the belted plaid was ideally suited to the climate and terrain of the Highlands, but the Frenchman took the opposite view, stating that 'this attire is certainly least adopted to a people who live in so cold and humid a climate as this'.[43]

By the end of the eighteenth century, Highland dress had been transformed into a stylised costume worn chiefly by men of the Highland regiments. In the Highlands themselves, according to Sarah Murray, 'the true Highland dress with the belted plaid, is now seldom worn; and even the kilt is discarded, except by sporting gentlemen, and farmers, who find it convenient for walking in all places and weathers'.[44] Writing in 1819, Robert Southey was pleased at the apparent victory of the trews over the kilt as the preferred dress of Highland men. 'It is proof of increasing decency and civilization that the Highland philabeg, or male-petticoat, is falling into disuse. Upon a soldier or a gentleman it looks well; but with the common people, and especially with boys, it is a filthy, beggarly, indecent garb.'[45] Had he known that his royal patron would shortly put his seal of approval on Highland dress, he might have tempered his stance; George IV began something of a craze in Britain with his brief appearance in a kilt. Southey then repeated the assertion first made in the March 1785 issue of the *Edinburgh Magazine* that the philabeg or 'little kilt' was invented by the Englishman Thomas Rawlinson in the 1720s to better clothe the Highlanders employed at his ironworks in Glengarry and Lochaber:[46]

> The more civilized chieftains before that time wore trouse. Those who came from the remote highlands to the rebellion of 1715 were all drest in a long loose garment, home-made, and of one colour, buttoned above and laced below down to the knees, which as the cobler's stall served him for parlour and kitchen and hall, served them for coat, waist-coat, breeches, and shirt.[47]

The effect of George IV's visit on attitudes towards Highland dress is apparent from John Eddowes Bowman's thoughts on the subject. He visited the Highlands in 1825 and remarked: 'The Tartan Plaid thrown gracefully over the shoulder, and indeed the whole dress, has a very captivating effect and is very splendid'.[48]

The accounts of those who ventured beyond the Highland line in the years after the Forty-Five reveal a preoccupation with the rebellion. Most travellers, especially those of the Whig persuasion, heaped abuse upon the Gaels for their dangerous folly and their backwardness in general. The publication of James Macpherson's Ossian in the early 1760s diverted attention from politics towards the idea of the Gaels as living examples of the noble savage.

With the arrival of the Romantic era in the early nineteenth century, the reputation of the Highlands and Islands as a mysterious and picturesque place worth visiting was established. By the 1820s an embryonic tourist industry was in place to meet the demand, created largely by the works of Walter Scott, and facilitated by improvements to the region's communications network.

Amidst the holiday atmosphere, there were voices of dissent. Some visitors were aware of the real problems facing Gaeldom and were unwilling to compose a pleasant travelogue of their experience. They gave their readers some idea of the desperate situation of ordinary Gaels, and protested against the hardship and migration which resulted from the squandering of human resources by Highland proprietors bent on short-term profit.

However, most nineteenth-century accounts consist of pretty descriptions of the brave Highlander and his rugged glen, revealing his altered status from an object of fear and contempt to that of the archetypal Scot.

NOTES

1. Sir Leslie Stephen and Sir Sidney Lee, eds., *The Dictionary of National Biography* (Oxford, 1917, reprinted 1973), XVI, p. 13.
2. Richard Pococke, *Tours in Scotland: 1747, 1750, 1760* (Edinburgh, 1887), p. 108.
3. Thomas Pennant, *A Tour in Scotland* (Warrington, 1769), p. 158. Johnson once said of Pennant: 'That dog is a whig'.
4. George Menary, ed., *The Concise Dictionary of National Biography* (Oxford, 2nd ed. 1906, reprinted 1979), I, pp. 696–7.
5. Dr Samuel Johnson, *A Journey to the Western Islands of Scotland* (London, 1775, reprinted Oxford, 1924), p. 96.
6. Mary Anne Hanway, *A Journey to the Highlands of Scotland . . . by a Lady* (London, c. 1775), pp. 59–61.
7. *The Dictionary of National Biography*, IX, pp. 702–3.
8. Robert Heron, *Scotland Delineated* (Edinburgh, 1799, reprinted 1975), p. 158.
9. Sarah Murray, *A Companion and Useful Guide to the Beauties of Scotland* (Hawick, 1982), p. 35.
10. James Hogg, *A Tour in the Highlands in 1803* (Edinburgh, 1986), p. 11.
11. Dorothy Wordsworth, *Recollections of a Tour Made in Scotland, A.D. 1803* (London, 1874), pp. 98–9.
12. *Ibid.*, p. 116.
13. *Ibid.*
14. Hogg, pp. 41–2.
15. *Ibid.*, p. 43.
16. *The Dictionary of National Biography*, V, p. 484.
17. William Daniell, *A Voyage Round Great Britain . . .* (London, 1814), III, p. 1.
18. *The Concise Dictionary of National Biography*, I, p. 1224.
19. Robert Southey, *Journal of a Tour in Scotland in 1819* (London, 1929), pp. 225–6.
20. John Eddowes Bowman, *The Highlands and Islands: A Nineteenth Century Tour* (Gloucester, 1986), p. 3.
21. *Ibid.*, p. 38.
22. *Ibid.*
23. James Boswell, *The Journal of a Tour to the Hebrides with Samuel Johnson, LL.D.* (London, 1786, reprinted Oxford, 1924), pp. 254–5.
24. *Ibid.*, p. 256. The chiefs' selling of tacks to the highest bidder, a practice which essentially abolished clanship at a stroke, earned this comment from Johnson: 'To banish the Tacksman is easy, to make a country plentiful by diminishing the people, is an expeditious mode of husbandry; but that abundance, which there is nobody to enjoy, contributes little to human happiness' (Johnson, p. 79).

25. Thomas Pennant, *A Tour in Scotland and a Voyage to the Hebrides* (Warrington, 1774), p. 293.
26. *Ibid.*, pp. 293–4.
27. *Ibid.*, p. 294.
28. Hanway, p. 126.
29. *Ibid.*, pp. 126–7.
30. Murray, p. 155.
31. Hogg, p. 92.
32. *The Concise Dictionary of National Biography*, I, p. 1224.
33. Southey, pp. 136–7.
34. Pococke, pp. 127–8.
35. Pennant, *A Tour in Scotland*, p. 117.
36. *Ibid.*, p. 193.
37. *Ibid.*, pp. 193–4.
38. Pennant, *A Tour in Scotland and a Voyage to the Hebrides*, pp. 228–9.
39. Barthélemy Faujas de Saint Fond, *A Journey through England and Scotland to the Hebrides* (English translation Edinburgh, 1784), I, pp. 240–3.
40. Hanway, pp. 132–3.
41. Johnson, p. 104
42. *Ibid.*, p. 104.
43. Faujas de Saint Fond, p. 266.
44. Murray, p. 155.
45. Southey, p. 139.
46. See J. Telfer Dunbar, *Highland Costume* (Edinburgh, 1977), pp. 33–4.
47. Southey, p. 139.
48. Bowman, p. 71.

5

Romanticists

AS CLANSHIP WITHERED under the commercialisation of estate management in the decades after the Forty-Five, Gaeldom became a focus for writers and artists. From the 1760s onward, the Gaels were considered less and less to be the dangerous barbarians who had threatened British civilisation, and adjectives such as 'dismal' and 'forbidding' used by earlier travellers to describe the Highlands and Islands were being replaced by more favourable terms. At a time when increasing numbers of Gaels had to choose between migration to the Lowlands or emigration, a highly romanticised vision of the Highlands' past developed, which endured to the Victorian era and beyond. The outside world never knew very much about Gaeldom to begin with, but with James Macpherson's alleged translations of ancient Gaelic poetry, and later with the poems and historical novels of Sir Walter Scott, both in turn providing inspiration for writers, musicians and artists in Scotland and elsewhere, it was to be fed a constant diet of heroic deeds and epic battles set in a place that never existed outside the vivid imaginations of the Romanticists.

Ossian and Romanticism

The important precursor of the Romantic movement was the work of James Macpherson, the cause of the greatest literary controversy Scotland has yet seen. Indeed, the controversy in time became more famous than the poetry itself. The affair began when Macpherson met the writer and dramatist John Home in 1759. Macpherson stated that he had several pieces of 'ancient poetry', and when Home asked to see them, Macpherson asked him if he knew Gaelic. Home replied that he did not, to which Macpherson asked: 'Then, how can I show you them?' 'Very easily,' said Home, 'translate one of the poems which you think a good one and I imagine that I shall be able to form some opinion of the genius and character of the Gaelic poetry.' Macpherson declined at first but after some pressure from Home, Macpherson 'in a day or two' handed him the 'translation' of a poem on the death of Oscar.[1] Home was pleased, and showed it to, among others, Dr Hugh Blair, Professor of Rhetoric and Belles

Lettres at Edinburgh University. With encouragement (and some say collaboration) from Blair, Macpherson published *Fragments of Ancient Poetry* anonymously in 1760; it sold so well that a second edition was published by the end of the year. The success of *Fragments* enabled Macpherson to make two tours of the Highlands, where he collected Ossianic ballads and manuscripts, and in 1761 he produced the epic *Fingal*. Macpherson's third and final Ossianic work, *Temora*, was published in 1763.

The authenticity of Macpherson's translations of the poems of Ossian, a legendary Gaelic bard, was questioned from the beginning by the *literati* of Edinburgh and London. It fell to Blair to offer a defence, which he provided in his treatise on the poems in 1763; he argued that the poems translated by Macpherson were proof of the existence of Gaelic epic poetry amidst a primitive and unsophisticated culture.[2] He sought to strengthen his argument by including with the treatise a number of documents supporting his view. He asked his friend David Hume, the great sceptic of the Scottish Enlightenment, for his opinion as to the type of evidence to be included. Hume did not mince his words, and writing from London informed Blair that most learned men there doubted the poems were the actual translations of ancient ballads. He did not think the poems would retain their popularity and esteem if their authenticity were questioned, for their 'beauty' was not in enough demand to ensure that, and, 'if the people be once disgusted with the idea of a forgery, they are thence apt to entertain a more disadvantageous notion of the excellency of the production itself'.[3]

Macpherson's apparent arrogance angered many of those who doubted his integrity in the first place; Hume wrote, 'the absurd pride and caprice of Macpherson himself, who scorns, as he pretends, to satisfy any body that doubts his veracity, has tended much to confirm this general scepticism'. Hume had reasons to believe in the authenticity of the poems, 'more than it is possible for any Englishman of letters to have', but told Blair of his reasons against it, namely that 'the preservation of such long and connected poems, by oral translation alone, during a course of fourteen centuries, is so much out of the ordinary course of human affairs, that it requires the strongest reasons to make us believe it'.[4]

Those who doubted the authenticity of Ossian were correct in that the poems were not the literal translations of ancient ballads as preserved in manuscript or taken *verbatim* from oral sources. However, their scepticism arose more from a general disbelief that a 'barbarous' culture such as Gaeldom could possess epic poetry than from an understanding of Gaelic oral tradition; this was a subject which few outside the Highlands, let alone in London, knew anything about. In the preface to *Fragments*, Macpherson claimed that he was translating from ancient Gaelic poems: 'The date of their composition cannot be exactly ascertained . . . they were certainly composed before the establishment of clanship in the northern part of Scotland, which is itself very ancient', adding that 'one circumstance' – he did not elaborate – 'seems to prove them coeval with the infancy of Christianity in Scotland'.[5] But Macpherson never complied with his critics' demand to show to the world the original Gaelic manuscripts from which he made his translations; naturally, this refusal to exhibit the original texts led many to disbelieve their existence.

Dr Samuel Johnson was the greatest of Macpherson's critics. During his visit to the Highlands and Islands in 1773 he took every opportunity to collect information that cast even more doubt on Macpherson's claims. Johnson and Boswell often found people with a knowledge of Ossianic poetry as it existed in the oral tradition, and with the help of their Gaelic-speaking hosts would compare their rendition of certain tracts with Macpherson's versions; sometimes they found similarities, but more often not.

After one such experiment, in which Macpherson's description of a detail closely matched that of the oral tradition, Boswell reminded Johnson that he had said that he did not require Macpherson's translation of Ossian to any more resemble the original than Alexander Pope's translation of Homer. Johnson replied, 'Well, sir, this is just what I always maintained. He has found names, and stories, and phrases, nay passages in old songs, and with them has blended his own compositions, and so made what he gives to the world as the translations of an ancient poem'. If this were the case, Boswell said, then it was 'wrong' for Macpherson to publish Ossian as a poem in six books. 'Yes sir,' Johnson said, 'and to ascribe it to a time too when the Highlanders knew nothing of *books*, and nothing of *six*; – or were perhaps got the length of counting six.'[6]

The controversy was at its height during the 1760s and 1770s, a time when no self-respecting man or woman of letters in Europe was without an opinion on the issue, and continued beyond the end of the century. Most dismissed the poems as a modern creation because they believed the Gaels were too backward to possess an ancient literary epic. A great number of books and pamphlets were published during those years supporting one side of the argument or the other; the most objective of these was the report published in 1805 by the Highland Society of Scotland.

This was based on thorough investigation and found that while the traditional Ossianic legends were indigenous to Scotland (some said they came from Ireland) and were still to be found in the Highlands, none were found to resemble the fragments produced by Macpherson closely enough to be a direct translation. Therefore, the report concluded, Macpherson had edited the original Ossianic poems wherever he found them and inserted his own compositions, the latter being by far the larger part. This conclusion is shared by modern critics: D.S. Thomson writes, 'Macpherson was neither as honest as he claimed nor as inventive as his opponents implied'.[7]

William Wordsworth was inspired by Ossian and a tour in Scotland with his sister Dorothy in 1803 to write a number of poems about the Highlands. While he dismissed James Macpherson as a forger and impostor, Wordsworth was familiar with Ossianic style and content and occasionally borrowed ideas from Macpherson.[8] It was from his visit to the area around Dunkeld that Wordsworth was moved to write 'Glen Almain; or the Narrow Glen', published in 1807. Wordsworth must have been alone in expressing the view that the authenticity of Ossian was unimportant:

> Does then the Bard sleep here indeed?
> Or is it but a groundless creed?
> What matters it? – I blame them not
> Whose Fancy in this lonely Spot
> Was moved; and in such way expressed
> Their notion of its perfect rest.[9]

Wordsworth wrote poems that were more firmly rooted in Highland history. His 'Sonnet in the Pass of Killicranky' was inspired by his visit there in 1803, and while the poem displays considerable political naïveté, it demonstrates that by the beginning of the nineteenth century, Jacobitism had shed its reputation for insurrection and had become not only a safe literary subject but one readily adaptable to Romantic writing:

> Six thousand Veterans practised in war's game,
> Tried men, at Killicranky were arrayed
> Against an equal host that wore the plaid,
> Shepherds and herdsmen. – Like a whirlwind came
> The Highlanders; the slaughter spread like flame;
> And Garry, thundering down his mountain-road,
> Was stopped, and could not breathe beneath the load
> Of the dead bodies. – 'Twas a day of shame
> For them whom precept and the pedantry
> Of cold mechanic battle do enslave.
> O for a single hour of that Dundee
> Who on that day the word of onset gave!

Like conquest would the Men of England see,
And her Foes find a like inglorious grave.[10]

Wordsworth was inspired by a visit to Balquhidder churchyard to write 'Rob Roy's Grave'. In the poem he calls Rob Roy the Scottish equivalent of Robin Hood, and makes the Jacobite into something of a Jacobin. In common with other Romanticists (an exception being Scott), Wordsworth was initially taken with the freedom that seemed to emanate from the French Revolution, and because Rob Roy was indeed a law unto himself, the poet saw Rob Roy as embodying a number of revolutionary ideals. For Wordsworth, Rob Roy came either too late or too early: too late because 'polity was then too strong' and too early because he died before the era of liberty that seemed to Wordsworth to be imminent. The first premise at least is demonstrably wrong, for during Rob Roy's life, 'polity' did not sufficiently exist in the Highlands to deter him from anything. Nevertheless, the poem is important if only for the influence it had on Scott – the title page of his novel *Rob Roy* carries a line from it:

> Heaven gave Rob Roy a dauntless heart
> And wondrous length and strength of arm:
> Nor craved he more to quell his foes,
> Or keep his friends . . . from harm.
> For Thou, although with some wild thoughts,
> Wild Chieftain of a savage Clan!
> Hadst this to boast of; thou didst love
> The *liberty* of Man.[11]

Scott and Celtification

Sir Walter Scott (1771–1832) played the biggest part in the cultural rehabilitation of the Gaels. It was from a number of influences in his youth that Scott received a Highland, and more particularly a 'neo-Jacobite', bias that would colour his work. He recalled as a child 'detesting the name of Cumberland with more than infant hatred', and recalled hearing of 'the cruelties exercised in the executions at Carlisle, and in the Highlands after the battle of Culloden'.[12] Although raised in the Church of Scotland, Scott was an Episcopalian convert and he quite probably sympathised with the non-juring element of the Jacobite movement. While admitting early in his literary career that he was largely ignorant of 'Celtic manners', he stressed that 'I have from my youth delighted in all the Highland traditions which I could pick up from old Jacobites who used to frequent my father's house', his father being an Edinburgh advocate whose clientèle included a number of them.[13] In addition to these impressions, Scott made several visits to the Highlands as a youth.

He made a tour of Highland Perthshire in 1793 during which he took in the scenery and met several Highland lairds, and from Abercrombie of Tullibody he heard anecdotes of Rob Roy Macgregor.[14] Scott was to build on these contacts with the Highland élite throughout his life. A Tory and a social climber (witness his mock-feudal creation of Abbotsford), he believed that everything good and distinctive about Gaeldom was embodied in the chiefs and clan gentry. The fact that they might be Eton-educated and permanently resident in London was immaterial to him. Such a perspective helps to explain Scott's tacit approval of emigration and the Clearances; chiefs such as Alastair MacDonell of Glengarry were to become Scott's collaborators in the substitution of myth for reality that was to underlie the cultural rehabilitation of Gaeldom.

Scott had been an enthusiastic reader of Macpherson's Ossian. '[These] tales were for a long time so much of my delight that I could repeat without remorse whole Cantos of the one & Duans of the other',[15] but in time, 'the tawdry repetitions of the Ossianic phraseology disgusted me rather sooner than might have been expected from my age',[16] explaining that 'Ossian . . . has more charms for youth than for a more advanced stage'.[17] On the authenticity of Ossian, he wrote that 'after making every allowance for the disadvantages of a literal translation & the possible debasement which those *now* collected may have suffered in the great & violent change which the Highlands have undergone since the researches of Macpherson', he concluded that 'incalculably the greater part' of Ossian was Macpherson's own creation.[18] But he clearly understood the tenacity with which learned Gaels held to the belief that Ossian was authentic: 'When once the Highlanders had adopted the poems of Ossian as an article of national faith you would far sooner have got them to disavow the Scriptures than to abandon a line of the contested tales'.[19]

Nevertheless, the influence which Macpherson had on Romantic writers such as Scott, not only in matters of style (an arcane subject for historians) but subject matter as well, cannot be overestimated. Ossian suggested to Scott that the Highlands and Islands could not be equalled as a Romantic setting, and only reinforced the persistent Lowland belief that Gaeldom in the days of clanship consisted of savagery, violence, heroism, some culture, but not much else – a misconception that Scott himself did little to remedy.

'The Lady of the Lake' was Scott's third long poem, appearing in 1810. Four years earlier, he had confided to his friend and correspondent Lady Abercorn about a work he had in mind:

This is a Highland romance of Love Magic and War founded upon the manners of our mountaineers with my stories about whom your Ladyship was so much interested. My great deficiency is that being born and bred not only a lowlander but a borderer I do not in the least understand the Gaelic language and am therefore much at a loss to find authentic materials for my undertaking.[20]

Whether Scott had really overcome this deficiency or not, 'The Lady of the Lake' proved to be not only a critical but a commercial success, and ensured that he would return to a Highland theme in later works. The keys to this success lay in Scott's Romantic depiction of 'Celtic manners', his accurate assumption that the reading public wanted 'light and natural poetry, but which would stir the heart',[21] and perhaps most importantly, his description of the Trossachs, that safe and picturesque gateway to the Highlands. Anyone who doubts that Scott helped create the Highland tourist industry should consider the words of Welsh tourist John Eddowes Bowman, who visited the area in 1825. 'Of all the fairy scenes which Scotland had hitherto presented to our observation,' he wrote, 'the Trossachs and Loch Katrine must undoubtedly be set down as the most enchanting.' He found the scene 'just as it is described in the first Canto of the Lady of the Lake'. He continued:

Who that has a mind the least sensible to the charms of Nature and of Poetry, can fail, while rambling here, to bear testimony to the spirited fidelity of the picture which Sir W. Scott has drawn of it in that bewitching gem of poetry? Though the scenery is new and enchanting, we recognize it at every turn, by his luxurious touches, and when we attempt to describe it, it is his glowing language.[22]

In a letter to Scott, the Anglo-Irish writer Maria Edgeworth explained the popular appeal of the poem. 'The novelty of the Highland world as discovered to our view powerfully excites curiosity and interest', and although 'it is all new to us it does not embarrass or perplex, or strain the attention. We never are harassed by doubts of the probability of any of these modes of life.' While the readers themselves did not know these details of Highland life before reading the poem, 'we are quite certain they did exist exactly as they are represented'.[23] In his poems and novels about the Highlands, Scott assumed that his readers knew little or nothing of the subject, which was wise considering that his works were not aimed specifically at the Scottish market, which was too small to support a writer of his ambition, but rather the entire British Empire, and by extension the rest of the English-speaking world. The notes which Scott included in his works, without which the average reader would have been lost, were based upon his researches and impressions, and these often reveal what he himself thought about his subject. In Canto

I, stanza XVI of 'The Lady of the Lake', the unnamed hero (who is later revealed to be King James V) is hunting a stag in the Trossachs when he muses: 'To meet with highland plunderers here / Were worse than loss of steed or deer'.[24] In his notes to the poem, Scott explained simply that the clans 'who inhabited the romantic regions in the neighbourhood of Loch Katrine, were, even until a late period, much addicted to predatory excursions upon their lowland neighbours'.[25]

Despite the success enjoyed by 'The Lady of the Lake', it was soon overtaken as Byron's romantic poetry not only perfected the genre but captured its market. Scott's response was to create his own genre. *Waverley*, published in 1814, is generally credited as being the first historical novel in the English language. It shares a number of elements with 'The Lady of the Lake', such as a heroic Highland chief as a central character, the setting just beyond the Highland line, and Highland-Lowland conflict, but whereas 'The Lady of the Lake' is set in the sixteenth century, *Waverley* is centred on the Forty-Five, and involves one of Scott's favourite themes, historical change. Scott drew on the many Jacobite anecdotes he had received over the years, which he supplemented with printed sources, namely John Home's *History of the Rebellion in the year 1745* (1802) and James Ray's *A Compleat History of the Rebellion* (1746).[26]

The plot involves a young English officer in the government army, Edward Waverley, who is sent to Scotland at the beginning of the Forty-Five. He meets a Jacobite laird in Lowland Perthshire, makes his way into the Highlands where he encounters a Highland chief, Fergus MacIvor, his sister Flora, and their clan, and soon becomes a Jacobite himself, pledging his loyalty to the cause and to Charles Edward Stuart. The novel follows the course of the rebellion up to the Jacobite retreat at Derby and the subsequent skirmish at Clifton, at which point Waverley becomes separated from the army. As a result, the circumstances and result of the battle of Culloden are described only at second hand, and the 'pacification' that followed not at all – Scott chose not to describe these events in detail. There is no romance in atrocity, and while Scott had a regard for facts uncommon in fiction writers, he was unwilling to let the truth spoil a good story. He had written several years before the publication of *Waverley*, 'the time is now past when the theme [Jacobitism] would have both danger and offence in it'.[27] However, Lorn Macintyre has suggested that for Scott to portray the more unseemly aspects of the battle such as the Duke of Cumberland's order of no quarter 'would be offensive to Hanoverian prejudices which Scott himself to some extent shared'.[28] In addition, for Scott to describe the battle in his characteristically painstaking manner, he may well have had to reveal the unpalatable fact the Cumberland's army included not only Scots but Highlanders (notably Campbells, Grants, and Munros) as well. But *Waverley* had, and still has for some, great appeal, and enjoyed even more critical acclaim and commercial success than 'The Lady of the Lake'. As a critic for the *Edinburgh Review* wrote in November 1814:

... one great source of the interest which the volumes before us undoubtedly possess, is to be sought in the surprise that is excited by discovering, that in our own country, and almost in our own age, manners and characteristics existed, and were conspicuous, which we had been accustomed to consider as belonging to remote antiquity, or extravagant romance.[29]

Byron's work notwithstanding, Scott returned to the long verse romance with 'The Lord of the Isles', published in 1815, which depicted power struggles and divided loyalties in the West Highlands and Hebrides in the years up to and including the Wars of Independence. The climax is a description of the Battle of Bannockburn, which is both realistic (he acknowledged John Barbour's *The Brus* [c. 1375] as his source) and romanticised; Scott wished to convey the impression to his readers that Highlanders and Lowlanders, or 'Celts' and 'Saxons' as he may have preferred, joined forces to preserve Scottish independence and eject the foreign invader. This alleged partnership is anachronistic as the distinction between the two cultures had not yet emerged. Scott's real purpose, however, was to suggest that the Gaels had always been capable of patriotism, that is, before the raising of Highland regiments of the British army in the decades after Culloden. From Canto VI, verse xxviii reads:

Bruce, with the pilot's wary eye,
The slackening of the storm could spy.
'One effort more, and Scotland's free!
Lord of the Isles, my trust in thee
Is as firm as Ailsa-rock;
Rush on, with Highland sword and targe,
I, with my Carrick spearmen, charge:
Now, forward to the shock!'
At once the spears were forward thrown,
Against the sun the broadswords shone;
The pibroch lent its maddening tone . . .[30]

Scott's next work with a Highland theme was *Rob Roy*, published in 1818. The novel shares several elements with *Waverley*: a Highlander as a central character; Highland-Lowland conflict, which in *Rob Roy* is represented by the gentleman outlaw himself; and the setting. The story is largely set in the area around Loch Lomond, once again a part of the Highlands easily accessible from the south. It is in *Rob Roy* that

Scott most successfully portrays the difference between Highland and Lowland: 'hordes of wild, shaggy, dwarfish cattle and ponies, conducted by Highlanders, as wild, as shaggy, and sometimes as dwarfish, as the animals they had in charge, often traversed the streets of Glasgow'.[31] Scott describes the sight of (and reaction to) Highland drovers at the Glasgow markets:

> Strangers gazed with surprise on the antique and fantastic dress, and listened to the unknown and dissonant sounds of their language, while the mountaineers, armed even while engaged in this peaceful occupation with musket and pistol, sword, dagger, and target, stared with astonishment at the articles of luxury of which they knew not the use . . .[32]

Scott no longer felt the need to supply his readers with innumerable details contrasting the two cultures; rather, he allowed his characters to express their particular loyalties and prejudices in their own voices. In doing so, he perpetuated a number of Highland myths, particularly with respect to the state of law and order in Rob Roy's time. Frank Osbaldistone, the Englishman who narrates the story, is reproved by the Lowland magistrate Bailie Nicol Jarvie for his erroneous assumptions about law enforcement in the Highlands:

> . . . the truth is, that ye ken naething about our hill country, or Hielands, as we ca' them. They are clean anither set frae the like o' huz; there's nae bailie-courts amang them – nae magistrates that dinna bear the sword in vain . . . But it's just the laird's command, and the loon maun loup; and the never another law they hae but the length o' their dirks – the broadsword's pursuer, or plaintiff, as you Englishers ca' it, and the target is defender; the stoutest head bears langest out – and there's a Hieland plea for ye.[33]

In explaining the appeal that crime has for the 'uncivilised' Gaels, Bailie Jarvie states that there was not work for up to half of them, and that 'the agriculture, the pasturage, the fisheries, and every species of honest industry about the country, cannot employ the one moiety of the population, let them work as lazily as they like, and they do work as if a pleugh or a spade burnt their fingers'.[34] He tells Frank Osbaldistone of the overcrowding and scarcity in Highland parishes (but not that this was a result of estate mismanagement). Allowing for a proportion of those who 'may make some little thing for themsells honestly in the Lowlands by shearing in harst, droving, hay-making, and the like', Bailie Jarvie said there remained 'mony hundreds and thousands o' lang-legged Hieland gilies that will neither work nor want, and maun thigging and sorning on their acquaintance, or live by doing the laird's bidding, be't right or be't wrang':[35]

And mair especially, mony hundreds o' them come down to the borders of the low country, where there's gear to grip, and live by stealing, reiving, lifting cows, and the like depredations! A thing deplorable in ony Christian country – the mair especially, that they take pride in it, and reckon driving a spreagh a gallant, manly action, and mair befitting of pretty men (as sic reivers will ca' themsells) than to win a day's wage by ony honest thrift.[36]

The chiefs were no better in this respect than their clansmen, Bailie Jarvie asserts, 'for if they dinna bid them gae reive and harry, the deil a bit they forbid them; and they shelter them, or let them shelter themsells, in their woods, and mountains, and strongholds, whenever the thing's done'.[37] Each and every chief tried to maintain the greatest number of clansmen he could, or, which was the same thing, as many clansmen as could maintain themselves 'in ony fashion, fair or foul'.[38] Anyone living just south of the Highland line and suffering the loss of cattle and other property at the hands of Gaels *would* be likely to believe the whole of Gaeldom was a den of thieves; and in reality these crimes *were* attributed to Highlanders in general. Unfortunately, Scott presented Bailie Nicol Jarvie as a reliable witness and in passing on his remarks without disclaimer, he merely enshrined the myth that cattle stealing was an enterprise conducted by entire clans with the chiefs acting in a Mafia 'Godfather' role.

The less-than-romantic truth was that such activities were carried out by the criminal element largely outwith the clan system, as the chiefs and clan gentry preferred legal (and more lucrative) means of obtaining additional income. But Scott left his readers in 1818 with the impression that the Gaels had been, until quite recently,

> ... wi' gun and pistol, dirk and dourlach, ready to disturb the peace o' the country whenever the laird likes; and that's the grievance of the Hielands, whilk are, and hae been for this thousand years by-past, a bike o' the maist lawless unchristian limmer that ever disturbed a douce, quiet, Godfearing neighbourhood, like this o' ours in the west here.[39]

Scott returned to Highland subject matter with two short stories, 'The Highland Widow' and 'The Two Drovers', which were included in *The Chronicles of the Canongate* published in 1827 and 1828. 'The Highland Widow' is the story of Elspat, the old widow of a Jacobite and infamous cateran, MacTavish Mhor, who learns that her son, Hamish Bean, has through necessity enlisted with a Highland regiment destined for America. The widow is aghast that her son has joined the army of the 'Saxons' and is intent on preventing his departure; Scott means her to represent the 'old order' in the Highlands and all it stood for such as

Jacobitism, cattle-stealing, barbarism, etc. The widow is ignorant and isolated from the rest of the world to the extent that 'she was quite unconscious of the great change which had taken place in the country around her, the substitution of civil order for military violence, and the strength gained by the law and its adherents over those who were called in Gaelic song, "the stormy sons of the sword"'.[40]

In contrast, her son is well aware of the new state of affairs in the Highlands. When his mother reproves him for enlisting and urges him to become a cateran like his father, he replies

> . . . how shall I convince you that you live in this land of our fathers, as if our fathers were yet living? When my father lived and fought, the great respected the man of the strong right hand, and the rich feared him. That is ended . . . the land is conquered – its lights are quenched, – Glengarry, Lochiel, Perth, Lord Lewis, all the high chiefs are dead or in exile – We may mourn for it, but we cannot help it. Bonnet, broadsword, and sporran – power, strength, and wealth, were all lost on Drummossie-muir.[41]

The widow manages to detain her son beyond the time he was to report for duty, and as a result, he is taken prisoner by his fellow Gaels and executed for desertion. Despite the obvious faults of the story, such as the contrived nature of the plot and the false, Ossian-like English spoken by the characters, it is Scott's only attempt to portray life in the Highlands in the aftermath of the Forty-Five, and his only story concerned exclusively with common folk in the Highlands as opposed to the chiefs and clan gentry.

'The Two Drovers' is a study of national character and concerns a dispute between friends that ends in tragedy. The 'Celt' is represented by Robin Oig, who is 'as light and alert as one of the deer of his mountains',[42] the 'Saxon' is represented by Henry Wakefield, 'the model of Old England's merry yeomen'. Friends from previous droves, they meet shortly after the Doune Fair and agree to travel together, with their herds, to the cattle markets in England. While south of the border, an argument between the men, both jealous of their honour, develops into a feud, which results in Robin Oig killing Henry Wakefield.

Robin Oig is taken prisoner, tried, and executed. Scott never makes it clear whether Robin Oig, a Gael, is to be taken to represent the Scottish people as a whole, or if Henry Wakefield, a 'Saxon', represents the Lowlands as well as England itself. Perhaps Scott himself provided the answer in 1822 when he chose to present Highland dress (itself an artificial device) to George IV and the world as the national garb of Scotland.

The state visit by George iv to Scotland in 1822 was the first by a

British monarch north of the border since 1650; no precedent existed for a royal visit since the Union. Walter Scott, the acknowledged expert on Scotland's heritage, was the natural choice as Master of Ceremonies for the occasion, for he alone had the reputation for boldness and imagination required to give the event all the pomp and pageantry it seemed to merit. That he had those qualities was amply demonstrated when he spearheaded the efforts to locate the Honours of Scotland (or Crown Jewels), and when these relics of Scottish nationhood were found in Edinburgh Castle in 1818, the waiting crowd was told of the discovery by a touch of theatre that only Scott could have planned, the raising of the royal standard.[43] A great deal of the pageantry planned by Scott for the visit was what his son-in-law John Lockhart called 'Sir Walter's Celtification of Scotland'.[44]

Using the trappings of Gaelic culture, mythical or simply concocted, Scott created a 'plaided panorama' (again Lockhart's words), casting a powerful spell which presented Scotland as a picturesque, homogeneous place draped liberally in tartan. By 1822, Gaeldom had become a minority culture in the process of marginalisation. Yet within a short time, Scott invented for it a bogus tradition that was taken at the time (and still is) to be both ancient and representative of Scotland as a whole. This development would not have been possible without the conscious co-operation of the chiefs and clan gentry eager to deflect criticism of their treatment of their erstwhile clans. Perhaps the most persistent myth created for George IV's visit was that of Highland dress. Scott had decided that the kilt and all its accoutrements, by this time a highly stylised costume which bore little resemblance to the clothing actually worn by Gaels in the days of clanship, was to be the national dress of Scotland for the purpose of the visit, and planned a number of events for which its use was to be obligatory; for one such event, a Grand Ball, Scott decreed that with the exception of those in uniform, 'no Gentleman is to be allowed to appear in any thing but the ancient Highland costume'.[45]

Scott's insistence on the matter of dress not only annoyed many of the Lowland élite who were most assuredly not Gaels (but who complied anyway), but members of the Highland gentry itself. Sir John Peter Grant of Rothiemurchas, father of Elizabeth Grant, complained of 'the whimsical affectation of a sort of highland costume', which he felt was worn 'with about as much propriety in the conception and execution as if it had taken place in Paris or Brussels'.[46]

Nevertheless, Scott had set the tone for the proceedings when he wrote to the Highland chiefs to procure their participation in a 'gathering of the clans' he had planned, not only for the King's benefit but for all to see. He wrote to John Norman MacLeod, 24th chief of his clan, urging him to come to Edinburgh 'and bring half-a-dozen or half-a-score of Clansmen, so as to look like an Island Chief as you are. Highlanders are what he will like most to see'.[47] David Stewart of Garth, the old soldier whose recently published *Sketches of the Character, Manners and Customs of the Highlanders of Scotland* had established him as an expert on the Highlands, was in charge of organising the martial aspects of the pageantry. Stewart was also in charge (or guilty) of planning and executing George IV's controversial, albeit brief, appearance in Highland dress. When the King, a large man by any standards, was presented in both kilt and stockings during a levée at Holyroodhouse at which more than twelve hundred people were introduced to him in the space of seventy-five minutes,[48] some were delighted while others were scandalised. 'The greatest offense given by that expensive and unfortunate costume was not to aesthetic taste,' John Prebble writes, 'but to Lowland pride, and to the self-esteem of those Highland gentlemen who wished to distance themselves as far as possible from the presumed savagery of their ancestors.'[49] Prebble quotes James Stuart of Dunearn, who seemed to sum up the feelings of many who witnessed the spectacle:

> The King did not seem to move a muscle and we all asked ourselves when we came away, what had made us take so much trouble. He was dressed in tartan. Sir Walter had ridiculously made us appear a nation of Highlanders, and the bagpipe and the tartan was the order of the day.[50]

While the falseness of Scott's 'Celtification' was apparent to many in 1822, the image he gave to the world has persisted to the present day, bolstered by, among other things, Queen Victoria's neo-Jacobitism and the contributions made by Sir Harry Lauder in the field of light entertainment. Because Scott has become the acknowledged preserver of Scotland's past, the myths he created were not only believed in but were also assumed to be rooted in antiquity. In presenting the Highland Laddie as the archetypal Scot, he not only reduced a country of rich cultural diversity to a one-dimensional caricature, but created a false and highly sanitised picture of Gaeldom, where cold commercialism, and not a romantic feudalism, was the reality. Edwin Muir called Scott 'a sham bard of a sham nation'.

Scott wrote about many aspects of Highland history – clanship, conflict with the Lowlands, Jacobitism, and even the clan fight at Perth in 1396 in *The Fair Maid of Perth* (1828) – but about clearance, emigration, and the chiefs' abandonment of *Dùthchas*, he let his readers remain ignorant. To ascertain Scott's views on the breakdown of the clan system and its causes, one must consult his personal correspondence. As these were not the official output of 'the author of *Waverley*', he could afford to express himself without causing public offence.

To his friend and regular correspondent the Countess of Sutherland (later Marchioness of Stafford), on whose estate the most radical 'improvement' programme was attempted, he wrote in November 1811 that he had little doubt that her 'patriotic attempts to combine industry with such reliques of ancient manners, as still dignify the highlanders who have the good fortune to be under your protection' would succeed, though perhaps not with 'the rapidity that your philanthropy may anticipate'.[51]

The Sutherland estate reorganisation, which meant the conversion of the interior to sheep walks and the decanting of the population to the coasts, proved controversial and led to accusations of greed and brutality. However, Scott believed the changes being undertaken in Sutherland were acceptable, and he reassured the Marchioness of Stafford of the benevolence of her actions:

> It has taken a generation to convert a race of feudal warriors (for such were highlanders previous to 1745) into a quiet and peaceable peasantry, perhaps it may take as long to introduce a spirit of action and persevering exertion necessary to animate them in their new profession. In the mean time, a new race is gradually arising who will be trained to those sentiments and habits which the present state of society requires, and which it is your ladyship's wish to introduce, and who will, in the course of twenty years, look back at the prejudices of their fathers, and with gratitude to their mistress who pursued their welfare in spite of themselves.[52]

Scott's attitude towards the Clearances seemed to alter somewhat with time, however. In a letter to Maria Edgeworth in July 1830 (in which he used the remarkable device of referring to chiefs and clan gentry as *H*ighlanders and the common Gaels as *h*ighlanders), he wrote, 'I am sorry to say that the Highland Lairds like the Irish have in many instances run the reckless course you describe and I would to God that gibbeting one of them would be a warning to the rest'.[53] But he told her that a Highland chief/proprietor 'is not and cannot be the man towards his vassals which their fathers were before the year 1745',[54] explaining that 'before that fatal year' a chief depended upon the number of his men he could raise, and calculated his wealth on that basis. The only time chiefs and clan gentry went to the Continent was to buy arms 'against the grand effort'. The Forty-Five ended this system, he wrote, and the descendants of the Jacobite chiefs were restored 'by the humanity of government but their ancient relation to their vassals could not and should not be renewed', and if anything remained of 'the old influence' it was reserved exclusively for the raising of men for the Highland regiments.[55]

When men were not needed for the army, Scott wrote, 'the Chief or Laird naturally enough found the immense herds of society which loitered on his estate rather a curse than a blessing'.[56] A single Lowland shepherd could offer ten times the rent for a place 'which the highlanders a hundred perhaps in number' could pay, and after the conversion to sheep walks, 'six shepherds and twelve dogs would often tenant the land which had maintained fifty families'.[57] Scott was well qualified to make such statements. A Borderer, he came from a sheep-owning family. Also, Scott's one-time friend and correspondent James Hogg, a shepherd himself, had toured the Highlands in 1803, and his account of his experiences there, which contained his views on the suitability and implications of sheep farming in the region, were communicated to Scott in a series of letters.[58]

In addition, Scott revealed to Maria Edgeworth that 'Highland gentlemen are fond of *spaglin* as they call it a sort of showy vanity – they are desirous to keep abreast of the English in expense and maintain their own privileges of chieftainship besides'.[59] Under the circumstances, he continued, the chiefs had no alternative but to convert their estates to sheep walks, despite the emigration that resulted adding, 'it is vain to abuse the gentlemen for this which is the inevitable consequence of a great change of things', but 'when the Highlander is driven on by a personal love of expense the change is attended with more ruinous circumstances and general distress'.[60] When this was the case, he wrote, 'the lands are bought on speculation often by men of Highland extraction or lowlanders who are kind enough to the people, sometimes to speculatists who wish to make the most of their purchase'. The latter situation was 'difficult and dangerous' in the Highlands, as 'there is a point beyond which the highlander cannot be driven. If an attempt is made to drive his cattle you must look for very lawless results. In return while they have anything they will submit to the hardest life [rather] than leave the glen'.[61] He then referred Maria Edgeworth to the writings of the Earl of Selkirk, that exponent of emigration in the early nineteenth century.

The cultural activities of the Highland societies

Scott was not the only would-be preserver of Gaelic culture. From the last quarter of the eighteenth century, a number of societies were formed in London, Edinburgh, and elsewhere to preserve and maintain the more picturesque aspects of Gaelic culture, a great stimulus being the popularity of Ossian. While some of these were little more than social clubs that gave gentlemen of Highland extraction or otherwise the opportunity of wearing Highland dress, others actively supported Gaelic through the collection and publishing of material, as well as sponsoring piping competitions.

The Highland Society of London was formed in 1778 to preserve the dress, music and 'martial spirit' of the Gaels. It was composed of chiefs, clan gentry and other interested parties resident in London, and among its immediate priorities was the encouragement of piping and the composition of Gaelic poetry. It arranged 'gatherings' beginning with the Falkirk Tryst in October 1781 at which piping competitions were held, attempted for twenty years to recruit a MacCrimmon piper in an effort to establish a professorship in the bagpipe at a Scottish university – without success – and encouraged a system of musical notation for the pipes.[62]

The Society also began, at the Falkirk Tryst of 1781, an annual Gaelic poetry competition on the fixed theme of the Gaelic language and the bagpipe. The first winner was the already established poet Duncan Bàn Macintyre (*Donnachadh Bàn Mac-an-t-Saoir*), who went on to win the prize on five further occasions by 1789. In his successful entry for 1781, Macintyre (1724–1812) praises the work of the Society and proceeds to make a laughable claim for the popularity of Gaelic south of the border. An English translation reads:

> London is full at present
> of the activity of Highland friends
> who are exalting Gaelic,
> each day as it comes round;
> and because of the excellence with which
> the heroes make frequent use of it,
> every man in England
> would fain have it in their midst.[63]

The task which Macintyre assumed in composing a poem every year on the same topic (in order to augment his income as a member of Edinburgh's City Guard, a job he held for many years after leaving the Highlands in 1766), neatly mirrored the commercialisation of estate management that was taking place in the Highlands. The artistic limitations imposed by the Society certainly affected an undeniably talented poet; in the opinion of a recent editor of Macintyre's poetry, 'it is to be regretted that the subject was not changed: even Macintyre, with all his resources of vocabulary and metrical variations, finds it difficult to produce new ideas on the same topic, year after year. This may account for some obscurities in thought and language to be found in the poems'.[64]

One stanza from Macintyre's unsuccessful entry for the competition of 1785 praises the valour of the Highland regiments, who fight in defence of 'Gaelic, pipe, and flag', the latter presumably the Union Flag, while another comments on the recent disannexation of the forfeited estates and makes the absurd assertion that once the descendants of attainted Jacobites have regained their estates, 'no farmer will be in distress'. Macintyre's reputation was not founded on such doggerel:

> London is very highly encouraged
> by the vigour of the gallant Gaels,
> who gained respect wherever they were sought out –
> those stalwart, handsome champions,
> who are assuming real responsibility
> for keeping the country powerful,
> and have decreed that, for all time,
> Gaelic, pipe, and flag shall be inviolable.
>
> Each incident that befalls them
> is more auspicious than the last;
> the lands of which they were dispossessed
> they have completely regained;
> all who have rights will come into their heritage,
> they are overlords of their own property;
> the heirs will be well to do,
> and no farmer will be in distress.[65]

The Highland Society of London played an important part in the belated legalisation of Highland dress. A Society committee consisting of General Simon Fraser (son of Lord Lovat), Lord Chief Baron Macdonald and others approached the MP and Pitt supporter the Marquess of Graham (later 3rd Duke of Montrose), who introduced the successful bill in 1782; this achievement was commemorated by Macintyre in his 'Song to the Highland Garb' (*Oran do 'n eideadh Ghaidhealach*), which won him the £5 prize offered by the Society on the subject of the 'Glorious Restoration of the Highland Dress' in 1784.[66] The Society further demonstrated its concern for 'the literature and language of the Gael' by subscribing to several collections of Gaelic poetry, resolving in 1788 to give 10 guineas annually in support of Raining's School, SSPCK's Gaelic teacher-training college in Inverness, and by making repeated (and unsuccessful) attempts to establish a Chair in Gaelic and Celtic Literature at a Scottish university.[67]

Not surprisingly, the Highland Society of London became embroiled in the Ossianic controversy, and in 1779 wrote to James Macpherson expressing its wish that he publish the original Gaelic manuscripts he used in his translation. Macpherson replied that he was ready to publish the poems as soon as an adequate fund was provided for printing the work 'in a elegant manner'. In 1782 Macpherson gave what Gaelic poems he had to the Society for their publication, as they had received £1000 for this purpose from 'patriotic Highlanders' in India.[68] By this time Macpherson was heavily involved in Indian affairs (he had become an MP in 1780), and it was clear he was fast losing interest in the whole matter. Nothing more was heard from him, and he died in 1796. His failure over three decades to publish the Gaelic manuscripts from which he allegedly translated should have been enough to convince everyone that no such manuscripts existed. But the Highland Society of London took care to acquire Macpherson's papers, a task simplified by the fact that John Mackenzie, the Society's secretary at the time, was also the executor of Macpherson's estate.[69]

In 1805 the Highland Society of Scotland published the results of its inquiry into the authenticity of Ossian, and in 1807 the Highland Society of London published what purported to be the original Gaelic Ossian with an introduction by Sir John Sinclair. These Gaelic poems were widely believed to be translated from Macpherson's English version and not originals at all, but the Society persevered: after the Battle of Waterloo the secretary was sent to France to find any ancient Celtic manuscripts in the colleges and libraries of Paris.[70]

The Highland Society of Scotland was founded in Edinburgh in 1784 by a group of prominent Improvers who had as their principal aim the economic betterment of the Highlands and Islands, but who were also resolved to 'pay a proper attention to the preservation of the Language, Poetry, and Music of the Highlands'.[71] In that same year a committee of the Society heard Duncan Bàn Macintyre sing his poem 'On the Restitution of the Forfeited Estates'.[72] The peak of the society's cultural activities was from the end of the eighteenth century to around 1825, during which time it acted as a Gaelic 'academy of letters', amassing a large collection of manuscripts, papers, and printed work. In the first few years of its existence the Society retained a bard, a piper, and a 'professor of Gaelic', as well as sponsoring Gaelic classes and piping.[73] Lasting achievements of the Highland Society of Scotland were its inquiry into the authenticity of Ossian, the results of which were published in 1805, and a Gaelic dictionary, launched by Sir John Sinclair in 1806 and completed eventually in 1828.[74]

The work of the Highland societies was important if only for the amount of Gaelic material they were able to collect. The considerable energy devoted by them to the Ossianic controversy would have been better spent helping to develop Gaelic into a language of industry and commerce, thereby ensuring for it a more secure future as well as countering its popular image as barbaric, obsolete and suited only to poetry.

The cult of the Forty-Five

Interest in the Highlands' past was not confined to the genteel society which read Scott's lengthy works and debated the authenticity of Ossian. While the reputation of Robert Burns rests mainly upon his Scots poetry, from 1787 he turned his attention to song-writing and contributed around 250 songs partly or wholly of his own composition to two collections while amassing many more.[75] Supplying lyrics to familiar tunes or improving already existing ones, Burns used both Scots and English. This was not merely an antiquarian exercise but afforded an opportunity for innovation. He was to present the Gaels and their Jacobite loyalties in a favourable light – indeed, Burns must have been one of the first Lowland songwriters to do so. He was on safe ground in that the Jacobite threat was extinct. But his was a sentimental neo-Jacobitism, and perhaps he was converted during his tour of the Highlands in 1787, which included a visit to the battlefield of Culloden. In his song 'The Chevalier's Lament', written in March 1788, Burns offers the thoughts of Charles Edward Stuart while in hiding after the battle. The idea that the prince mourned the ruin of his 'gallant' Highlanders more than his own is not only romantic but quite absurd. The myth of 'Bonnie Prince Charlie' was in the making:

> The deed that I dar'd, could it merit their malice,
> A king and a father to place on his throne?
> His right are these hills, and his right are those valleys,
> Where the wild beasts find shelter, tho I can find none!
>
> But 'tis not my suff'rings this wretched, forlorn-
> My brave gallant friends, 'Tis your ruin I mourn!
> Your faith prov'd so loyal in hot bloody trial,
> Alas, can I make it no better return?[76]

Not all of Burns's Jacobite songs are mere myth-making, however. 'The Battle of Sherramuir' is ostensibly concerned with the battle of Sheriffmuir in the 1715 rebellion, but Burns admired the Jacobites' defiance of 'Whigs and Covenant true blues' and perhaps saw a parallel between this and his own dispute with the ministers and elders of the Auld Licht persuasion in Ayrshire. For him, the Jacobites fought not for the restoration of the autocratic and anglicising rule of the Stuarts but represented a bold and direct challenge to established authority.

> But had ye seen the philibegs,
>   And skyrin tartan trews, man;
> When in the teeth they daur'd our Whigs,
>   And Covenant true blues, man!

In lines extended lang and large,
When baignets o'erpower'd the targe,
    And thousands hasten'd to the charge,
Wi Highland wrath and frae the sheath,
Drew the blades of death, till, out a breath,
    They fled like frightened daws, man![77]

Another composer of Jacobite songs was Baroness Carolina (1766–1845), better known as Lady Nairne. Her songs appeared after those of Burns, and her devotion to Jacobitism was more sincere. Her most famous song, 'Will ye no come back again?', is a plea for the return of Charles Edward Stuart and is typical of the sentimentalism that abounds in her work. The transformation of the 'young pretender' who had endangered British civilisation in 1745 into the 'Bonnie Prince Charlie' who fought for Scotland was mirrored by the rehabilitation of the Gaels. A race formerly believed to be pagan barbarians whose delight in the theft of cattle was exceeded only by that provided by the indiscriminate slaughter of women and children, had become the faithful followers of the Prince and the resolute defenders of Scottish nationhood. The real issues that surrounded the Forty-Five were forgotten, and Lady Nairne (among others, it must be said) was perhaps wilfully ignorant of the fact that while some of the clansmen who joined the rebellion may well have believed they were fighting for Scotland in some undefined way as well as for their chief, Charles Edward Stuart most certainly had a different agenda.

However, for Lady Nairne's Jacobite songs to have gained the enduring popularity they have enjoyed, myth had to replace fact. A song commemorating Donald Cameron of Lochiel's threat to burn the houses of his clansmen reluctant to join the Jacobite army would hardly have achieved much pathos. Typical of Lady Nairne's output is 'My Bonnie Hieland Laddie':

Prince Charlie he's cum owre frae France,
    In Scotland to proclaim his daddie;
May Heaven still his cause advance,
    And shield him in his Hieland Plaidie!
But tho' the Hieland folks are puir,
    Yet their hearts are leal and steady;
And there's no ane amang them a',
    That would betray their Hieland laddie.[78]

Lady Nairne's song 'Charlie is my darling' emphasises how the clansmen in the Forty-Five fought for 'Scotland's right', though what is meant by this is not revealed, nor, predictably, what it meant for 'the young chevalier'. With minor changes, the song could easily have sung the praises of the Gaels who fought and died in far greater numbers in British wars of colonisation around the world:

> Wi' Hieland bonnets on their heads,
>   And claymores bright and clear,
> They came to fight for Scotland's right,
>   And the young chevalier.
>
> They've left their bonnie Hieland hills,
>   Their wives and bairnies dear,
> To draw the sword for Scotland's lord,
>   The young chevalier.[79]

While it may appear ironic that the cult surrounding Charles Edward Stuart did not begin in earnest until after his death in 1788, it could not have taken place while there was any chance, however remote, that Jacobite aspirations could be revived. If anything, the popularity of the myth of Bonnie Prince Charlie grew with the passing years, and was exploited by some who should have known better. James Hogg, the 'Ettrick Shepherd' of Scottish literature who is now credited with writing some of the best fiction of the nineteenth century, nevertheless felt obliged to indulge in neo-Jacobite fancy. His song 'McLean's Welcome', published in his 1821 collection *Jacobite Relics*, is one such work:

> Come o'er the stream, Charlie, dear Charlie, brave Charlie;
> Come o'er the stream, Charlie, and dine with McLean;
> If aught will invite you, or more will delight you,
> 'Tis ready, a troop of our bold Highlandmen,
> All ranged on the heather, with bonnet and feather,
> Strong arms and broad claymores, three hundred and ten![80]

Gaeldom and the fine arts

The appeal of the Highlands as a subject for Romantic artists extended to composers of 'serious' music as well. Felix Mendelssohn (1809–1847) visited Britain in 1829–30, and in a letter written from London in June of 1829 he told a friend, 'I have bought a ticket for a long trip and am setting out for Scotland, which I long to visit because I expect to compose a good deal there. The bagpipes and the echoes are said to be altogether strange'. He had found the Metropolis less than inspiring: 'There is no music in London, and the art itself is alien to the people'.[81]

Mendelssohn's visit to the Hebrides, and Staffa in particular, resulted in the celebrated 'Hebrides' Overture (Fingal's Cave) in 1830. It was in Fingal's Cave itself that Mendelssohn wrote the first twenty bars of the work, apparently with little subsequent amendment.[82] According to a biographer, Mendelssohn was 'a great reader, and literary associations with Ossian, Macpherson, and Fingal may have had a part to play' in the composing of the work. In his opinion, however, 'this was fairly negligible. Wind, water and rocky beach directly shaped Felix Mendelssohn's 'Hebrides' overture'.[83]

A more certain influence upon Mendelssohn was Scott, to whom the composer and a travelling companion paid homage at Abbotsford in 1830. They had a letter of introduction, but when they arrived Scott paid them scant attention – he was ill and hard at work on a new edition of his novels in an attempt to clear his debts – and they were shown the door after half-an-hour.[84] Mendelssohn's attempt to learn about Scott's musical preferences ended in failure, but he and his friend 'might have been surprised by their discoveries, for the great novelist who was supplying half of Europe with musical subjects was himself entirely unmusical'.[85]

An artist whose inspiration can be more easily traced is the painter Alexander Runciman (1736–1785). Runciman was an associate in Rome of the painter Gavin Hamilton who is said to have begun an association between painting and Scottish literature in the later eighteenth century,[86] and Runciman was to apply this approach in his most famous work, known as the *Hall of Ossian* (1772). Ossian was then at the height of its popularity and must have inspired Runciman and his patron Sir John Clerk who commissioned the painter to decorate the cupola of his hall at Penicuik in 1772. Despite the scepticism that surrounded Macpherson's poetry, Runciman persevered and in time completed twelve large subjects which were not based upon actual scenes from Ossian but were interpreted rather more liberally. According to a twentieth-century critic, Runciman 'gave full reign to the idea of the intensity and naturalness of ancient Gaelic poetry . . . as transmitted very imperfectly by Macpherson, rather than to any authentic manifestation of Gaelic culture'.[87] In the opinion of a late nineteenth-century critic who viewed the paintings before they were destroyed by fire in 1899, the *Hall of Ossian* suffered from 'too much violent action and heroic posing of the figures'; Runciman was said to have dreamt of rivalling Michelangelo's painting of the Sistine Chapel at the Vatican.[88]

Painting Highland subject matter remained popular well into the nineteenth century. Scott's work was a spur to tourism in the Highlands and suggested that the land and seascape there were beautiful and atmospheric rather than ugly and sterile. In the opinion of one critic, 'there is little doubt that the art received its greatest impetus' from Scott; the poem 'Lady of the Lake' (1810) in particular 'awakened such an enthusiasm for the Highlands that crowds flocked to enjoy the beautiful scenes' he had described.[89]

The appeal of Highland scenery was not confined to Scots artists. The English painter J.M.W. Turner (1775–1851), who in the words of a critic was 'especially attracted to the sublime scenery of mountains and to those river, lake, and coastal sites which would allow him to explore the broad and luminous effects of sky reflected in water',[90] was naturally enough drawn to the Highlands and toured the region during his visit to Scotland in 1815. A painting inspired by the visit, *Loch Fyne, Argyllshire* (1815), depicts Highland fishing folk drawing in nets from the loch in the foreground, dwarfed by the scale of the mountains that surround them.

The acknowledged master of Highland landscape painting, Horatio MacCulloch (1805–1867), was most active in the 1850s and 1860s and paintings such as *Highland Deer-Forest* (1856) and *Glencoe* (1864) encapsulate the appeal of Highland scenery as popularised by Scott, although Runciman was probably the greater influence. Sir Edwin Landseer (1802–1873), the popular painter of Highland scenes from the 1820s onward, presented the Victorian ideal of the Highlands in such works as *The Monarch of the Glens* (1851) and *Rent Day in the Wilderness* (1868), the latter indulging in neo-Jacobite sentimentality.

Romantic perspectives: Anne Grant and Elizabeth Grant of Rothiemurchus

A woman whose ideas about the Highlands were very much influenced by Ossian and Romanticism in general was Anne Grant (1755–1838). A Lowlander born and bred, her life in the Highlands began when she married the minister of Laggan, on Speyside. As was common in her time, Anne Grant was an avid correspondent and her letters were published by her son in book form, as *Letters from the Mountains*, in 1806.[91] Her viewpoint was that of a 'white settler', a perspective she first gained when as a young woman her family lived among the Mohawks in America; the feelings she expressed for the Gaels were affectionate but condescending in the extreme, for she had no doubt of her cultural (and with it intellectual) superiority.

Although the clan gentry in the area were adopting southern forms of gentility, she wrote in a letter of June 1791 that they were not particularly rich. However, 'they have been mostly in the army, are socially and kindly disposed, and have more both of spirit and good-breeding than is usually met with in people of their pitch'. She waxed more romantic about the common people: 'I am very fond of the lower class of people; they have sentiment, serious habits, and a kind of natural courtesy'.[92] But she was under no delusions as to their lack of sophistication. Concerning an outbreak of disease in Laggan in 1793, Anne Grant wrote that a certain young woman had recently died from what she put down to a fever, 'yet every one insisted that her death was caused by grief for the loss of her brother', and she recounted the tale of another young person with similar symptoms who was said by local people to be dying of love 'though no mortal can say of whom. Thus primitive and romantic are the notions of our mountaineers'.[93]

In a letter written in 1794, she related an episode in which her dairymaid claimed to have spoken to a cow, adding, 'could you have believed that there existed manners and opinions so primitive as those which are still preserved in the parish of Laggan?' But the 'quaint notions' of the people of Laggan were a constant joy to her; she wrote that 'the lower class of Highlanders excel all other low classes, being possessed of a superior degree both of fancy and feeling'. She explained that 'their pastoral cares [include] more, both of leisure and variety, than falls to the lot of other peasants'.[94] She remarked that people 'adopt the habits and prejudices of those about us, even while we pity their ignorance, and fancy ourselves more enlightened', and admitted that she had learned 'to rejoice at the birth of people's fifteenth child, and to listen to stories of apparitions and predictions'.[95]

When recalling her life among the Gaels in a letter of February 1821, Anne Grant asserted, 'I am convinced there does not exist a person in decent station with a mind in any degree cultivated or capable of refinement who has had more intercourse with the lower classes' in the Highlands than herself; this was due to her assiduity 'in learning the language of the country where my lot was thrown'. She closely scrutinised those around her: 'Long days have I knit my stocking or carried an infant from sheaf to sheaf, sitting and walking by turns on the harvest-field, attentively observing conversation which for the first years of my residence I was not supposed to understand'. She believed her ability to converse with the people in their native language made her popular, as 'seldom a day passed that I did not find two or three petitioners in the kitchen respectfully entreating for advice, medicine, or some petty favour. Often I sat down with them, and led them to converse, captivated with the strength and beauty of their expressions in their native tongue'. She added, 'it would not be easy to make you comprehend how often the duties of a Highland housewife subject her to the necessity of communion with her inferiors'.[96]

Writing in July 1795, Anne Grant described the kind nature of the people of Laggan, which she attributed to their lack of intellectual sophistication. This kindness manifested itself even in hard times. People who had no means of supporting their children nevertheless 'continue to rejoice at every addition, and consider the loss of offspring as the greatest misfortune that can possibly befall a family', and since bad weather and what she described as 'new modes of farming' had 'impoverished' the people, every poor tenant in the parish was supported in some way by the children:

> Without reasoning or reflecting, such hearts find the strongest and most pleasurable emotions excited, merely by the exercise of tender and laudable affections. Strangers to false refinement, and incapable, from want of cultivations, of that exalted enjoyment that arises from sentimental attachment grounded on intellectual excellence, the ties of nature, the 'charities' of life, are the great sources of their comfort, and sweeten all their hardships.[97]

The simple qualities of the Gaels were not to be of much use in the changing conditions in the Highlands, according to Anne Grant. In a letter written in December 1792, she declared: 'The only cause of complaint in Scotland is the rage for sheep-farming'. Those at the sharp end of Highland 'improvement' were unprepared for what lay ahead of them; they had 'neither language, money, nor education, to push their way anywhere else', although 'they often possess feelings and principles that might almost rescue human nature from the reproach which false philosophy and false refinement have brought upon it'. She defended those who had attempted to drive the newly arrived Great Cheviot sheep out of Ross-shire earlier that year; they were 'driven to desperation by the iron hand of oppression', but nevertheless 'acted under a sense of rectitude, touched no property, and injured no creature'.[98]

Writing in January 1793, Anne Grant expressed her belief that 'the only real grievance Scotland labours under, originates with landholders'. The newly found wealth of the merchant class had led them 'to contend with our gentry, in all the exterior elegancies of life. The latter seem stung with a jealous solicitude to preserve their wonted ascendancy over their rivals'. The landlords could only accomplish this, she explained, by greatly increasing their rents. As a result, 'the ancient adherents of their families are displaced'. She seemed unaware that the Highland chiefs and clan gentry vied not with the merchants but with their aristocratic counterparts in the south. The dispossessed clansmen were 'accustomed to a life of devotion, simplicity, and frugality, and being bred to endure danger, fatigue, and hardship, while following their cattle over the mountains, or navigating the stormy seas that surround their islands', were the 'best resort of the state' when it encountered 'difficulties', that is, war.[99] Critics of the high rents and evictions that led to emigration often argued that through such a policy, men who would otherwise be available for military service were lost to the country.

Anne Grant believed herself to be an expert on Gaelic culture and history, although her understanding of these subjects seems to have been largely derived from Macpherson's Ossian. In a letter written in April

1802, she informs her correspondent that 'in the progress of Highland society, there was a kind of intermediate state, to which a great deal of pleasing, fanciful poetry owes its origin'. This was a 'heroic age' which consisted of hunting and warfare. Romance, a secondary pursuit, 'gave scope to those pursuits that elevated the minds of the Highlanders into that sublime melancholy with which their love, their poetry, and their music were so strongly tinctured'. But alas, this age was not to last:

> When their extravagant and restless knight-errantry had almost occasioned the extinction of the Fingalian race of heroes, a new tribe appeared, more industrious, and less enterprising. In short, the pastoral age commenced; and the first tenders of cattle were regarded by heroic bards and lovelorn maidens (who were of course musical and poetical) as a degenerate race, who had not spirit or ability to encounter the hazards and fatigues of a life of hunting.[100]

Anne Grant was by nature a believer in the authenticity of Ossian, as it conformed to her conception of the Highland past. In a letter written in September 1802, she attacked Malcolm Laing, whose *History of Scotland* included an appendix which sought to expose Macpherson's deception. 'Indeed,' she wrote, 'his etymologies, in which the whole strength of his detections lie, fall to the ground with a touch, like a house of cards, as I shall hereafter prove to your conviction.' She then pledged to defend Ossian by writing 'the Dissertation on Ossian's Poems, by which I shall live and die'.[101]

Anne Grant herself wrote poems and songs on Highland themes. One such song was composed in 1799 to commemorate the Gordon Highlanders' departure for Holland; in it the 'Highland Laddie' makes an appearance, ready to die for King and Country. A stanza from the song will more than suffice:

> Suppose, ah, suppose, that some cruel wound
> Should pierce your Highland Laddie,
>   and all your hopes confound!
> The pipe would play a cheering march,
>   the banners round him fly,
> The spirit of a Highland Chief would lighten in his eye.
> The pipe would play a cheering march,
>   the banners round him fly,
> And for his king and country dear
> with pleasure he would die![102]

Perhaps one reason for Anne Grant's sensitivity concerning the authenticity of Ossian was that some questioned the authenticity of *her* poems. It seemed that some of those who had read her poems doubted whether her depiction of idyllic scenes and the simple goodness of the Gaels could exist in an area which was well known for its deprivation. In a letter to her publisher of December 1802, Anne Grant made the following reply:

> Do not you be concerned about the people's imputing exaggeration to me, with regard to the Utopian scenes and Arcadian virtues of my Alpine regions. What would you have? You know I have always represented the country as wild and barren to the last degree, and the inhabitants living in a state of great poverty and hardship. When I describe particular glens and sylvan scenes as possessed of wild and singular beauties, – when I impute to the natives tenderness of sentiment, ardour of genius, and gentleness of manners beyond their equals in other countries, – every one that knows anything of them must know that these have always characterized them.[103]

A woman who shared some of Anne Grant's Romantic ideals but from a very different perspective was Elizabeth Grant of Rothiemurchus (1797–1885), whose *Memoirs of a Highland Lady*[104] provide a glimpse into the lives of an upper-class Highland family in the early nineteenth century. Elizabeth Grant wrote her memoirs from 1845 to 1854 strictly for the perusal of her family, which was typical of Highland gentry at the time; they were dedicated to Improvement and were fully assimilated with the rest of the British aristocracy. Although quite anglicised, they retained a considerable attachment to their Highland 'heritage'. Elizabeth Grant and her siblings were raised in London, where her father pursued a legal and political career, and her brothers attended Eton. In their absence, the family estate of Rothiemurchus on Speyside had undergone improvements. Elizabeth Grant recalled her aunt's reaction to the changes effected:

> She said the whole romance of the place was gone. She prophesied, and truly, that with the progress of knowledge all the old feudal affections would be overwhelmed, individuality of character would cease, manners would change, the highlands would become like the rest of the world, all that made life most charming there would fade away, little would be left of the olden time, and life there would become as uninteresting as in other little remarkable places.[105]

Elizabeth Grant experienced 'culture shock' upon her return to Speyside in 1812. 'We had been so long in England,' she wrote, 'that we had to learn our highland life again. The language, the ways, the style of the house, the visitors, the interests, all were so entirely different from what had been latterly affecting us . . .'[106] Her recollections of life at Rothiemurchus have a strongly Romantic flavour to them, especially regarding the relationship between her family and the people on the estate. Clanship was most certainly extinct by the period she described, yet she seemed enchanted by 'the old feudal feelings' that the people showed to them, which she referred to as 'Duchas' – perhaps she did not know that the concept of *Dùthchas*, or hereditary trusteeship, was an integral part of the clan system that bound a chief to pursue the clan's interest and not simply his own:

> Such was our Highland home; objects of interest all round us, ourselves objects of attention all round, little princes and princesses in our Duchas, where the old feudal feelings get paraded all in their deep intensity. And the face of nature so beautiful – rivers, lakes, burnies, fields, banks, braes, moors, woods, mountains, heather, the dark forest, wild animals, wild feathers, wild fruits; the picturesque inhabitants, the legends of our race, fairy tales, the raids of the Clans, haunted spots, the cairns of the murdered – all and everything that could touch the imagination, there abounded and acted as a charm on the children of the Chieftain who was so adored; for my father was the father of his people, loved for himself as well as for his name.[107]

She was extraordinarily frank about her family's expensive lifestyle and its effects on their finances. Her father returned to Scottish legal practice in 1814–15, and 'the fees came in I know usefully, though certainly not in sufficient quantity to authorize our expensive way of living'. They entertained often, and she admitted that 'my dress and my Mother's must have cost a fortune, it all came from London'; her mother wore 'velvet, satin, rich silks, costly furs and loads of expensive lace while the variety of my nets, gauzes, Roman pearl trimmings and French wreaths, with a few more substantial morning and dinner dresses must have helped to swell up the bills to some very large amount'.[108]

The growing popularity of the Highlands as a playground for the rich was attested by Elizabeth Grant's recollection of a visit made about 1815 by two 'stupid specimens' from England, a merchant and a barrister whose sporting foray ended in failure 'for they waited for the late breakfast, came in dress coats to it, and were so long afterwards fitting on all the astonishing variety of their sportsman accoutrements, the day was too advanced by the time they were completely equipped for the keepers to be able to take them to the best ground'.[109] These sportsmen did not have to pay for their recreation, but such visits presaged the eventual conversion of Rothiemurchus to a sporting estate in 1827.

Elizabeth Grant may have viewed the Highlands through Romantic eyes, but she was no fan of Sir Walter Scott. Of his novel *Waverley* she wrote, 'I did not like it'. In addition to her dislike of the novel's plot and style, she found 'the whole idea given of the highlands so utterly at variance with truth'.[110] She was hardly more charitable concerning the man himself, and in her appraisal of him, she exhibited more than a little social snobbery but more revealingly indicated that his efforts to join the ranks of the aristocracy were less than successful: 'His family were all inferior. I have often thought that this was the reason of the insipidity of his ideal gentlemen and ladies – he knew none better'.[111] She much preferred David Stewart of Garth, whom she met around 1817–18 when he was writing his history of the Highland regiments. He had been taken with her piano renditions of Highland military music, and gave her a copy of his book upon its publication. 'He was a fine old soldier,' she wrote, 'though a little of a bore sometimes, so very enthusiastic about the deeds of his warrior country men.'[112]

The Rothiemurchus estate saw another round of improvements from 1820 to 1823 under the direction of Elizabeth Grant's brother William. The haste with which these changes were made testifies to the extent to which the family depended more and more on the income provided by the estate. Her comment below that a woman would have proceeded with more 'delicacy' betrays her ignorance of the evictions carried out in 1785 by Marjorie, widow of the 14th chief of Glengarry, and those of her daughter, Elizabeth Chisholm of Strathglass, who evicted the majority of her tenants in 1801.[113] Perhaps the lack of enthusiasm shown by the people of the Rothiemurchus estate for these latest improvements showed that they were apprehensive about their future:

> They were changed times to the highland idlers. The whole yard astir at five o'clock in the morning, himself perhaps the first to pull the bell, a certain task allotted to every one, hours fixed for this work, days set apart for that, method pursued, order enforced. It was hard up hill work, but even to tidiness and cleanliness it was accomplished in time. He overturned the old system a little too quickly, a woman would have gone about the requisite changes with more delicacy; the result, however, justified the means.[114]

The Grants of Rothiemurchus rose to the occasion provided by the visit of George IV to Edinburgh in 1822. Elizabeth stayed at home to care for her sick mother, but her father, brother, and two sisters made the trip. Her father was most certainly glad he did, notwithstanding his comments on the lack of taste that attended the wearing of Highland dress, for his timely presentation of a dozen bottles of Glenlivet whisky and fifty brace of ptarmigan to the King at Holyroodhouse was to be instrumental in his appointment to an Indian judgeship in 1827, making possible his escape from the clutches of his many creditors. Elizabeth Grant's comment on the 'Celtification' that marked the king's visit was typical of those made by Scott's detractors. 'A great mistake was made by the Stage Managers,' she wrote, 'one that offended all the southron Scots; the King wore at the Levee the highland dress. I daresay he thought the country all highland, expected no fertile plains, did not know the difference between Saxon and Celt.'[115]

She was altogether more tolerant of the Highland-derived fantasy provided by the Sobieski brothers, who paid a visit to Rothiemurchus about 1825. They claimed to be the sons of the legitimate son of Charles Edward Stuart, by his wife Princess Louise Stolberg, and because of the current popularity for things Jacobite, the brothers were enthusiastically received by Highland gentry. The men cashed in on the tartan frenzy that followed in the wake of George IV's visit and claimed to possess special knowledge of tartans; in time they published *Vestiarium Scoticum* (1842) which was said to be based on a sixteenth-century manuscript, and *The Costumes of the Clans* (1845), a work held in great esteem by tartan devotees.[116]

These claims earned them the wrath of Scott, and coincidentally with their ill-received conversion to Roman Catholicism, it seemed that another dead-end controversy along the lines of Ossian was in the making. Their deception was a clever one but lacked the pernicious nature of Scott's 'Celtification'. As Elizabeth Grant described the Sobieski brothers: 'They always wore the Highland dress, kilt and belted plaid, looked melancholy, spoke at times mysteriously. The effect their pantomime produced was astonishing; they were *feted* to their hearts' content; half the Clans actually believed in them; for several years they actually *reigned* in the north country'.[117] Elizabeth Grant's life in the Highlands was to come to an end in 1827 when her father lost his parliamentary seat and the protection it afforded from his creditors – he was forced to flee to London and then abroad. 'He never returned to his Duchas,' she wrote. 'When he drove away to catch the Coach that lovely summer morning, he looked for the last time on those beautiful scenes I do believe he dearly loved, most certainly was proud and vain of', but, she added, 'he never valued his inheritance rightly.'[118] When word came of his appointment as an Indian judge, the rest of the family prepared to leave. 'There was a good deal to be done,' she wrote, 'for the house was to be left in a proper state to be let furnished with the shootings, a new and very profitable scheme for making money out of bare moors in the highlands. We were to take nothing with us but our wardrobes, all else was to be left for sale . . .'[119] Elizabeth Grant was evidently more concerned with the fate of her household furnishings than the fate of the estate tenants adversely affected by the conversion – she wrote nothing of this.

NOTES

1. *Report of the Committee of the Highland Society of Scotland, appointed to inquire into the nature and authenticity of the Poems of Ossian*, Henry Mackenzie, ed. (Edinburgh, 1805), pp. 68–69.
2. Hugh Blair, *A Critical Dissertation on the Poems of Ossian, the son of Fingal* (London, 1763).
3. *Report of the Highland Society of Scotland*, pp. 4–5.
4. *Ibid.*, pp. 5–6.
5. James Macpherson, *Fragments of Ancient Poetry* (Edinburgh 1760, reprinted 1979), p. 10.
6. James Boswell, *Journal of a Tour to the Hebrides with Samuel Johnson, LL.D.*, R.W. Chapman, ed. (Oxford, 1924, reprinted 1984), p. 332.
7. *The Companion to Gaelic Scotland*, D.S. Thomson, ed. (Oxford, 1983), p. 190.
8. John Robert Moore, 'Wordsworth's Unacknowledged Debt to Macpherson's Ossian', *Publications of the Modern Language Association of America*, 40 (1925), pp. 362–378.
9. Dorothy Wordsworth, *Recollections of a Tour to the Highlands of Scotland* (London, 1803), pp. 213–214.
10. *Ibid.*, pp. 207–208.
11. *Ibid.*, p. 229.
12. J.G. Lockhart, *Memoirs of the Life of Sir Walter Scott, Bart.* (Edinburgh, 1862), pp. 5–6.
13. *The Letters of Sir Walter Scott*, H.J.C. Grierson, ed. (London, 1932–1936), 11 vols., I, p. 324.
14. Lorn Macintyre, 'Walter Scott and the Highlands' (Glasgow University Ph.D. thesis 1976), 2 vols., I, p. 122.
15. Grierson, I, p. 319.
16. Lockhart, p. 11.
17. Grierson, I, p. 320.
18. *Ibid.*, I, p. 321.
19. *Ibid.*, I, p. 322.
20. *Ibid.*, I, p. 303.
21. Macintyre, I, p. 139.
22. J.E. Bowman, *The Highlands and Islands: a Nineteenth Century Tour* (Gloucester, 1986), p. 81.
23. *The Life and Letters of Maria Edgeworth*, A.J.C. Hare, ed. (London, 1814), I, pp. 226–231 (quoted in Macintyre, I, p. 320–321).
24. Sir Walter Scott, *The Lady of the Lake* (Edinburgh, 1810), p. 21.
25. *Ibid.*, p. 297.
26. Sir Walter Scott, *Waverley, or, 'Tis Sixty Years since*, Claire Lamont, ed. (Oxford, 1986), p. xix.
27. Grierson, II, p. 37.
28. Macintyre, I, p. 329.
29. *Edinburgh Review*, November 1814, p. 209.
30. Sir Walter Scott, *The Lord of the Isles* (Edinburgh, 1815, reprinted 1977), p. 211.
31. Sir Walter Scott, *Rob Roy* (Edinburgh, 1830), p. 24.
32. *Ibid.*, pp. 24–25.
33. *Ibid.*, pp. 124–125.
34. *Ibid.*, p. 127.
35. *Ibid.*, pp. 127–128.

36. *Ibid.*, pp. 128–129.
37. *Ibid.*, p. 129.
38. *Ibid.*
39. *Ibid.*, p. 130.
40. Sir Walter Scott, *The Two Drovers and Other Stories*, Graham Tulloch, ed. (Oxford, 1987), p. 142.
41. *Ibid.*, pp. 159–160.
42. *Ibid.*, p. 224.
43. John Prebble, *The King's Jaunt* (London, 1988), p. 11.
44. *Ibid.*, p. 18.
45. *Ibid.*, p. 103.
46. Elizabeth Grant of Rothiemurchus, *Memoirs of a Highland Lady* (Edinburgh, 1988), 2 vols., I, p. 166.
47. Prebble, p. 105.
48. *Ibid.*, p. 263.
49. *Ibid.*, p. 269.
50. *Ibid.*
51. Grierson, III, p. 23.
52. *Ibid.*
53. *Ibid.*, XI, p. 377.
54. *Ibid.*
55. *Ibid.*
56. *Ibid.*, XI, p. 379.
57. *Ibid.*
58. See the section on Hogg's Highland visit in Chapter 3.
59. Prebble, *ibid.*, p. 105.
60. *Ibid.*
61. *Ibid.*
62. Alastair Campbell of Airds, Yr., *The Highland Society of London, 1773–1978* (London, 1978), p. 25.
63. *Songs of Duncan Bàn Macintyre*, Angus Macleod, ed. (Edinburgh 1952), p. 273. The full title of the poem is 'Ode to Gaelic and the Great Pipe in the Year 1781' (*Rann do 'n Ghaidhlig 's do 'n phiob-mhoir, 'sa' bhliahhna 1781*).
64. *Ibid.*, p. 512.
65. *Ibid.*, pp. 293–295. 'Ode to Gaelic and the Great Pipe in the Year 1785'.
66. Campbell, pp. 7–9.
67. *Ibid.*, p. 9.
68. *Ibid.*, pp. 9–11.
69. *Ibid.*, p. 11.
70. *Ibid.*, p. 26.
71. *Prize Essays and Transactions of the Highland Society of Scotland* vol. I, first series (Edinburgh, 1799), p. iii.
72. *Songs of Duncan Bàn Macintyre*, p. xxxi.
73. Ronald Black, 'Highland Society of Scotland', *A Companion to Gaelic Scotland*, p. 121. Black expands on this topic in his article, 'The Gaelic Academy: The cultural commitment of the Highland Society of Scotland', *Scottish Gaelic Studies*, XIV (2), pp. 1–38.
74. *Ibid.*, p. 122.
75. T. Crawford, 'Robert Burns', *A Companion to Scottish Culture*, David Daiches, ed. (Edinburgh, 1982), p. 48.
76. Robert Burns, *The Complete Works of Robert Burns*, (Alloway, 1986), p. 322. The song is sung to the tune 'Captain O'Kean'.
77. *Ibid.*, p. 394. The song is sung to the tune 'Cameron Kant'.

78. *Life and Songs of the Baroness Nairne with a memoir and poems of Carolina Oliphant the Younger*, Charles Rogers, ed. (Edinburgh, 1905), pp. 201–202.
79. *Ibid.*, p. 204.
80. James Hogg, 'McLean's Welcome', *The Oxford Book of Scottish Verse*, John MacQueen and Tom Scott, eds. (Oxford, 1966, reprinted 1989), p. 427.
81. Heinrich Eduard Jacob, *Felix Mendelssohn and his times* (London, 1959), p. 168: entry for 23 June 1829.
82. Shima Kaufman, *Mendelssohn* (London, 1934), p. 113.
83. Jacob, p. 200.
84. Kaufman, *ibid.*, p. 113.
85. Jacob, p. 241.
86. J.D. MacMillan, 'Painting, 1700–1900', *A Companion to Scottish Culture*, p. 274.
87. J.D. MacMillan, 'Gaelic Art in Modern Times', *The Companion to Gaelic Scotland*, p. 12.
88. Robert Brydall, *Art in Scotland* (Edinburgh, 1989), p. 164.
89. *Ibid.*, p. 219.
90. John Gage, 'J.M.W. Turner', *The Thames and Hudson Encyclopedia of British Art*, David Bindman, ed. (London, 1985), p. 271.
91. Anne Grant, *Letters from the Mountains* (London, 1806), 2 vols.
92. *Ibid.*, I, p. 13.
93. *Ibid.*, II, p. 55.
94. *Ibid.*, II, p. 81.
95. *Ibid.*
96. Alexander Macpherson, *Glimpses of Church and Social Life in the Highlands in olden times* (Edinburgh and London, 1893), pp. 106–107.
97. Anne Grant, II, p. 97.
98. *Ibid.*, II, pp. 46–47.
99. *Ibid.*, II, pp. 47–50.
100. *Ibid.*, II, pp. 174–175. Given her affection for Ossian, it may not be coincidence that James Macpherson was a Speyside man.
101. *Ibid.*, II, p. 200.
102. Alexander Macpherson, p. 77. The song is sung to the tune 'The BlueBells of Scotland'.
103. Anne Grant, *Ibid.*, II, p. 223.
104. Elizabeth Grant of Rothiemurchus, *Memoirs of a Highland Lady* (Edinburgh, 1988), 2 vols.
105. *Ibid.*, I, p. 98.
106. *Ibid.*, I, p. 210.
107. *Ibid.*, II, p. 223.
108. *Ibid.*, II, p. 10.
109. *Ibid.*, II, p. 36.
110. *Ibid.*, II, p. 72.
111. *Ibid.*, II, p. 73.
112. *Ibid.*, II, pp. 79–80.
113. Alexander Mackenzie, *History of the Highland Clearances* (Inverness, 1883), p. 285.
114. Elizabeth Grant, *Ibid.*, II, p. 156.
115. *Ibid.*, II, pp. 165–166.
116. J. Telfer Dunbar, *Highland Costume* (Edinburgh, 1977), pp. 34–35.
117. Elizabeth Grant, II, p. 187.
118. *Ibid.*, II, p. 199.
119. *Ibid.*, II, p. 200.

6

Militarists

IT WAS CHIEFLY due to the military participation of Jacobite clansmen in the Forty-Five that the popular image of Gaeldom reached its nadir in the 1740s. Yet in a relatively short time, the service of the Highland regiments in the British army completed the rehabilitation of the Gaels in the eyes of the rest of Britain. During the seventy years between the Battles of Culloden and Waterloo, the common view of the Gaels as bloodthirsty rebels bent upon the destruction of the British constitution had changed to a belief that they were among its most staunch defenders.

The first suggestion that Highland men be brought into the British service was made by John Campbell, 1st Earl of Breadalbane, who proposed to William III in 1690 that they be used 'to take up arms for your majesty in case of any insurrection at home, or invasion from abroad, or that your majesty think fit to use some of them in foreign parts'.[1] The Government did raise two regiments from the Whig clans, and one of these, the Argyll regiment, was used against the MacDonalds of Glencoe in 1692.

The large-scale recruitment of Highland soldiers was yet to come, but Breadalbane's proposal anticipated the future of the Highland regiments: the 'fencible' regiments would be used at home to defend against foreign invasion or to quell rebellions (notably in Ireland), while the 'line' regiments would be used in Continental wars as well as being sent to win and defend British colonies abroad. While many Highland men joined (or were pressed into) the navy, they were not formed into distinctly Highland units as were soldiers; between the beginning of the Seven Years' War in 1756 and the end of the Napoleonic Wars in 1815, over 48,300 men were recruited from the Highlands and Islands to serve in twenty-three line regiments and twenty-six fencible regiments of the British army, not including the Black Watch, which first saw service in 1743.[2] This figure is remarkable given the total population of the region, which rose from about a quarter of a million in 1755 to stand around 350,000 in 1830.[3]

The first Highland line regiment of the British army was the 43rd (later 42nd 'Royal Highland') Regiment, better known as the Black Watch, formed in 1739 with the addition of four companies to the original six independent companies raised in 1725 by General Wade to police the Highlands. Initially the regiment remained in Scotland. In his *History of the Scottish Regiments in the British Army* (1862), A.K. Murray recounts the words of an anonymous English historian who was evidently surprised to find men of the Black Watch exhibiting civilised behaviour and

> ... to see these savages, from the officer to the commonest man, at their several meals, first stand up and pull off their bonnets, and then lift up their eyes in the most solemn and devout manner, and mutter something in their own gibberish, by way, I suppose, of saying grace, as if they had been so many Christians.[4]

The Black Watch was sent first to England and then to the Continent in the war with Spain. The mutiny of the regiment in 1743 has been described elsewhere,[5] but briefly, the men attempted to return to the Highlands upon concluding that with the Government's breaking of pledges over their terms of enlistment, the 'contract' between themselves and the army was terminated. In the opinion of David Stewart of Garth, 'it is impossible to reflect on this unfortunate affair without feelings of regret, whether we view it as an open violation of military discipline on the part of brave, honourable, and well meaning men, or as betraying an apparent want of faith on the part of government'. Stewart (1772–1829) was an officer in the Black Watch and served in Flanders, the Caribbean, Minorca, the Peninsula, and Italy, and eventually retired due to wounds received in battle; his *Sketches of the Character, Manners, and Present State of the Highlanders of Scotland* (1822) was the first history of the Highland regiments.

If anything, the mutiny had impressed upon the Government that Highland regiments should in future be ordered out of Britain soon after recruitment – in short, they were not to be entrusted with arms at home. Stewart believed the mutiny had an effect upon the Gaels as well:

> The indelible impression which it made on the minds of the whole population of the Highlands, laid the foundations of that distrust in their superiors, which was afterwards so much increased by various circumstances ... and latterly still more confirmed by the mode of treatment by northern landholders towards their people.[6]

Later in 1743 the Black Watch joined the British army in Flanders, and their conduct there moved the Elector Palatine to thank George II 'for the excellent behaviour of the regiment while in his territories, and for whose sake I will always pay a respect and regard to a Scotsman in future'.[7] The Black Watch fought its first battle at Fontenoy, and while the British lost, the French commander Marshal Saxe said of the regiment: 'These furies rushed in upon us with more violence than ever did a sea driven by a tempest'.[8] At the beginning of the Forty-Five, the Black Watch was ordered back to Britain and was stationed with other forces in the south of England, ostensibly to contest any French landing there, but clearly the Government did not trust the men of the regiment to remain loyal in such a conflict; three companies newly raised for the regiment were kept in Scotland to join the Government effort, but a number of men from these companies switched to the Jacobite side at the Battle of Prestonpans.

The question of trust was quite probably involved in the decision to station the Black Watch in Ireland in 1749, where it was to remain for the next six years.[9] Indeed, it was to become standard Government policy to station Highland troops, especially those of the fencible regiments, in Ireland rather than Scotland or England, and conversely, Irish regiments of the British army were stationed in Scotland – the imperial principle of 'divide and rule' was first tested at home.

Highland Regiments and the Seven Years' War

The first large-scale use of Highland soldiers in the British army came with the Seven Years' War, and the recruitment of the 78th Fraser's Highlanders in 1757 in particular set a precedent that others would follow. The regiment was raised and commanded by Simon Fraser (1726–82), the chief of the Frasers and son of Lord Lovat. Fraser led his father's clan to defeat in the Forty-Five, and while Lovat himself was executed and the Lovat estate was annexed to the Crown, Fraser managed to switch to the Government side. He shrewdly calculated that by recruiting badly needed men for the British army, he might win back the estate and rebuild his fortune. Regimental historians often cite the incentive of wearing the Highland dress and bearing arms (banned in 1747) that enlistment offered in explaining the success with which Fraser gained his 1400 men, most of them Frasers, in such a short time. Less romantic perhaps but no less important was the coercion exerted in Fraser's behalf by the factors of the once-Jacobite estates, at the behest of the Commissioners for the Annexed Estates. In a letter to the factors dated 7 January 1757, the Commissioners told them that the King had ordered 'a Body of Forces to be raised in the Highlands of Scotland', and as Lt. Col. Simon Fraser had asked the Treasury (ultimately responsible for the Annexed Estates) for their co-operation in the recruitment process, the Commissioners ordered that 'you do give your utmost aid and assistance towards the raising of said troops'.[10]

The Annexed Estates Board was to use its power over its tenants to help those also disinherited in 1752 to follow Fraser's example in gaining respectability through raising men, especially for the British effort in the American War of Independence. The tenants and their dependents who were not recruited in this way often found themselves displaced to accommodate the demobilised soldiers and sailors whose resettlement was among the Board's chief functions. In 1774, the Lovat estate was restored to Simon Fraser (by that time a major-general) for his services to the Crown, a full decade before the other estates were disannexed.

The 78th regiment played a crucial role in the British victories at Louisbourg, Nova Scotia, and the Heights of Abraham in Quebec in 1759, helping to secure the defeat of the French under Montcalm and immortality for the British commander General James Wolfe. But alas, Wolfe was no friend of the Gaels. As a young officer Wolfe had fought the Jacobites at Culloden and took part in the pacification that followed, and while he respected the Highlanders' bravery in battle, he did not trust them nor did he have much regard for their lives. He once wrote of Highland soldiers: 'I should imagine that two or three independent Highland companies might be of use; they are hardy, intrepid, accustom'd to a rough Country, and no great mischief if they fall. How can you better employ a secret enemy than by making his end conducive to the common good?'[11] While stationed at Fort Augustus in 1751, Wolfe devised a plan along the lines of the Glencoe massacre to eliminate any remaining residue of Jacobitism in the Highlands: he proposed that one of his patrols be sent on a suicide mission to assassinate the chief of the Macphersons, believing that the resulting uproar would in turn justify the destruction of the entire clan and act as a warning to others.[12] Fortunately for the Macphersons, Wolfe was then but a major.

Notwithstanding previous efforts to recruit Gaels into the regiments of the British army, William Pitt claimed in a speech in the House of Commons in 1766 that he had been the first Government minister to discover the potential of the Highland regiments. He asserted that he had no prejudices regarding the Gaels. 'I have no local attachments: it is indifferent to me, whether a man was rocked in his cradle on this side or that side of the Tweed. I sought for merit wherever it was to be found . . . it is my boast,' he continued, 'that I was the first minister who looked for it, and I found it in the mountains of the north. I called it forth, and drew it into your service, a hardy and intrepid race of men! men, who, when left by your jealousy, became prey to the artifices of your enemies and had gone nigh to have overturned the state in the war before last.' An important factor in the changing attitudes towards the

Gaels was the emergent though not yet fashionable belief, here expressed by Pitt, that they were not solely responsible for the upheaval created by the Forty-Five. It was implicit in Pitt's argument that Highland soldiers were loyal and trustworthy and therefore deserved respect; referring to the service of the Highland regiments in the Seven Years' War, Pitt noted, 'these men, in the last war, were brought to combat on your side: they served with fidelity, as they fought with valour, and conquered for you in every part of the world'. He condemned the remaining prejudices against the Gaels with the declaration, 'Detested be the national reflections against them! they are unjust, groundless, illiberal, unmanly'.[13]

The Black Watch

When fighting broke out between French and British colonists in North America in 1756, the Black Watch formed part of the army sent there. When the regiment arrived in New York it attracted much attention, 'particularly on the part of the Indians, who, on the march of the regiment to Albany, flocked from all quarters to see strangers, whom, from the singularity of their dress, they considered to be of the same extraction as themselves, and whom they therefore regarded as brothers'.[14] In 1758 the regiment formed part of the force sent to attack the French fort of Ticonderoga on Lake Champlain. It was something of a suicide mission, and the losses of the British, especially of the Black Watch, were great; the regiment lost 314 killed and 333 wounded.[15] These are the words of an eyewitness to the battle:

> With a mixture of esteem, grief, and envy, I consider the great Scots Highlanders in the late bloody affair. Impatient for orders, they rushed forward to the entrenchments, which many of them actually mounted. They appeared like lions, breaking from their chains. Their intrepidity was rather animated than damped by seeing their comrades fall on every side. I have only to say of them, that they seemed more anxious to revenge the cause of their deceased friends, than careful to avoid the same.[16]

In October 1758 a second battalion of the Black Watch was raised at Perth and was soon on its way to the Caribbean to join the attack against Martinique, then under French control. The attack was unsuccessful, and the army was sent instead to make an attempt upon the island of Guadaloupe, also a French colony. The British fared better there, and after four months' fighting the island succumbed.[17] According to David Stewart of Garth, the mere sight of the Highlanders struck terror into the hearts of the defenders:

By private accounts, it appears that the French had formed the most frightful and absurd notions of the '*Sauvages d'Ecosse*'; they believed that they would neither take nor give quarter, and that they were so nimble, that, as no man could catch them, so nobody could escape them; that no man had a chance against their broadswords; and that, with a ferocity natural to savages, they made no prisoners, and spared neither man, woman, nor child; and as they were always in the front of every action in which they were engaged, it is probable that these notions had no small influence on the nerves of the militia, and perhaps regulars of Guadaloupe.[18]

The two battalions of the Black Watch were united in America during the early 1760s, and for the next few years were engaged in sporadic fighting with the 'ancient possessors' of that country.

When the regiment was ordered to Ireland in the summer of 1767, it was praised in an article appearing in the *Virginia Gazette*. The article said the Black Watch had 'since its arrival been distinguished for having undergone the most amazing fatigues, made long and frequent marches through an inhospitable country, bearing excessive heat and severe cold with an alacrity and cheerfulness, frequently encamping in deep snow [and] continually exposed in camp and in their marches to the alarms of a savage enemy, who in all their attempts were forced to fly'. The article continued, 'the freemen of this and the neighbouring provinces have most sincerely to thank them for that resolution and bravery with which they . . . defeated the enemy and insured us peace and security from a savage foe; and . . . they have our thanks for that decorum in behaviour which they maintained during their stay in this city'.[19]

The Black Watch arrived in Cork in October 1767. Referring to the regiment's earlier posting in Ireland of 1749–56, military historian James Browne wrote, 'the utmost cordiality existed between them and the inhabitants of the different districts where they were quartered; a circumstance the more remarkable, when it is considered that the military were generally embroiled in quarrels with the natives'. Perhaps the 'natives' found Highlanders less objectionable than other British troops, for 'upon the return of the regiment from America, after an absence of eleven years, applications were made from the towns and villages where they had been formerly quartered, to get them again stationed with them'. While Browne conceded David Stewart of Garth's point that a shared culture promoted friendly relations between the regiment and the people, he asserted that 'nothing but the most exemplary good conduct could have overcome the natural repugnance of a people who, at that time, justly regarded the British soldiery as ready instruments of oppression'.[20]

Some years later the Black Watch was to be given a similar task, but this time closer to home. In 1792 the entire regiment was ordered to Ross-shire to put down the disturbance caused when recently evicted men of the area drove out the sheep which had replaced them in the belief that they would then regain their land. The action was remarkable not merely for its naïveté but for the fact that no one was hurt and no property (including the sheep) was damaged. The Black Watch was ordered to resolve a situation which in Stewart's words 'occasioned little less alarm among the gentlemen of Ross than the Rebellion of 1745'.[21] Fortunately for all concerned, the affair had blown over before the regiment's arrival; most relieved of all would have been the men of the Black Watch, because the regiment was largely recruited from Ross-shire and many of the men would have had local connections:

> Happy, indeed, it was that the affair was concluded in this manner, as the necessity of turning their arms against their fathers, their brothers, and their friends, must have been in the last degree painful to the feelings of the soldiers, and dangerous to their discipline, – setting their duty to the King and country in opposition to filial affection and brotherly love and friendship.[22]

During the subsequent winter of 1792–3, the men of the Black Watch were, in the words of Stewart, 'actively employed against the Lowlanders, who were rioting, and hanging, drowning, and burning the effigies of those they called their political oppressors'. It is interesting to find Stewart referring to Lowlanders *en masse* in the same way that others referred to Highlanders; more importantly, however, he saw Highland soldiers in general as an ideal counter-revolutionary asset. This belief, shared by others, originated in the idea that the 'clannish' Gaels revered their 'superiors' in a way that other people in Britain did not, and further, that the Gaels were intellectually not up to grasping the abstract notions of liberty and equality that had spread with the French Revolution. Stewart wrote: 'The inhabitants of Perth, Dundee, and some other towns amused themselves with planting the tree of liberty, dancing round it, and threatening vengeance on all who should oppose it. The regiment was hurried south as rapidly as it went north, and during the winter and spring, garrisoned the town of Dundee, and all the coast as far as Fort George.'[23]

When the Black Watch was assembled at Montrose in April 1793 in preparation for the coming war with France, around 750 additional men were needed to bring the regiment to full strength. But according to Stewart:

> ... the regimental recruiting parties were not successful. The late transactions in Ross-shire began to show their baneful influence. It was not now, as in 1756 and 1776, when the regiment was completed

to more than 1100 men, in a few weeks, as quickly, indeed, as they could be collected from their distant districts.[24]

The rising fame of the Highland regiments

In time, the reputation of the Highland soldier as a loyal and courageous defender of British interests was to grow to the point where even critics of the established order displayed pride in the glorious exploits of the Highland regiments. In particular, those critical of the 'improvements' undertaken on Highland estates would point to the service of the regiments in underlining the injustices suffered by the Gaels as a result of rising rents and evictions. The writer of the pamphlet *The Present Conduct of the Chieftains and Proprietors of Lands in the Highlands of Scotland, Towards their Clans and People* (1773) identified himself simply as 'a Highlander', and intriguingly, he dedicated his work to Sir James Adolphus Oughton, the English general and Gaelic learner who was to become Commander-in-Chief of North Britain (*sic*) in 1773. The writer argued that the landlords' conduct, that is, the dramatic rent increases which forced many to leave their holdings, was not only 'against their own personal and family interest' and 'against religion, justice, and humanity' but was injurious to the state as well. 'The Highlanders are a hardy, active, spirited people,' he wrote, 'and have a natural genius for arms. Our officers in general are fond of them as soldiers.'[25] In the recent war with France, he noted, Britain had no fewer than fourteen battalions of Highlanders in its service:

> They were often tried and proved, and were always found to be firm, and resolute, and trusty troops. Our commanders in different parts of the world, reposed the highest confidence in them, upon the most hazardous and hardy services, and never were disappointed by them. Nay, it may be truly said, that they had no inconsiderable share in making our most important conquests: The reduction of Louisburgh, Quebec, Crown Point, Montreal, Niagra, and Fort du Quesne, the taking of Guadaloupe, the conquest of Martinico, and the Havanna, the plains of Germany and our conquests in India, will all tell what assistance the government received from the Scots Highlanders.[26]

The writer asked whether those Highland proprietors who raised rents beyond the ability of people to pay were in fact 'friends to the constitution' when they were engaged in 'breaking the spirits of those who have showed themselves so fit for supporting its honour? They are really, tho' unintentionally, undermining it'. By their actions they drove the people to America, he argued, 'perhaps to be some day dangerous to the mother country'. A rebellion there could not be ruled out, for 'our colonies in America are daily growing in power, wealth and science'. In any future conflict between the colonies and Britain, 'the genius of the Highlander will fall in at once with the nature of the country, where all men are hunters, and bred to the use of arms'. If the Gaels' emigration to America were allowed to continue as a direct result of the rent increases, the writer warned, 'they will make excellent partizans for the first enterprising genius that shall aspire to form an independent establishment. This prospect may be very distant but it is not altogether imaginary'.[27]

At the onset of the American War of Independence two years later, both sides went to great lengths to recruit Highland men. Their numbers in the colonies were considerable and increasing, and their reputation as fearless soldiers was well established. After being forced off his possession in Skye by his chief Sir Alexander McDonald in 1774, Allan McDonald of Kingsburgh settled (with his wife Flora) in North Carolina. He bought a 500-acre plantation on Barbecue Creek in the upper Cape Fear area and by the outbreak of fighting was well-off by local standards. Cape Fear had been home to a number of Highland settlements since the 1730s, and more Highlanders had arrived recently. When the war began Allan McDonald was one of the first to offer his services to the British governor Josiah Martin. Under Martin's first plan for combating the rebellious colonists, McDonald and his son-in-law were to serve directly under him, because 'besides being men of great worth, and good character, [they] have most extensive influence over the Highlanders here, [a] great part of which are of their own names and families'.[28] The colonists in North Carolina were equally determined to enlist the help of the erstwhile clansmen. In a letter dated 1 December 1775, their delegates to the Continental Congress reported to the North Carolina Provincial Congress on their efforts to recruit Highlanders through 'the power of the pulpit, reasoning and persuasion':

> We know the respect which the Highlanders entertain for the clergy; they still feel the impressions of a religious education, and truths to them come with irresistible influence from the mouths of their spiritual pastors . . . The Continental Congress have thought proper to direct us to employ two pious clergymen to make a tour through North Carolina in order to remove the prejudices which the minds of the Highlanders may labor under with respect to the justice of the American controversy.[29]

This approach was inevitably hindered by the fact that John MacLeod, the one Gaelic-speaking minister in North Carolina, was a staunch loyalist.[30] Several months earlier, the Provincial Congress of North Carolina had appointed a deputation 'to confer with the Gentlemen who have lately arrived from the Highlands in Scotland to settle in this Province', in order to give them the American perspective on 'the Nature of our Unhappy Controversy with Great Britain, and to advise and urge them to unite with the other Inhabitants of America in defence of those rights which they derive from God and the Constitution'.[31] Thousands of Highlanders fought in the war on both sides, but most of them as soldiers of the Highland regiments of the British army. The penchant of Highlanders for choosing the losing side was evident in the colonists' victory at the Battle of Moore's Creek Bridge near Wilmington, North Carolina in February 1776, in which Highland courage could not overcome poor leadership and American guile – 50 Highlanders were killed and 880 captured with the deaths of only two 'patriots'.[32] Following the war, Canada became the favoured destination of Highland emigrants, and while some prejudice towards Highlanders lingered in the United States due to their general adherence to the British cause, George Washington could write to Robert Sinclair on 6 May 1792, telling him: 'Your idea of bringing over Highlanders appears to be a good one. They are hardy, industrious people, and will, in time, become valuable citizens'.[33]

Resistance to recruitment and the Militia Act

The seemingly bottomless pool of one-time clansmen for the line and fencible regiments of the British army was quickly evaporating by the 1790s. Heavy recruiting in the past, especially in the years 1757–61 for the Seven Years' War and 1775–78 for the American War of Independence, combined with the migration and emigration of the young and fit, meant that fewer men were available (or willing) than previously, notwithstanding the general increase in population in the Highlands in the second half of the eighteenth century. The writer of a report on Gairloch to the Lord Lieutenant of Ross in 1798 confirmed this: 'Though this Parish be among the most extensive Parishes in the Highlands of Scotland, yet Recruiting parties being so frequent among us for years past, have left us but few young men; so that our Parish at this period chiefly consists of Children, women, and old men'.[34] In addition, the old enticements offered to prospective recruits, those of serving under officers of their own name and the privilege of wearing Highland dress and bearing arms, had lost their appeal. The *Statistical Account* contains evidence that the military ardour widely attributed to the Gaels was abating. In his description of the parish of Portree in 1794–5, schoolmaster Alexander Campbell wrote

Some spirited young men are fond of the military profession: but here, as likewise in the country, the generality seem to have lost that martial disposition which was so characteristic of their fathers. When any is enlisted for the service, his relations are, for some time, inconsolable; and in particular the mothers, sisters, and wives would rather have their respective relations to pass the most miserable and wretched life with themselves at home, than see them go into the army.[35]

Those men who did enlist would go without worry, Campbell wrote, 'were it along with their chief, his connections or dependents, with whom they are acquainted; and who, they are impressed with the idea, have a greater right to them, and would be more careful and tender of them'.[36] Despite the assimilation of chiefs and clan gentry into the ranks of the British aristocracy and the commercialisation of estate management throughout the Highlands and Islands, many Gaels continued to believe that the hereditary duty of a chief to protect his clan from any threat was still in force. This extended to believing that men serving in Highland regiments under officers of their own name would continue to receive protection. Most chiefs merely exploited these sentiments for the purposes of recruitment, but at least one was concerned that his prestige in the Highlands might suffer if he were seen to abandon his men in foreign parts. Lt. Col. Norman MacLeod of Harris raised the second battalion of the Black Watch in 1780 and embarked with it to India in December of that year as its commander. When the Government decided in 1786 to send home the officers and non-commissioned officers of the battalion and draft the privates into other, non-Highland regiments also serving in India, MacLeod wrote to the Commander-in-Chief of the British forces there, Sir Eyre Coote, K.B., begging him to intervene. 'I have to observe to Your Excellency,' he wrote, 'that it is the first time ever that this regiment was drafted, and that we were raised upon the idea of being exempted from that misfortune.' He continued:

My own Company are all of my own name and Clan, and, if I return to Europe without them I shall be effectually banished from my own home, after having seduced them into a situation from which they thought themselves spared when they enlisted into the service. They are now much reduced, and being on a brisk and actual service, will be still more so before they can be drafted; their numbers will not then exceed 30 or 40 men. I must entreat Your Excellency to allow me to carry them home with me, that I may not forfeit my honour, credit, and influence in the Highlands, which have been exerted for His Majesty's service.[37]

In February 1797 a proposal was made at the instigation of William, Duke of York, to enlist sixteen thousand men for a Highland corps 'to be employed in Great Britain or Ireland in Case of Actual Invasion or Civil Commotion, or the imminent danger of both or either'. The men would be recruited as clan levies to serve under their own chiefs in brigades 'which are mutually attached from local situation or otherways, to one another, as well as to their Brigadier'. How Campbells and Stewarts of Appin, never great friends at the best of times, were thought to feel 'mutual affection' for each other escapes comprehension; nevertheless the author claimed the plan was formed 'upon the principles which seem calculated to obtain the unanimous approbation, and support of all ranks of people in the Highlands and to make it a popular measure'. In explaining the logic of the plan, the author assumed the old ties of clanship still existed:

> The Highlanders have ever been, and still are warmly attached to their Chiefs, and Ancient Customs, particularly in regard to the Ranking and Marshalling [of] the Clans. The present arrangement completely embraces these views; as each Clan forms a distinct Battalion commanded by their natural Chief or Leader, more or less in a number according to the strength of the Clan, and proprietors are equally well supported each at the head of a Brigade.[38]

In times of war, the necessity of putting men into uniform would have to be balanced against the possible economic costs of labour shortages, but the author dealt with any objection on that score with this assertion: 'From the ordinary vocations of the Highlanders in general, it is obvious that no equal number of men in any one district of the Kingdom can be employed with as little injury to agriculture and manufactures'. As the contribution of Gaels to the British economy was minor to begin with, it was reasoned, the loss of their labour was of little concern. What made the raising of the Highland corps even more attractive, the author argued, was that

> . . . at the moment they may be justly considered, the only considerable Body of Men, in the whole Kingdom who are as yet absolutely Strangers to the levelling and dangerous principles of the present age, and therefore they may be safely trusted indiscriminately with the knowledge and use of arms. They admire the Warlike exploits of their Ancestors to a degree of Enthusiasm and proud to see the Ancient order of things restored, they will turn out with promptitude & alacrity.[39]

The reaction of the 5th Duke of Argyll to the plan was typical of chiefs. He wrote in a letter dated 10 March 1797 to Henry Dundas (political manager of Scotland for the Tory Government), 'I cannot encourage any attempt of that sort, especially as I think that in place of assisting the service, I would have the contrary effect, by raising suspicions in the minds of the people, and perhaps making them refuse to inroll under the Volunteer Act'.[40] However, Dundas himself was enthusiastic about the plan. He commended it in a letter to Walter Ogilvy of Clova dated 22 February 1797, writing that although laws had been passed 'for restraining the Spirit of Clanship in the Highlands of Scotland, the system might be justifiable by the recent Circumstances which gave rise to that Policy. It has for many years been my opinion that those reasons, whatever they were, have ceased, and that much good, in place of mischief may on various occasions arise from such Connection among persons of the same Family and Name'.[41]

In reply Ogilvy poured cold water on the scheme. While 'it would afford me much pleasure to say anything satisfactory on the subject of his Royal Highness the Duke of York's plan for embodying the highland Clans,' he told Dundas that 'you know much better than I can express that the disarming, the highland dress & Jurisdiction acts have much weakened the influence over their vassals and namesakes', and as a result 'it will be extremely difficult if not impossible to make the proposed Levies' without concerted Government action.[42]

Although the Duke of York's fanciful plan was abandoned, the desire remained for a force in addition to the already established line and fencible regiments that could suppress civil disturbances as well as defend the country against French invasion. The Militia Act was passed in July 1797 and provided for the compulsory enlistment of men chosen by ballot from parish records. The measure was fiercely resisted in the Lowlands, culminating in the killing of eleven recalcitrant miners in Tranent, East Lothian by English dragoons. Resistance in the Highlands soon came in Perthshire, when the authorities' fear that radical 'incendiaries' from the Lowlands would contaminate the innocent Gaels with notions of democracy was realised in the form of Angus Cameron and James Menzies, two Highlanders from Glasgow. Their well-intentioned resistance was eventually put down by force,[43] and although the Gaels' detestation of compulsory military service was apparent for all to see, the Militia Act remained in force.

Further evidence that the 'warlike nature' of the Gaels was fast dying out can be found in comments in the *Statistical Account* of 1791 by the Rev. Charles Stewart of the united parish of Strachur and Stralachlan, on Loch Fyne, who reported that within the past thirty years, especially since the introduction of sheep farming, a number of men from the parish had become sailors, 'but it appears, that necessity, and not choice, has been the cause'. Each time that two, three, or more farms were converted into a single sheep walk, '12 or 16 tenants, with their families, were thrown out of their usual line of employment'. However, he wrote, 'the sea opened its arms to the young and active'.[44] From the time sheep farming began, 'a very great change is observed in the people'. Before that time, 'they showed no predilection for a seafaring life', but instead, 'their sentiments were generally warlike. Round every fireside, the entertainment of the evening was rehearsing tales of former times, the actions of brave men, the warlike feats of their ancestors':

> By such a conversation, the young mind, fired with the spirit of great examples, eagerly panted after an opportunity of being signalized, by surmounting difficulties, by encountering dangers. Attachment to the chief, and a jealousy of his honour, were reckoned primary virtues. When the chief, or any of his family stepped forward to serve in the army, all the young men readily followed him, as their fathers had done on previous occasions.[45]

The minister cited as examples of this eagerness to enlist the first raising of the Black Watch and in particular when two members of the local clan gentry, Ardkinglass and Strachur, were made officers in Lord Loudon's regiment in 1745. He pointed out that although it was not then customary for an officer's commission to depend upon his raising a certain quota of men, the two had no difficulty in recruiting the requisite numbers, but, he observed, 'how different the sentiments of the people in 1778!' In that year, the clan gentry of Argyllshire had stepped forward to raise men for the planned Western Fencible Regiment, but despite the fact that the men of the parish 'had an express promise from Government, that they should not be called out of the Kingdom, nor even into England, excepting in case of an invasion, the heritors were obliged to bribe them high'.[46] By the 1790s, there were apparently few men left to recruit:

> The district is now thinned of its inhabitants. The people have been forced to leave their native hills. Such as have gone have changed their manners, and the old spirit of the Highlander is extinguished in those that remain. The sheep have banished the people.[47]

It was not of course sheep but the policies of estate management pursued by chiefs and clan gentry that had 'banished' the tenantry. As the Rev. Stewart related, 'a military spirit prevails much among the gentlemen; but their lands give them so much more rent by stocking them with sheep, that they cannot withstand the gain'.[48] The new breeds of sheep being introduced in the Highlands and Islands required the best of grazings and winter pastures, and were incompatible with the rearing of black cattle and the traditional system of settlement based on the township. Nevertheless, landlords were determined to keep people somewhere on their estates to facilitate military recruitment. The reorganisation of Highland estates along commercial lines, combined with the need to raise men for the army, indispensable for the Highland gentry's integration with the British aristocracy, led proprietors to promote congestion in the newly created crofting communities.[49]

When the Militia Act was brought into effect in 1797, it was resisted in Argyllshire despite the arbitrary power held by the Argyll estate over its tenants. Niel Douglas, a Relief Synod lay preacher who toured parts of Argyllshire in the summer and autumn of 1797, wrote of meeting 'a number of poor people, both men and women, who were going of foot to Inverary, about their sons, whose names had been given in for the militia':

> Their anxiety and distress of mind were visible in their very looks. They lamented the loss of such an opportunity of hearing sermon, and especially the occasion of their journey. The day fixed for their appearance was at hand, and they found it inconvenient to go sooner, and impossible longer to delay. They much dreaded their sons would be sent abroad when raised, and would not believe their clergy, or Gentlemen, asserting the contrary; having been so often deceived by fair promises when levies were formerly made.[50]

Douglas tried to persuade the people that 'they had no cause of alarm, that there was no such thing intended in the present case', and commented, 'it is an unhappy state of society when the lower orders lose all confidence in the word of their superiors, and are apt to suspect every measure which they recommend'. However, Douglas clearly understood the resentment caused by the Militia Act: 'The many levies of young men from the Highlands in all our wars, few of whom return; and the visual mode of raising them, have made impressions that will not soon or easily be forgotten'.[51]

If people on traditional Campbell lands were unhappy with the Militia Act, those living in places more recently acquired by the House of Argyll were even less pleased. The Duke wrote in a letter of October 1797 to the chamberlain (or steward) of Mull that 'while almost every person able to bear arms is turning out in one shape or other in the service of their country, I cannot but greatly blame the people of Icolmkill [Iona] for refusing to allow their sons to go into the militia . . . a service so mild and at the same time so necessary for the protection of ourselves and our property'.

> . . . as a mark of my displeasure I desire that Archd. McInnes and his son, Hugh McDonald and Donald McKillop, all of that island, who were concerned in beating and abusing Hector McPhail, employed to take up the lists of young men for the militia, be removed from their possessions at Whitsunday next, as I will suffer no person to remain on my property who does not respect and obey the laws, and let it be

understood that whoever harbours any of these person in the island after that time will be served in the same way.[52]

Alastair MacDonell and the Glengarry Fencibles

Diana Henderson has written, 'To raise any regiment the prime mover had to have influence, ambition and financial backing ... it is in the area of recruiting that the Highland Regiments were unique.'[53] The great majority of senior officers in the regiments during this period were Highland gentry and used their power as landlords to procure the necessary recruits; essentially tenants and others residing on a certain estate gave up their sons for military service in exchange for promises that they would not be evicted.

However, for a chief to recruit men for a regiment from an estate upon which evictions had already taken place was a different task altogether, as was demonstrated by the efforts of Alastair Ranaldson MacDonell the 15th chief of Glengarry, to lead the men of his name in a fencible regiment.

The 12th chief of Glengarry had rallied to the Jacobite cause with 600 men in 1745–6, and in 1777, 750 MacDonells were recruited into the 76th (Macdonald) Regiment to join the British effort against the American colonists.[54]

The inhabitants of Glengarry, a Catholic enclave, were struggling to pay recently increased rents when the first sheep farmer arrived from the Borders in 1782, and evictions were begun in 1785 by Marjory, wife of Duncan MacDonell, the 14th chief, when 500 people were cleared to accommodate a sheep farm on Loch Quoich.[55] Marjory Grant MacDonell, the daughter of Sir Ludovic Grant of Dalvey, is credited with being the moving force behind the 'improvement' of Glengarry; she must have set an example for her daughter Elizabeth, who married William Chisholm of Chisholm in 1795 and managed the estate of *her* ailing husband. Under Elizabeth Chisholm's direction, much of Strathglass was cleared to make way for sheep farms, and the displaced people emigrated to Nova Scotia.[56] A similar policy was followed by her brother, Alastair Ranaldson MacDonell, the 15th chief. The idea of raising a Highland regiment composed of Roman Catholics originated with a young priest stationed in Badenoch, Father Alexander MacDonell. Upon learning in 1792 that a large number of Barra Catholics bound for America had been marooned and left destitute in Greenock when their emigrant ship was disabled in a gale, he went to Glasgow and managed to procure manufacturing work for some 600 of them. When war broke out with France in 1794, the manufacturers were unable to export to the Continent, and the Barra people (among others) were made redundant.

Their situation was grim indeed; most could speak only Gaelic, and they received a great deal of sectarian abuse from the people of the city. Father MacDonell then devised a plan for raising a regiment of Catholic Highlanders with his own chief, Alastair MacDonell of Glengarry, as colonel.[57] He wrote to the Earl of Fife explaining his proposal, and the earl expressed his reservations concerning the religious complexion of such a regiment to Henry Dundas:

> All the Roman Catholicks here I believe are Jesuits, the preasts had 'till lately some allowances from forreign Societys, that is now at an end, they must therefore have their support intirely on keeping poor people in a state of ignorance and disunion, which I have always considered a great misfortune. I humbly think the arming a distinct Roman Catholick Regt. a very dangerous measure, tho' allowing them to enlist in a Protestant corps is a very different matter.[58]

Although MacDonell was not entrusted with his own regiment, the hundred men he raised from the remaining tenants on his estate for a company of the Strathspey Fencibles were gladly accepted by Sir James Grant, who was raising the regiment. He was to regret MacDonell's gift, however, for the Glengarry company was to play a prominent part in the mutiny of the regiment at Linlithgow in March 1794 over plans to send it to England in violation of assurances given at the time of recruitment.[59] MacDonell's lackadaisical attitude towards the mutiny did not endear him to many, but the Government's need of soldiers was overwhelming; as soon as recruiting restrictions for Catholics were abandoned, MacDonell was given permission to raise men for his own fencible regiment. He went to Glengarry and began his efforts at Loch Quoich and Loch Garry, and reportedly 'some young men took to the high braes to escape his urgent drums and others came in unwillingly, forced into service by threats of eviction against their kindred'.[60] The numbers thus recruited must have been insufficient, for MacDonell was soon agitating for the transfer of the Glengarry company of the Strathspey Fencibles to his own regiment. Grant was understandably happy to be rid of the men, provided MacDonell either replace them or pay compensation. MacDonell believed the men were his by right, and petitioned Henry Dundas in a letter dated 27 October 1794, informing him that 'I brought about a hundred men into the Grant Fencibles, *all* my own Tenants Sons who follow'd me from mere attachment', and no one should be surprised 'if I should have every inclination to have as many of them or any others of that Regt. as would choose to follow me to the number permitted by Government.' MacDonell argued that this would be 'the means not only of *compleating* my Regt. but also of *disciplining* my Regt. in a very short time.'[61] Dundas approved the transfer, and MacDonell thanked him in a letter of 9 November, and took the opportunity to acquaint Dundas of the special attachment the Glengarry men had for him as their chief: 'to convince you of the attachment of those men to me, & their willingness to enter on a more extensive Service' he enclosed a copy of a letter he had received from the men from their station at Stranraer.[62]

In the letter, dated 27 October 1794, the men acknowledged that the Government had given its permission to soldiers of the Strathspey Fencibles to join other regiments, and told MacDonell, 'it is our most earnest desire and ardent wish to follow you to any part of the earth his Majesty may order you to lead us'. They wrote that they sought 'no Bounty or any other recompense from Government but the satisfaction of being under your Banners and sharing with you every danger in the service of our King and Country as it was our attachment to you alone that made us forsake our friends and families'. The men admitted that they had not been ill-treated by their officers but stated rather pathetically, 'our minds can never be content separated from you; our fore Fathers pertained to your fore Fathers and we wish to pertain to you that we may in like manner receive protection from you'. What followed was a plea for a renewal of the reciprocal obligations of clanship. Although they had not sought any terms upon their enlistment in his company of the Strathspey Fencibles, as he was not yet of age,

... we hope now that you are your own master and have it in your power that our aged parents our wives and Children and such of our friends as depend upon us should have something for our sake during our absence and if we chance to return home ourselves that we may know where to betake ourselves indeed expect to enjoy those possessions which our ancestors so long enjoyed under your ancestors though now in the hands of Strangers ...[63]

Aware that commercial interest rather than hereditary obligation was now the prime consideration of estate management in the Highlands, the men promised to pay 'as high Rent as any of your Lowland Sheepherds ever gave' and further undertook that all would 'become bound for anyone whose circumstances may afford you room to mistrust'. The letter went on to repeat their attachment to MacDonell and was signed by the men of the company.[64] According to James Browne, 'this offer was very acceptable to the government, as it formed a precedent to all Fencible corps raised after this period' in that such regiments could herceforth be stationed outwith Scotland.[65]

In November 1794 MacDonell proposed to Henry Dundas that he be allowed to recruit for his regiment from amongst the Highlanders in Glasgow, MacDonells and others, aided by the MacDonell Society (one of the numerous Highland societies that existed in Lowland towns), and also promised the co-operation of the MacInnes Society.[66] A fierce critic of the plan was John Dunlop, then Lord Provost of Glasgow. Dunlop regarded with horror the prospect of a predominately Catholic Highland regiment commanded by MacDonell that would most likely be stationed in his city. He wrote to the 3rd Duke of Portland, then Home Secretary, and told him that he had 'no hesitation in giving my opinion that Col. MacDonell's proposals ought not to be listened to'. He continued:

> There have been many doubts, about the propriety of his conduct on several occasions, especially at Linlithgow, and at Paisley, and whatever his construction may admit of it, it cannot be denied to have been that of a hotheaded, weak, young Man – I should be very sorry to see a person of this description or indeed any man whatever, have an armed Corps in this City, which would in all probability, look up to their Chieftain, rather than to the Magistrates, and which indeed, from the tenor of his proposals would be entirely under his command; an idea absurd in the highest degree.[67]

Dunlop doubted whether the 'people in Business' referred to in the MacDonell Society would be able to leave their homes 'for any length of time', but the root of his objection to the proposal was the state of revolutionary fervour then believed to exist in Glasgow. 'There are four or five people here who come from Glengarrys Country,' he wrote. 'They are infernal Democrats, and very likely they may have put this nonsense in his head, either with a view to deceive him with respect to their Loyalty, thinking the matter would go no further, or with a worse intention.'

> There are not three men of the name of McDonald, that as Depute Lieutenant, I would entrust with Arms, and as to the McInnis's, they are still less respectable – upon the whole I should think the short answer to Col. McDonell ought be, that Government wished to arm people of respectability only, and . . . in Glasgow, only men of that description, and of sound principles. . . .[68]

John Dunlop's warning was evidently ignored, for MacDonell was allowed to recruit in Glasgow, and he finally received the Glengarry company from the Strathspey Fencibles in December 1794. However, MacDonell was enraged that any of his remaining tenants should refuse to join his regiment, and accordingly he wrote to his agent in Inverness on 27 November 1794:

> Enclosed you have a list of small tenants belonging to my Knoydart property – their leases being expired by Whitsunday first – and having refused to serve me, I am fully determined to warn them out, and turn

them off my property, without loss of time; and as this is the first order of the kind I have given you since I came of age, I have only to add that your punctuality and expedition on the present occasion will be marked by me.[69]

The new Glengarry (British Highland) Fencible Regiment was sent to Guernsey where it served until 1798, when it was sent to Ireland to be used along with other Highland regiments to put down the rebellion there against British rule. For a 'fencible' it was certainly stationed far from home – the Government's distrust of Highland regiments was still evident. The regiment returned to Glengarry for disbandment in 1802. MacDonell's ostentatious lifestyle had left him some £80,000 in debt, sixteen times the annual rent he received from his tenants, and much of the land he had promised to the returning soldiers had already been leased to Lowland shepherds.[70] The future for the men of the Glengarry Fencibles and their families was bleak indeed. The regiment's chaplain, the same Father Alexander MacDonell who had first proposed the raising of the regiment, procured grants of land in Canada, and the majority of the disbanded soldiers and their dependents followed him.[71] Whether MacDonell regretted his treatment of the regiment or not, the departure of the men and their dependents did not affect the success of the 'improvements' undertaken on the Glengarry estate: rents increased from £700 in 1786 at the beginning of the evictions to stand between £6000 and £7000 in 1825.[72]

The Sutherland estate and the 93rd Highlanders

The proprietors of the Sutherland estate were to have different difficulties in raising men for the Highland regiments, but the task was relatively straightforward while something remained of the old ties of clanship. The first Sutherland Fencibles were raised in 1759 by Lord Sutherland, and were disbanded after the Peace of Paris in 1763. When the suggestion was made in 1769 that a second fencible corps be raised, the thirteen-year-old Countess gave the reply, 'I have no objection to raising a Sutherland Regiment; I am sorry I cannot command it myself'.[73] It was disbanded in 1783. The third Sutherland Fencibles were raised by Lt. Col. William Wemyss (a cousin of the countess and nephew of the last Earl of Sutherland) in 1793 to serve in Ireland, as were the Reay Fencibles, also raised from men on the estate. While the Sutherland Fencible Regiment was involved in the suppression of the rising in Ireland in 1798, an event occured that would sour relations between the Sutherlanders and Wemyss. At one point during the rebellion, the regiment was marching in the middle of a column which came upon a stream. While the other regiments marched straight through the water, the Sutherlanders broke ranks to use stepping stones; as a result, 'the rear of the Column was much retarded'. The men believed the officers were at fault, but when the column next came to a river, Wemyss ordered his men to wade through the water while the rest of the column used a bridge.[74]

The third fencible regiment was disbanded in January 1799, but by the summer of that year the decision had been made to raise a regiment of the line from Sutherland, which unlike the fencibles would serve outwith the British Isles. The response from the members of the disbanded Sutherland Fencibles, and the population at large, was poor. By July the Countess (now the Marchioness of Stafford) was worried, and hinted in a letter to factor John Fraser that a list of 'defaulters' be kept.[75] In September and October of 1799, the Sutherland estate manager Colin Mackenzie and Wemyss conducted a tour of the estate. Mackenzie wanted to discover the causes of the poor response to the recruitment of the new 93rd regiment and a means by which to remedy the situation. He suspected the men had been 'contaminated' by revolutionary ideas during their time in Glasgow and Ireland, and believed they had a strong dislike of Wemyss (now a Major-General) following the 'stepping stones' incident in Ireland. He wrote to the Marchioness expressing his fears:

> I imagine that the Men of the late Fencibles who came home were the root of the business. Some of them I believe had imbibed in the South, particularly at Glasgow and also perhaps in Ireland, Crude and undigested Notions quite inapplicable to a Country like Sutherland which I dare say tainted some of their Neighbours here; and many or most of the Old Regiment (I mean the last) had conceived a foolish and absurd prejudice against General Wemyss of which I believe they are now ashamed . . .[76]

Mackenzie also considered the estate's tacksmen to be a hindrance to recruiting, and was unwilling to promise them security of tenure in exchange for volunteers, a practice from the days of clanship which had no place in commerce.[77] In a letter to the tacksmen dated 23 September 1799, Mackenzie requested a list of the names of all men on their farms 'whose age and size qualify them to be soldiers', and asked the tacksmen to indicate any man whose circumstance 'seems to you to afford them grounds for exemption, and to each of these names I beg of you to annex the precise circumstance on which you ground your opinion'. Secondly he requested a list of those men who had already enlisted, and thirdly, a list of

> . . . the remainder; being persons who have hitherto declined to enlist tho' in your own opinion they are called on to come forward in the service of their Country. As to the last class I know I need not enforce

the propriety of your making them feel and understand that unless they immediately alter their course they are not to expect any favour or indulgence or be permitted to remain on the Sutherland Estate any more then the Countess's own immediate tenants who are in the same predicament.[78]

According to R.J. Adam, the difficulties involved in the raising of the 93rd Sutherland Highlanders in 1799 'played a considerable part in turning the minds of the proprietors and managers towards changes in the arrangement of the estate. In addition, measures were adopted to aid recruitment which themselves produced considerable complications for the future'.[79]

The 93rd regiment was finally embodied at Inverness in August 1800 and for the next two years served in Scotland, Ireland, and the Channel Islands. The good behaviour evidently displayed by the Sutherlanders earned them considerable, albeit condescending, praise. The *Digest of Service* described the exemplary conduct of the 93rd:

... in such a regiment not only did each individual feel accountable for his own character but in some degree responsible for the conduct of his comrades; and, as in order to increase wholesome rivalship between the different companies of the battalions they were at first classified by parishes, an arrangement which naturally excited the greatest emulation, it followed that each soldier became speedily convinced that by behaving ill he should not only be covered with personal disgrace, but would in some measure bring dishonour upon the parish to which he, in common with all his comrades in the same company with himself, belonged.[80]

In 1802, the 93rd was about to be disbanded, and 50–60 men had already been discharged, when the countermanding of General Wemyss' orders forced him to recruit in Sutherland to make up the difference. The estate's policy of 1799 that promised land in return for service was not to be renewed; Colin Mackenzie wrote to the new factor David Campbell in November 1802 telling him not to 'include any promise of farms etc.'[81] In 1804–05 the estate did nothing more than 'recommend' regiments to the men and threaten not to give new leases to tenants who gave recruits to other regiments. No further attempts were ever made to raise a regiment from the Sutherland estate alone.[82]

The 93rd regiment was included in a force sent in 1805 to attack the Dutch colony at the Cape of Good Hope. Thirty-five men of the regiment drowned when their landing boat was over-turned, but the 93rd soon saw its first battle and won its first battle honour.[83] The Sutherlanders were also first in the advance on the Dutch stronghold, and according to David Stewart of Garth, when the men received the order to attack,

... the charge was so impetuous, and apparently so irresistible, that the enemy, appalled and panic-struck, fired the last volley in a manner without aim or effect, gave way at all points, and fled in great confusion, having sustained a loss of more than 600 men killed and wounded, while that of the British was only 10 killed, and 191 wounded.[84]

The regiment was to remain at the Cape for the next eight years, but soon after the fighting was over the Sutherlanders were, according to Stewart, 'anxious to enjoy the advantages of religious instruction agreeably to the tenets of their national church', and accordingly formed themselves into a congregation, appointed elders, and paid a stipend 'to a clergyman of the Church of Scotland, and had divine service performed agreeably to the ritual of the established Church'.[85]

The author of a twentieth-century history of the Sutherland regiments includes a quotation from Donald MacLeod's *Gloomy Memories of the Highlands* (1840–1) in explaining the piety of the soldiers: 'the Highlander . . . was taught to revere parents and ancestors, to be faithful to trust, to despise danger, to be respectful to superiors, to fear God and honour the King'.[86] Alas, military historians are as oblivious to social issues as social historians are to military issues. Any further reference to *Gloomy Memories* would have disclosed some unsavoury truths about the situation back in Sutherland; referring to the human cost of the large-scale reorganisation of the Sutherland estate, MacLeod wrote:

> ... the children and nearest relations of those who sustained the honour of the British name in many a bloody field were ruined, trampled upon, dispersed, and compelled to seek an asylum across the Atlantic; while those who remained from inability to emigrate, deprived of all the comforts of life, became paupers – beggars – a disgrace to the nation whose freedom and honour many of them had maintained by their honour and cemented with their blood.[87]

During the evictions of 1811, the Sutherland estate managers responded to an imagined case of armed defiance by requesting that a military force be sent from Fort George. Accordingly, the 21st Regiment of Foot, an Irish regiment, was ordered to Sutherland 'by forced marches, night and day, a distance of fifty miles, with artillery, and cart-loads of ammunition'. Upon their arrival, some of the Irish soldiers reportedly declared that they 'would now have revenge on the Sutherlanders for the carnage of their countrymen at Tarahill and Ballynamuck',[88] but the expected uprising did not materialise. It was no mistake that the British military authorities chose to use Irish Gaels to suppress Scottish Gaels in this way, and the remarks of the Irish soldiers would confirm that such a divide-and-rule strategy was working. Had the 93rd regiment been available for the task, it is inconceivable that the Government would have sent it to Sutherland to act as the strong arm of frightened estate managers, as the Black Watch had been ordered to do in Ross-shire in 1792.

The 93rd regiment eventually returned from Africa and the behaviour of the Sutherlanders upon their arrival at Plymouth in August 1814 must have startled the inhabitants. Instead of spending their pay in the 'taverns and gin shops' of the port as did other new arrivals, David Stewart of Garth reported that 'the soldiers of Sutherland were seen in booksellers' shops, supplying themselves with Bibles, and such books and tracts as they required'.[89] The people of Plymouth would probably have been similarly charmed by the knowledge that during the regiment's short stay there, 'upward of £500 were lodged in one banking-house, to be remitted to Sutherland, exclusive of the many sums sent home through the post-office and by officers. Some of these sums exceeded £20 from an individual officer'.[90] Taking out of context, as Stewart does, the sight of soldiers sending money home rather than spending it on drink might seem odd, but considering the dire situation of the people of Sutherland, the action of the men can be seen in its true light. As for the soldiers' pursuit of religion instead of intoxication, the people of Plymouth might have been surprised to discover that by that time an increasing number of Gaels (soldiers included) were evangelical Presbyterians of the first order who would have viewed the prospect of spending any time in a Plymouth 'gin-shop' with unease.

Within a month of arriving at Plymouth the 93rd regiment was on its way across the Atlantic, first to Jamaica and then to join the British attack against New Orleans, which took place on 8 January 1815. The battle went badly for the British side, and the Sutherlanders, who formed the front line, suffered great casualties, with around 500 killed.[91] An American officer present at the battle described the conduct of the 93rd:

> Whatever was the name of that regiment they were the most surprising instance of cool determined bravery and undaunted courage I ever heard of, standing in the midst of a most destructive fire, firm and immovable as a brick wall.[92]

The Sutherlanders had been reluctant to join the 93rd regiment when it was first raised in 1799, well before the reorganisation of the Sutherland estate. As men of the regiment were nearing the end of their term of service in 1816, the *Military Register* reported that they had refused to re-enlist in the regiment, giving as their reason the evictions in Sutherland, specifically those in Strathnaver, and had requested to be re-mustered in regiments raised in Argyll and Ross.[93] This discontent in the regiment was not demonstrated at New Orleans, however. Stewart pointed out that although many Gaels had emigrated to America, 'there was not an instance of desertion; nor did one of those who were left behind wounded or prisoners, forget their allegiance, and remain in that country, at the same time that desertions from the British army were but too frequent'. Stewart continued, 'men like these do credit to the peasantry of their country, and contribute to raise the national character'. If this was so, he argued, 'the removal of so many of the people from their ancient seats, where they acquired those habits and principles, may be considered a public loss of no common magnitude'.[94]

Stewart doubted that with the changes effected by the Sutherland estate (which involved the removal of the population from the interior of Sutherland to stations along the coast to make way for sheep walks) the people could 'resume their ancient character and principles, which, according to the reports of those employed by the proprietors, have been so deplorably broken down and deteriorated'.[95] This alleged 'deterioration' may well have been misinformation spread by the estate managers to deflect criticism from themselves. However, Stewart believed the reports and declared them 'entirely unknown till the recent changes in the condition of the people, and the introduction of a new system, and every way opposite to the probity, religious and domestic habits of the same people':

> It is only when parents and heads of families in the Highlands are moral, happy, and contented, that they can instil sound principles into their children, who, in their intercourse with the world, may once more become what the men of Sutherland have already been, – 'an honourable example, worthy of the imitation of all'.[96]

Assessing the Highland soldier

Stewart of Garth attributed the Gaels' talent for war to their 'peculiar character and distinctive manners' which 'naturally originated' from their rugged surroundings. The Romantic notion of 'national character' held that the people of a given country or culture displayed common qualities. Sir Walter Scott subscribed to this idea and many of his poems, novels, and short stories are concerned with the allegedly warlike nature of the Gaels. His short story 'The Two Drovers', in particular, appears to have been influenced by Stewart's analysis:

> The ideas and employments, which their seclusion from the world rendered habitual, – the familiar contemplation of the most sublime objects of nature, – the habit of concentrating their affections within the narrow precincts of their own glen, or the limited circle of their

own kinsmen, – and the necessity of union and self-dependence in all difficulties and dangers, combined to form a peculiar and original character. A certain romantic sentiment, the offspring of deep and cherished feeling, strong attachment to their country and kindred, and in consequence disdain of submission to strangers, formed the character of independence; while an habitual contempt of danger was nourished by their solitary musings, of which the honour of their clan, and of losing descent from brave and warlike ancestors, formed the frequent theme.[97]

Stewart believed the formation of the 'military character' of the Highland soldier was influenced by harsh living conditions in the Highlands. 'Nursed in poverty, he acquired a hardihood which enabled him to sustain severe privations,' and 'as the simplicity of his life gave vigour to his body, so it fortified his mind.' Thus resolute in mind and body, the Highland soldier was taught 'to consider courage as the most honourable virtue, cowardice the most disgraceful failing; to venerate and obey his chief, and to devote himself for his native country and clan; and thus honour and duty called him'. As every man held these principles, and regarded 'any disgrace he might bring on his clan and district as the cruellest misfortune', the individual soldier had 'a peculiar motive to exertion'.[98] Stewart was annoyed that many based their attitudes towards Highland soldiers upon stories illustrating the 'barbarity' of their ancestors. The true character of the Highlanders, he argued, ought to be judged by their actions and not by 'collecting anecdotes two and three hundred years old, and giving them as specimens of what was supposed to have occurred within the fifty years preceding the Rebellion of 1745'. In that episode, he asked his readers, 'did they display any blood-thirsty atrocity?'[99]

In her book, *Highland Soldier 1820–1914*, Diana Henderson describes two currently held views on the use of Highland soldiers. The first holds that the Government set out 'not only to disarm the Highlands but to depopulate them, draining the manpower permanently to an army destined for foreign stations and wars, where it would inevitably be ravaged by disease and battles'; the men of the Highland regiments 'were frequently abused, abandoned and betrayed by a distant and unfeeling Government, who made no attempt to understand their Highland culture and motivation'.[100] This view is argued passionately by John Prebble in his book *Mutiny* (1975). A second point of view is that the recruitment of large numbers of Highland men for service in the British army was not only inevitable but desirable; that clanship was no longer a 'realistic' system in the light of serious overpopulation in the Highlands, and military service 'saved many from starvation and restored the credibility of the Highlander as the loyal fighting man'.

The argument that military service was somehow good for Highland men because it saved many of them from starving at home is bizarre. The experience of one regiment suggests otherwise. In 1781 the 78th Seaforth Highlanders embarked for India with 973 rank and file. Scurvy broke out *en route*, and by the time they reached Madras, 247 had died, and of the 726 survivors, only 369 were fit for service.[101] In addition, Henderson writes, as Britain was almost continuously at war between 1725 and 1800, the Government could not tolerate 'a rebellious and potentially open Northern flank', and this was 'a view supported by English, Lowland Scots and even Highlanders'. Instead, British military service gave the Gaels a 'realistic outlet' for their natural fighting abilities, and no other British regiments recruited at home were similarly indulged with regard to uniform (Highland dress). 'Fighting under their own officers to whom many of them had a personal relationship, the Highland regiments formed an elite, proud of their service, second to none and would have greeted any suggestion of abuse with anger and disdain.'[102]

This view ignores the coercive nature of military recruitment and the cynical use of Highland soldiers to put down revolts in Ireland or as expendable 'shock troops' in foreign wars while promises of land rights in return for service were betrayed by those recruiting the men. Even before the end of the Napoleonic Wars, it was not any vestigial tie of clanship but rather sheer necessity that made Highlanders enlist in a regiment. In his *General View of the Agriculture of the Counties of Ross and Cromarty* (1813), Sir George Steuart MacKenzie wrote that 'it is notorious that the inhabitants [of the Highlands] have a strong aversion to a military life.' He recounted that although a battalion of the 78th Seaforth Highlanders (commanded by his brother-in-law) was raised in a short time, 'this was not owing by any means to the spirit of the people. Indeed some bands of young Highlanders who went to join the regiment, declared, rather indiscreetly perhaps, that they had enlisted merely to save their parents from being turned out of their farms'.[103]

The mortality rate of Highland soldiers was very high, and losses in battle were much worse in defeat, such as those suffered by the Black Watch at Ticonderoga and the 93rd regiment at New Orleans. During the course of the Napoleonic Wars, many Highland regiments lost the majority of their men. One badly depleted regiment was the 79th Cameron Highlanders, raised in 1793 with a complement of around one thousand. By 1809 it had lost 737 officers and men in battle or from wounds, disease, or accident.[104] However, it was during the Napoleonic Wars that the transformation in attitudes towards the Highland soldier was made complete.

The belief that the Gaels were a disloyal, savage and warlike race at the disposal of foreign powers was banished forever. Replacing it was the belief that the Highland soldier was religious, sober and well behaved in peace, fierce and utterly fearless in battle, and loyal to the end. The Highland regiments were showered with affection and praise in the swell of self-congratulation that followed the victory at Waterloo. In its reporting of the fighting of 17 June 1815, *The Times* referred to 'the brave Highlanders',[105] a great change indeed from 1745–6. In recognition of their conduct in battle, three Highland regiments, the Black Watch, the 79th Cameron Highlanders and the 92nd Gordon Highlanders, received the battle honour, 'Waterloo', a highly coveted prize in military circles. The previous year (1814) had seen the publication of the novel *Waverley*, in which Sir Walter Scott created a romantic vision of the Gaels as a race of fierce and fearless warriors whose only failing was a misplaced loyalty to a deserving albeit hopeless cause. It seemed to many that in the seventy or so years between the Battles of Culloden and Waterloo, the Gaels' talent for war had been at last redirected towards the British national interest. For some, the rehabilitation of the Highland soldier had already taken place, and this change was celebrated in the song 'The Highland Character' by Sir Harry Erskine, a Black Watch officer. According to tradition, the words are translated from a Gaelic composition by a soldier of the Black Watch:

> In the garb of old Gaul, wi' the fire of old Rome,
> From the heath cover'd mountains of Scotia we come,
> Where the Roman endeavour'd our country to gain,
> But our ancestors fought, and they fought not in vain.
> Such our love of liberty, our country, and ancestors,
> That, like our ancestors of old, we stand by Freedom's cause;
> We'll bravely fight, like heroes bold, for honour and applause,
> And defy the French, with all their art, to alter our Laws.[106]

The rehabilitation of the Highland soldier took place in just over sixty years. Whereas an English officer at the time of the Forty-five would have regarded him with hatred and dread, by the 1820s a commission in a Highland regiment was a much sought-after prize. Henderson relates that Thomas Creevey MP wrote in his diary on 26th March 1828, 'We have an event in our Family. Fergy [Sir Ronald Ferguson] has got a regiment – a tip top crack one – one of those beautiful Highland Regiments that were at Brussels, Quatre Bras and Waterloo'.[107] The Gaels' experience of gaining a measure of 'respectability' through military service was later shared by ex-slaves and their descendants in the United States; and the long and distinguished service of the Highland regiments earned the 'Hielan laddie' a place in the folklore of the British Empire, thereby setting an example for Sikhs and Gurkhas, other conquered races of 'warlike' character who joined the British cause.

NOTES

1. 'Proposals Concerning the Highlanders' (1690), quoted in John Prebble, *Mutiny* (Harmondsworth, Middx., 1975), p. 21.
2. A.I. Macinnes, 'Scottish Gaeldom: The First Phase of Clearance', *People and Society in Scotland*, i (Edinburgh, 1988), p. 83. Macinnes derives this figure from statistics contained in J. Browne, *History of the Highlands and of the Highland Clans*, iv (Glasgow, 1832), pp. 132–384. Although no contemporary account deals exclusively with Highland sailors, John Knox discusses the subject in his *View of the British Empire* (London, 1785).
3. Macinnes, p. 74.
4. A.K. Murray, *History of the Scottish Regiments of the British Army* (Glasgow, 1862), p. 253.
5. John Prebble, *Mutiny*; H.D. MacWilliam, ed., *The Official Records of the Mutiny of the Black Watch ... 1743* (London, 1910).
6. David Stewart of Garth, *Sketches of the Character, Manners, and Present State of the Highlanders of Scotland: with details of the military service of the Highland Regiments* (Edinburgh, 1822), I, pp. 243–4.
7. Murray, p. 253.
8. *Ibid.*, p. 254.
9. *Ibid.*, pp. 254–5.
10. Scottish Record Office, E. 727/61/2.
11. Jenni Calder, *The Story of the Scottish Soldier, 1600–1914* (Edinburgh, 1987), p. 16.
12. Prebble, p. 94.
13. *Hansard's Parliamentary History 1766* (London, 1813), xvi, p. 98.
14. James Browne, *History of the Highlands and of the Highland Clans* (Glasgow, 1838), iv, p. 155.
15. Stephen Wood, *The Scottish Soldier* (Manchester, 1987), p. 36.
16. Murray, p. 256.
17. *Ibid.*, p. 257.
18. Stewart, i, p. 303.
19. *Virginia Gazette*, 30 July 1767; quoted in *Scots Magazine*, November 1767, pp. 605–6.
20. Browne, iv, p. 154.
21. Stewart, i, p. 393.
22. *Ibid.*, i, p. 394.
23. *Ibid.*, i, pp. 394–5.
24. *Ibid.*, i, pp. 395.
25. Anonymous, *The Present Conduct of the Chieftains and Proprietors of Lands in the Highlands of Scotland, Towards their Clans and People, considered impartially* (1773), p. 5.
26. *Ibid.*, p. 6.
27. *Ibid.*, p. 7.
28. Duane Meyer, *The Highland Scots of North Carolina, 1732–1776*, (Chapel Hill, North Carolina, 1961), p. 155.
29. J.P. Maclean, *Settlements of Scotch Highlanders in America prior to the peace of 1783* (Cleveland, Ohio, 1900), p. 116.
30. *Ibid.*
31. *Ibid.*, p. 117.
32. Meyer, pp. 158–60.
33. Maclean, from [?] Spark, *Writings of Washington*, xii, p. 304.
34. SRO GD 46/6/45.

35. *The Statistical Account of Scotland, 1791–99, edited by Sir John Sinclair*, D.J. Withrington and I.R. Grant, eds. (reprinted Wakefield, 1973–83), 20 vols., xx, p. 204 (parish of Portree).
36. *Ibid.*
37. Frank Adam, *The Clans, Septs and Regiments of the Scottish Highlands* (Edinburgh, 1934), pp. 307–8. The men were not drafted into other regiments, but were formed into the 73rd (Perthshire) Highlanders, and remained in India until ordered back to Britain in 1805. However, those men who were still fit for service after 25 years of duty and wanted to remain in India were given a bounty, and according to Adam, 'so many accepted the offer that few came home'. (*Ibid.*, p. 308.)
38. SRO GD 46/6/34.
39. Ibid.
40. SRO GD 51/1/670/2.
41. SRO GD 16/34/355.
42. SRO GD 16/34/356.
43. See Prebble, pp. 402–32.
44. *The Statistical Account of Scotland, 1791–99*, viii, p. 416 (united parish of Strachur and Stralachlan).
45. *Ibid.*, viii, p. 417.
46. *Ibid.*
47. *Ibid.*, viii, pp. 417–18.
48. *Ibid.*, viii, p. 418.
49. See Macinnes, pp. 70–90.
50. Niel Douglas, *Journal of a Mission to part of the Highlands of Scotland, in summer and harvest 1797, by appointment of The Relief Synod, in a series of letters to a friend, designed to shew The State of Religion in that country, and The claim the inhabitants have on the compassion of fellow Christians* (Edinburgh, 1799), pp. 102–3.
51. *Ibid.*, p. 103.
52. Eric Cregeen, *Argyll Estate Instructions, 1771–1805*, (Edinburgh, 1964), p. 195.
53. Diana M. Henderson, *Highland Soldier, 1820–1920* (Edinburgh, 1989), p. 6.
54. Alexander Mackenzie, *The History of the Highland Clearances* (Inverness, 1883, reprinted 1986), p. 195.
55. Charles Fraser-Mackintosh, *Antiquarian Notes* (Inverness, 1897), p. 126–7.
56. Mackenzie, pp. 284–6.
57. Rev. Father MacDonell, 'The Glengarry Fencibles', *Transactions of the Gaelic Society of Inverness*, XXVI (1910), pp. 342–4.
58. SRO GD 51/1/831.
59. See Prebble, pp. 289–318.
60. *Ibid.*, p. 360.
61. SRO GD 51/1/844/1.
62. SRO GD 51/1/844/2.
63. SRO GD 51/1/844/3.
64. Ibid.
65. James Browne, *History of the Highlands and of the Highland Clans* (London, 1848), iv, p. 380.
66. SRO GD 51/1/849/1.
67. SRO GD 51/1/849/2.
68. Ibid.
69. Charles Fraser-Mackintosh, *Letters of Two Centuries* (Inverness, 1890), pp. 328–9.
70. Prebble, p. 363.

71. Father Alexander MacDonell was appointed vicar apostolic of Upper Canada in 1810 and became Bishop of Kingston (Canada) in 1826. The emigrants settled in Glengarry County (between present-day Ottawa and Montreal), founded by a number of loyalist Highlanders forced out of New York during the American War of Independence. During the war with the United States in 1812–15, according to James Browne, 'they gave a proof [that] their allegiance to their sovereign was not impaired in their adopted country, by enrolling themselves along with other emigrants and the sons of emigrants, in a corps for the defence of the province, under the old designation of Glengarry Fencibles' (Browne, iv, p. 381).
72. James Barron, *The Northern Highlands in the Nineteenth Century* (Inverness, 1903–13), i, p. xxvi.
73. Douglas Sutherland, *The Argyll and Sutherland Highlanders* (London, 1969), p. 26.
74. R.J. Adam, ed., *Papers on Sutherland Estate Management* (Edinburgh, 1972), 2 vols., ii, pp. 4–5.
75. *Ibid.*, i, p. xxvi–xxvii.
76. *Ibid.*, ii, p. 4.
77. *Ibid.*, i, p. xxvi.
78. *Ibid.*, ii, p. 10.
79. *Ibid.*, i, p. xxvi.
80. Quoted in Sutherland, p. 30.
81. Adam, *Papers on Sutherland Estate Management, i*, p. xxvi.
82. *Ibid.*
83. Sutherland, pp. 30–1.
84. Stewart, ii, pp. 282–3.
85. *Ibid.*, ii, pp. 287–8.
86. Quoted in Sutherland, p. 31.
87. Mackenzie, p. 2.
88. *Ibid.*, p. 12.
89. Stewart, ii, p. 289.
90. *Ibid.*, ii, pp. 289–90.
91. Murray, p. 413.
92. Michael Brander, *The Scottish Highlanders and their Regiments* (London, 1971), p. 170.
93. Prebble, p. 167.
94. Stewart, ii, pp. 290–1.
95. *Ibid.*, ii, p. 291.
96. *Ibid.*
97. *Ibid.*
98. *Ibid.*, i, p. 7.
99. *Ibid.*, ii, appendix p. xxxvi.
100. Henderson, p. 5.
101. Frank Adam, p. 303.
102. Henderson, *ibid.*, p. 5.
103. Sir George Steuart Mackenzie, *General View of the Agriculture of the Counties of Ross and Cromarty* (London, 1813), p. 298.
104. Henderson, p. 7.
105. *Ibid.*, p. 9.
106. 'The Highland Character', by Sir Harry Erskine, from Thomas Crawford, 'Political and Protest Songs in Eighteenth Century Scotland', *Scottish Studies XIV* (1970), p. 30. See Stewart, i, p. 347.
107. Henderson, p. 8.

Conclusion

IT WAS DURING the Jacobite rebellion of 1745–6 that attitudes towards the Gaels were at their most hostile. They were then believed to be bloodthirsty savages who under the guidance of hostile powers were bent upon the destruction of the British way of life. The Highland Jacobites received some indication of their unpopularity during their advance into England. James Johnstone (better known as 'the Chevalier de Johnstone'), *aide-de-camp* to Charles Edward Stuart during the Forty-Five, wrote in his memoirs that 'the fright of the English' at their presence 'was inconceivable, and to a degree that seemed as if their heads were turned altogether'. He went on to relate the horror of an Englishwoman upon learning that Donald Cameron of Lochiel was to be quartered in her house. According to Johnstone, the poor soul appealed to Lochiel, 'supplicating him with hands joined, and with a flood of tears, to take away her life, but to spare those of her little children'. The chief was understandably bewildered at the woman's plea, and demanded whether she was mad, and to explain herself. She replied that every one said that the Highlanders ate children, and made them their ordinary food.[1] The hysteria in England was produced largely through Government propaganda, and as the people there knew nearly nothing of the Gaels, such rumours were taken at face value. In the Lowlands, however, hatred of the Gaels was well established and needed no encouragement from London.

While the defeat of the Jacobites at Culloden spelt the end of Stuart pretensions, Lowland and other commentators believed the Gaels to be inherently rebellious and made the establishment of 'law and order' in the Highlands their first priority. The Government agent (believed to be Edmund Bruce) who produced a report on the political situation in the Highlands in 1750 declared that it was 'evident to all men of common understanding' that 'the Disaffected and Savage Highlanders need to be Bridled and kept in awe by Garrisons and Standing forces 'till the present Generation wears out', and that 'those unhappy deluded people will still Continue Savages if nothing else is done to recover them from their Ignorance and Barbarity'.[2] When it became clear to even the most paranoid that Jacobitism was indeed a spent force, attention turned towards the rehabilitation of the Gaels, which meant the 'improvement' of the Highland economy and the 'civilisation' of the people.

Evidence that the processes of 'improvement' and 'civilisation' were believed to be inextricably linked comes from a report by the Rev. John Walker, sent by the General Assembly of the Church of Scotland in 1765 to inquire into the religious state of the Highlands. By that time, the Gaels were no longer thought to be under the sway of France or Spain but Walker believed that if they were 'lost' to the Roman Catholics, all attempts to reform them would fail. In the Catholic districts of Gaeldom, he asserted, 'not only the morals and manners of the People, but the very soil, is more rude and uncultivated'. He explained that 'the Popish inhabitants are as tenacious of the old customs, as they are of the old Religion', and argued that without the better provision of schools in particular, 'it is scarce to be expected, that the state of the Country is ever to be much altered for the better, or that Religion, Industry, and civilized manners, are ever to make considerable progress'.[3] While Walker stressed that the Gaels were industrious, most schemes took no account of the human population of the Highlands and Islands as potential beneficiaries.

'Improvement' included the introduction of trades and manufactures, the encouragement of fisheries, the building of roads and bridges, the establishment of towns and villages and, crucially, the modernisation of agricultural practices. The Annexed Estates Board (most of whom were Edinburgh lawyers) was the main interventionist agency in the years following the Forty-Five and sought through the exemplary management of the estates of attainted Jacobites to introduce improved communications and agricultural practices and to instill Lowland/English values of 'industry' and 'loyalty' into its tenants. Following the disannexation of the forfeited estates in 1784, the London-based British Fisheries Society became the most prominent outside agency charged with bringing prosperity to the region, but its efforts were misguided and ultimately little more successful than those of the Annexed Estates Board. When such schemes failed, for a host of reasons, the obstinacy and backwardness of the Gaels were usually blamed.

Whig ideology stressed the need to replace traditional relationships with modern (commercial) ones, and Whig polemicists argued that this change would 'free' the Gaels from the allegedly tyrannical power of their chiefs, who were thought to keep their people in 'slavish dependence'. For their part, the chiefs were to be relieved of the responsibilities of hereditary trusteeship or *Dùthchas* that bound them to pursue the interests of their clans as well as their own. They and other clan gentry were to live by the legalistic concept of *Oighreachd* which gave them absolute rights as proprietors to operate their estates along commercial lines. The selling of tacks to the highest bidder (notably in Argyll from 1737) pointed the way forward; and the emergence in the 1780s of the Highland Society of Scotland as an influential forum for the exchange of ideas on Improvement reflected the growing preference of Highland proprietors for capital-intensive enterprises such as sheep-farming to more diversified, non-agricultural projects.

The overthrow of communal agriculture based on the traditional township or *bàile* that marked the first phase of Clearance began in the 1730s and was more or less complete in the years following the Napoleonic Wars; crofting communities were created on marginal land and sought to derive their incomes variously from kelp manufacture, fishing, quarrying, supplemented by seasonal migration to the Lowlands for work. In addition, the illicit distilling of whisky could provide a source of much-needed cash. The vulnerability of the crofting communities to market forces was made evident with the post-1815 recession that came with the end of the war economy. The recession also exposed the folly of many chiefs and clan gentry who had opted to exploit their estates for short-term profits to subsidise conspicuous expenditure rather than adopting a balanced approach to the use of human and landed resources, and who found themselves in a perilous financial situation as a result.[4] The fall in agricultural prices for kelp and black cattle resulted in the accumulation of rent arrears, leading to eviction and ultimately to the bankruptcies of a number of proprietors, thus marking the general breakdown of the Highland economy[5] and setting the stage for the second phase of clearance from the 1830s.

This period saw the migration of large numbers of Gaels to the Lowlands in search of waged labour. Migrants from the relatively prosperous southern and eastern Highlands generally opted for permanent relocation in the growing industrial towns, especially in the west; while those from the Hebrides and West Highlands, where crofting communities were becoming the norm, preferred seasonal migration to the rural Lowlands to take part in the harvest or fishing ancillary work, thereby enabling the north-west 'to support a much larger population than could have survived from indigenous resources'.[6] This process began in the later eighteenth century but intensified with the economic pressures faced by many as a result of rent arrears and falling prices after 1815. Migration, whether permanent or temporary, had social implications as well. Not only were increasing numbers of Gaels becoming bilingual, but their presence in the Lowlands, for the purposes of employment and not for cattle-stealing or rebellion as in former times, undoubtedly made them appear less 'foreign' in Lowland eyes and helped to break down old antagonisms. Thus impersonal economic forces played a part in the ongoing rehabilitation of the Highlander.

The success of all schemes to bring the Gaels into the main-stream of British society was believed to depend upon the reformation of the Gaelic character. Before the Forty-Five, relatively little interest was shown in the religious state of the Gaels. However, in order to ensure that hostile powers could never again use the clans to attack the British state, increased efforts were made in the years after 1746 to eliminate Roman Catholicism and non-juring Episcopacy in the Highlands and to spread the English language and the established kirk to all parts. To effect this change, external agencies sought to bring about the moral and spiritual transformation of the Gaels. During the eighteenth century this task was left for the most part to the Society in Scotland for Propagating Christian Knowledge. The Society was a Lowland-based body which sought to spread literacy (to facilitate the reading of the Bible) in the Highlands and Islands through the operation of ambulatory schools, and the attitudes of its officials towards those they would 'civilise' can be taken as a reflection of contemporary Lowland thinking towards the Gaels. While the SSPCK's unrealistic English-only policy was abandoned in 1767, its efforts were hampered as much by prejudice as by the sheer scale of the task.

Nevertheless, by the early nineteenth century Gaels were in increasing numbers embracing the tenets of evangelical religion. This change was brought about not through the efforts of outside agencies intent upon deracinating the Gaels but rather through the work of local lay preachers known as Na Daoine, evangelical Gaelic poets, and the Gaelic school societies. Their success at 'civilising' the Gaels came through their use of the Gaelic language would not have been possible without the confusion and despair that attended the overthrow of clanship. In addition to aiding the spread of evangelicalism throughout Gaeldom, education had another (and not wholly unintended) result: as the secretary of the Committee for Destitute Highlanders wrote in 1837, 'Highlanders when educated become migrants'.[7]

Changing attitudes towards the Gaels were documented by visitors to the Highlands in the years after the Forty-Five, who felt safe to venture there after the clans had been 'tamed'. Most eighteenth-century accounts were written from a Whig perspective and condemned the Gaels for their primitiveness while wholeheartedly approving of the 'improvements' being undertaken upon Highland estates. Samuel Johnson's account of his tour of 1773 is a notable exception; however, his ill-informed remarks about the Gaelic language were seized upon by critics (and still are), while his strident attack on improvements which produced evictions and emigration were conveniently ignored. Interestingly, later critics of the chiefs' conduct were English as well, notably Sarah Murray and Robert Southey. But in the main, travellers after Johnson wanted to discover the 'noble savage' first proclaimed by Martin Martin in 1703 and later with more artistic license by James Macpherson and Sir Walter Scott. The Welsh tourist John Eddowes Bowman described the motive for his tour of the Highlands in 1825 as a search for 'their wild and romantic scenery, and the traces of primitive manners which still might remain among their simple and secluded inhabitants'.[8]

James Macpherson's alleged translations of the poetry of the legendary Gaelic bard Ossian first appeared in the 1760s and are seen today as a precursor of Romanticism – to such an extent that they are excluded from discussions of the Scottish Enlightenment. But Macpherson's work should be not considered in isolation from that movement, nor was he alone in his interest in Scotland's history, however transmogrified. William Robertson's *History of Scotland* (1759) represented an entirely more rational approach and demonstrated that the forward-looking literati were beginning to regard the study of the past as a natural extension of their interest in human nature. According to a recent writer, 'Ossian was a herald of the Romantic movement. For readers not entirely satisfied by the prevailing attitudes of the Scottish Enlightenment, Ossian offered an emotional and imaginative release'.[9] Despite that, confirmed sceptics like David Hume wanted to believe in the authenticity of Macpherson's poetry, more so 'than it is possible for an Englishman of letters',[10] but their interest in history was purely theoretical: they did not believe the past offered any advantages over their 'enlightened' present.

The considerable interest in the Highlands that resulted from the popularity and controversy of Ossian combined with the growing interest in antiquities to produce the cultural activities of the Highland Societies of London and Scotland. It was no accident that the first quarter of the nineteenth century, which saw the full flowering of the Romantic movement, also witnessed the peak of the Highland Society of Scotland's cultural activities when it acted as 'a Gaelic academy of letters'.[11]

The 'rational' approach to history as typified by the Scottish Enlightenment and the more recent antiquarian movement came together in the work of Walter Scott. He lived at a time when interest in the past was no longer an innocent pastime or a mere academic exercise. The French Revolution had seemed to many to herald a new age of chaos and social upheaval, and Scott's historical novels were seen across Europe as a rediscovery of past glories. While Scott followed in the footsteps of the Enlightenment *literati* in supporting the oligarchy of the landed élite,[12] reformers were increasingly looking to history for examples of stable, harmonious and above all ordered societies.

To embark upon reform was to be heading into the unknown, and a new understanding of historical processes was thought to be crucial in bringing about rational change and averting anarchy. Scott's fiction (especially relating to the Highlands) is about historical change, but the man himself would have no truck with reform. His letters to the *Edinburgh Weekly Journal* under the pseudonym 'Somnambulus' in 1819 predicted that anarchy would inevitably follow reform, which instead of being 'the cause of enlightened progress' would become 'a nightmare founded in collective madness'.[13] For T.C. Smout, Scott 'is not and does not want to be a realist dealing with living people in the Scotland of his day. There is, underlying all his art, a nostalgia for the Scottish past that seems to say that that which is Scottish and that which is past must therefore be admirable'.[14]

But in choosing to ignore the decidedly unromantic history of the Gaels after the Forty-Five, Scott did nothing to inform public opinion of the traumatic changes that were taking place throughout Gaeldom. As the man chiefly responsible for the 'rediscovery' of Scotland's past, he was put in charge of the visit of George IV to Edinburgh in 1822. Scott decided upon a Highland theme for the occasion, and so the myths he had created about the Gaels became institutionalised. Not only was an elaborate Highland costume established as the national dress of all Scotsmen but, at a more pernicious level, Scott created a 'plaided panorama' which to this day has bound perceptions of Scottish culture in a tartan straitjacket. His success in perpetrating this deception relied upon the assistance of a Highland élite eager to assume any role other than that of greedy proprietor, as well as that of their Lowland counterparts, who clutched at anything even remotely Scottish with the realisation that their Anglophile approach to respectability had failed.

Scott's first novel, *Waverley*, was published in 1814 and was a landmark in the rehabilitation of the Highlander. The book set forth the Gaels as a race of fearless warriors whose involvement in the Forty-Five resulted not from barbarity but loyalty to a romantic, albeit hopeless, cause. As it was the participation of some clans in the Jacobite cause that largely accounted for their disgrace, so too it was in the redirection of the Gaels' undoubted fighting abilities in the interests of the British Empire that their rehabilitation was made complete.

The idea that Gaels were 'loyal' would have been thought absurd in the 1740s, but in the seventy years between the Battles of Culloden and Waterloo (the latter marking the height of the Highland regiments' fame) over 50,000 men were recruited by their chiefs-cum-landlords into the Highland line and fencible regiments of the British army. In those years, the Gaels had gone from being the most feared and detested people in Britain, considered to be a threat to law and order and the British constitution, to being seen as among the chief defenders of these very things. William Pitt could boast to the House of Commons in 1766 that he had been the first to look to the Highlands for soldiers, and 'they served with fidelity, as they fought with valour, and conquered in every part of the world'. Nevertheless, Pitt felt compelled to counter the persistent prejudices against the Gaels: 'Detested be the national reflections against them! they are unjust, groundless, illiberal, unmanly'.[15]

Because the Gaels' contribution to the defence of Britain was so conspicuous, their advocates could pull the patriotic heartstrings of those in a position to take influential action. In 1773 an anonymous essayist charged that Highland proprietors acted against the public interest by raising rents and thus forcing the people to emigrate. He pointed out that in the Seven Years' War, Britain had fourteen battalions of Highlanders in her service: 'They were often tried and proved, and were always found to be firm and resolute, and trusty troops. Our commanders in different parts of the world reposed the highest confidence in them'. But the chiefs' actions drove the people to America, and once there,' the genius of the Highlander will fall in at once with the nature of the country, where all men are hunters, and bred to the use of arms . . . perhaps to be one day dangerous to the mother country'.[16] Conversely, an early prize essayist of the Highland Society of Scotland, Dr James Anderson, could argue in 1785 that notwithstanding existing prejudices against the Highlands, the exemplary conduct of the Highland regiments in the American War of Independence had meant that 'the region now had a well-founded claim to national attention' with regard to Improvement.[17]

Far from being regarded as dangerous, by the end of the eighteenth century Gaels were seen in official circles to be an ideal counter-revolutionary asset. The proposer of a plan in 1797 to create a Highland Corps to be used in case of invasion 'or Civil commotion' asserted that 'at the moment, they may be justly considered, the only considerable Body of Men, in the whole Kingdom who are as yet absolutely Strangers to the levelling and dangerous principles of the present age, and they may be safely trusted indiscriminately with the knowledge and use of arms'.[18] But the engineer Thomas Telford warned in a report to the government in 1802 that unless it prevented landlords from converting their estates into sheep-walks, 'that Race of People which has of late Years maintained so honourable a share in the Operations of our Armies and Navies will be no more'.[19]

In an age when loyalty to King and Country was not assumed but had to be demonstrated, the Gaels had done so in a way that left no doubters. The Whig polemicists who argued in the aftermath of the Forty-Five for the transformation of a race of barbarous rebels into loyal and God-fearing British subjects would have been pleased. By the 1820s the Highlands and Islands constituted a peaceful but distressed internal colony, favoured by tourists and artists and productive of wool, mutton and emigrants but, to a decreasing extent, of soldiers.

NOTES

1. James Johnstone, *Memoirs of the Chevalier de Johnstone*, 3 vols. (English translation Aberdeen, 1870–71), I, p. 60.
2. *The Highlands of Scotland in 1750*, Andrew Lang, ed. (Edinburgh, 1898), p. 144.
3. SRO CH.1/1/55. 'The Rev. John Walker's Report to the General Assembly on the state of the Highlands and Islands' (1765).
4. See A.I. Macinnes, 'Scottish Gaeldom: The First Phase of Clearance', *People and Society in Scotland*, I (Edinburgh, 1988).
5. Malcolm Gray, *The Highland Economy* (Edinburgh, 1957), pp. 149–59.
6. T.M. Devine, 'Highland Migration to Lowland Scotland, 1760–1860, *Scottish Historical Review*, LXII (1983), p. 149.
7. Ibid., p. 141.
8. J.E. Bowman, *The Highlands and Islands: a Nineteenth Century Tour* (Gloucester, 1986), p. 171.
9. Fiona Stafford, *Sublime Savage* (Edinburgh, 1988), p. 177.
10. *Report of the Committee of the Highland Society of Scotland, appointed to inquire into the nature and authenticity of the Poems of Ossian*, Henry Mackenzie, ed. (Edinburgh, 1805), p. 5.
11. Ronald Black, 'Highland Society of Scotland', *Companion to Gaelic Scotland*, D.S. Thomson, ed. (Oxford, 1983), p. 121.
12. T.M. Devine, 'The Failure of Radical Reform in Scotland in the late Eighteenth Century', in *Conflict and Stability in Scottish Society 1700–1850: Proceedings of the Scottish Historical Studies Seminar, University of Strathclyde 1988–90*, T.M. Devine, ed. (Edinburgh, 1990), p. 56.
13. Stana Nenadic, 'Political Reform and the Ordering of Middle Class Protest', in *Conflict and Stability in Scottish Society, 1700–1850, op. cit.*, p. 72.
14. T.C. Smout, *A History of the Scottish People, 1560–1830* (London, 1969, reprinted 1985), p. 467.
15. *Hansard's Parliamentary History 1766* (London, 1813), XVI, p. 98.
16. Anonymous, *The Present Conduct of the Chieftains and Proprietors of Lands in the Highlands of Scotland, Towards their Clans and People, considered impartially* (1773), p. 5.
17. Dr James Anderson, *An Account of the Present State of the Hebrides and Western Coasts of Scotland* (Edinburgh, 1785), pp. xi–xii.
18. SRO GD.46/6/34. Seaforth Papers (1797).
19. Parliamentary Papers 1803, IV, pp. 16–17. 'Survey and Report on the Coasts and Central Highlands of Scotland. Made by the Command of the Right Honourable the Lords Commissioners of His Majesty's Treasury, in the Autumn of 1820: Thomas Telford, Civil Engineer, Edin. FRS.'

Bibliography

I. ORIGINAL SOURCES

(i) Manuscripts

—National Library of Scotland,

Anonymous, 'Some Remarks on the Highland Clans, and Methods proposed for Civilizing them', date, Adv.MS.16.1.14.

Anonymous, Excerpts from 'Informations' regarding the Highlands, c. 1747, addressed to the Duke of Newcastle, MS 98, ff. 39–40.

Col. Robert Anstruther, Memorial in relation to the Roads of Communication made at the Public Expence through the Highlands of Scotland, Edinburgh, 25 March 1799, Adv.MS.33.4.19.

Letters to Sir Walter Scott, MS 3881, f. 89.

—Scottish Record Office,

—Church Records,

Report of Drs Hyndman and Dick, appointed by the General Assembly to visit the Highlands and Islands, 1760, CH.8/212/1.

The Rev. John Walker's Report to the General Assembly on the state of the Highlands and Islands, 1765, CH.1/1/55.

—Forfeited Estates Papers (1745),

Factors' reports, c. 1755: Report from Capt. John Forbes, factor upon the annexed estates of Lovat and Cromartie (in answer to the Commissioners' orders and instructions of 30 July 1755), E.729/1/12.

The Report of Mr Francis Grant General Riding officer and Inspector, 1756, E.729/7/3–4.

Memorial by Colin MacDonald of Boisdale, Esq., February 1771, to the Commissioners for the Annexed Estates, E.728/39/2.

Journal of Archibald Menzies, General Inspector, concerning estates of Perth, Struan, and Strathyre (Arnprior), with commissioners' instructions to him, 1767, E.729/8/17–18.

—Board of Trustees for Manufactures and Fisheries Papers, A

representation to the Lords Commissioners of His Majesty's Treasury, from the Trustees of the Board, in Edinburgh 21 January 1763, NG.1/1/17/76.

—Gifts and Deposits,
British Fisheries Society Papers: John Knox, 'A Discourse on the Expediency of Establishing Fishing Stations, or Small Towns, in the Highlands of Scotland and the Hebride Islands', London 1786, GD.9/1/16–17.
British Fisheries Society Papers: 'Incorporation of the British Society', 1786, GD.9/1/299.
British Fisheries Society Papers: A journal of the tour of the Hebrides by the Committee of Directors of the Society by Lachlan MacTavish (agent of 5th Duke of Argyll), July-August 1787, GD.9/1/25–26.
Melville Castle Muniments: Letter from Lord Fife to Henry Dundas, 7 October 1794, GD.51/1/831.
Melville Castle Muniments: Letters from Alastair MacDonell of Glengarry to Henry Dundas, November 1794, GD.51/1/849/1–2.
Macdonald Papers: John Blackadder, 'Survey, description, and valuation of Lord Macdonald's estates of Skye and North Uist', 1799, RH.2/8/24/139–140.
Ogilvy of Clova Papers: Letter from Henry Dundas to Walter Ogilvy, 22 February 1797, GD.16/34/355.
Ogilvy of Clova Papers: Copy letter from Walter Ogilvy to Henry Dundas, 4 March 1797, GD.16/34/356.
Seaforth Papers: Returns to the Lord Lieutenant of Ross, 13/2 to 19/7 1798, GD.46/6/45.

—Society in Scotland for Propagating Christian Knowledge Papers,
Minutes of Committee Meetings, 5 March 1751, GD.95/2/7.
Patrick Butter, 'Journal of a Visit to the Schools of the Society in Scotland for Propagating Christian Knowledge', 1824, GD.95/9/3.
Schools visits by John Tawse, 1827–1830, GD.95/9/4.
John Tawse, 'Report on a visitation of Schools in Skye, Lewis, and mainland parishes of Inverness-shire', 1830, GD.95/14/24.
'Report on and Journals of two visits to the Island of St Kilda by the Rev. John Macdonald, minister of Urquhart', 1822–24, GD.95/11/12.

(ii) Pamphlets and Broadsheets

—National Library of Scotland,
Anonymous, 'The Rise of the Present Unnatural Rebellion Discover'd; and the EXTRAORDINARY Power and Oppression of the HIGHLAND CHIEFS Fully Display'd. Being an Attempt to prove, that the

Common HIGHLANDERS act by Compulsion, and not by Inclination. TOGETHER with some Proposals for encouraging these unhappy Men, to return to their Duty; and screening them from the future Resentment of their Chiefs' (London, 1745), ABS.1.86.46.

Anonymous, 'State of Emigration from the Highlands of Scotland, its extent, causes, and proposed remedy' (London, 21 March 1803), Adv.MS.35.6.18.

Anonymous, 'Eight Letters on the Subject of the Earl of Selkirk's Pamphlet on Highland Emigration' (Edinburgh, 2nd edition, 1806), BCL.D5583(4).

Brown, Robert, 'Strictures and remarks on the Earl of Selkirk's Observations on the Present State of the Highlands' (Edinburgh, 1806), BCL.D5583(4).

'The Chevalier's Market, or, Highland Fair', a broadsheet with polemic and caricature (London, 1745), PDP 10/23(8).

Duick, John, 'A Memorial for Britons, a broadsheet with polemic and caricature (London, 1745), R.B.1.60.

'Bonnie Prince Charlie', a caricature by Richard Cooper (Edinburgh, 1745), P/BW/17.

Jacobite broadsheet with alleged comments of Charles Edward Stuart and Sir John Cope prior to the battle of Prestonpans (c. 1745), PDP 10/23(4).

—University of Glasgow,

Anonymous, 'The Present Conduct of the Chieftains and Proprietors of Lands in the Highlands of Scotland, Towards their Clans and People, considered impartially' (1773).

(iii) Printed texts

Adam, R.J., ed., *Papers on Sutherland Estate Management, 1802–1816* (Scottish History Society, Edinburgh, 1972), 4th series, VIII.

Anderson, Dr James, *An Account of the Present State of the Hebrides and Western Coasts of Scotland* (Edinburgh, 1785).

Anonymous, *An Account of the Society in Scotland for Propagating Christian Knowledge, From its commencement in 1709. In which is included, The present state of the Highlands and Islands of Scotland with regard to Religion* (Edinburgh, 1774).

Anonymous, *A Short Account of the Society in Scotland for Propagating Christian Knowledge in the Highlands and Islands* (London, 1809).

Anonymous, *An Account of the Present State of Religion throughout the Highlands of Scotland ... by a Lay Member of the Established Church* (Edinburgh, 1827).

Associate Synod, *Report on the Religious State of the Highlands & Islands of Scotland; with a plan for its amelioration* (Edinburgh, 1820).

Blair, Hugh, *A Critical Dissertation on the Poems of Ossian, The Son of Fingal* (London, 1763).

Boswell, James, *The Journal of a Tour to the Hebrides with Samuel Johnson, LL.D.* (London, 1786, reprinted Oxford, 1924), pp. 254–255.

Browne, James, *A Critical Examination of Dr MacCulloch's Work* (London, 1825).

Browne, James, *A History of the Highlands and of the Highland Clans*, 4 vols. (Glasgow, 1838).

Burns, Robert, *The Complete Works of Robert Burns* (Alloway, 1986).

Campbell, J.L., ed., *Highland Songs of the Forty-Five* (Scottish Gaelic Texts Society, Edinburgh, 1984).

Craven, J.B., ed., *Records of the Dioceses of Argyll and the Isles, 1560–1860* (Kirkwall, 1907).

Craven, J.B., ed., *Journals of the Episcopal Visitations of the Right Rev. Robert Forbes, M.A., of the Dioceses of Ross and Caithness, and of the Dioceses of Ross and Argyll, 1762 & 1770* (London, 1923).

Cregeen, Eric, *Argyll Estate Instructions: Mull, Morvern, Tiree, 1771–1805* (Scottish History Society, Edinburgh, 1964).

Daniell, William, *A Voyage Round Great Britain* ... (London, 1814).

Douglas, Niel, *Journal of a Mission to part of the Highlands of Scotland, in summer and harvest 1797, by appointment of The Relief Synod, in a series of letters to a friend, designed to shew The State of Religion in that country, and The claim the inhabitants have on the compassion of fellow Christians, by Niel Douglas, minister of the Gospel* (Edinburgh, 1799).

Douglas, Thomas, 5th Earl of Selkirk, *Observations on the Present State of the Highlands of Scotland, with a view of the causes and Probable Consequences of Emigration* (London, 2nd edition, 1806).

Duff, H. Robert, *Culloden Papers* (London, 1815).

Faujas de Saint Fond, Barthélemy, *A Journal through England and Scotland to the Hebrides*, 2 vols (English translation, Edinburgh, 1784).

Fea, James, *Considerations of the Fisheries in the Scotch Isles ... A General Account Elucidating the History, Soil, Productions, Curiosities, etc. of the Same, the Manners of the Inhabitants, etc.*, printed privately (London, 1787).

Forbes-Leith, William, ed., *Memoirs of Scottish Catholics During the Seventeenth and Eighteenth Centuries*, 2 vols (London, 1909).

Fraser-Mackintosh, Charles, *Letters of Two Centuries*, (Inverness, 1890).

Grant, Anne, *Letters from the Mountains*, 2 vols (London, 1806).

Grant, Elizabeth of Rothiemurchus, *Memoirs of a Highland Lady*, 2 vols (Edinburgh, 1988).

Gray, John, ed., *Some Reflections intended to promote the success of the Scotch Fishing Company* (London, 1789).

Grierson, H.J.C., ed., *The Letters of Sir Walter Scott*, 11 vols (London, 1932–36).

Haldane, J.A., *Journal of a Tour through the Northern Counties of Scotland and the Orkney Isles, in Autumn 1797. Undertaken with a view to promote the knowledge of the Gospel of Jesus Christ* (Edinburgh, 1798).

Hanway, Mary Anne, *A Journey to the Highlands of Scotland . . . By a Lady* (London, c. 1775).

Hare, A.J.C., ed., *The Life and Letters of Maria Edgeworth* (London, 1814).

Henderson, Andrew, *The History of the Rebellion, 1745 and 1746. Containing, A Full Account of its Rise, Progress and Extinction; The Character of the Highlanders, and their Chief-tains . . . By an Impartial Hand, who was an Eye-witness to most of the facts* (London, 2nd edition, 1748, reprinted from Edinburgh edition).

Henderson, Capt. John, *General View of the Agriculture of the County of Sutherland* (London, 1812).

Heron, Robert, *Scotland Delineated* (Edinburgh, 1799, reprinted 1975).

Hogg, James, *A Tour in the Highlands in 1803* (Edinburgh, 1986).

Home, John, *History of the Rebellion in the Year 1745* (London, 1802).

Inverness Society for the Education of the Poor, *Moral Statistics of the Highlands and Islands of Scotland* (Inverness, 1826).

Johnson, Samuel, *A Journey to the Western Islands of Scotland* (London, 1775, reprinted Oxford, 1924).

Johnstone, James, *Memoirs of the Chevalier de Johnstone*, 3 vols. (English translation, Aberdeen, 1870–71).

Knox, John, *A View of the British Empire, more especially Scotland; with some proposals for the Improvement of that Country, Extension of the Fisheries, and the Relief of the People* (London, 3rd edition, 1785).

Lang, Andrew, ed., *The Highlands of Scotland in 1750* (Edinburgh, 1898).

Loch, James, *An Account of the Improvements on the Estates of the Marquis of Stafford* (London, 1820).

Lockhart, J.G., ed., *Memoirs of the Life of Sir Walter Scott, Bart.* (Edinburgh, 1862).

MacBean, Lachlan, ed., *Buchanan, the Sacred Bard of the Scottish Highlands* (London, 1919).

MacCulloch, Dr John, *The Highlands and Western Islands of Scotland* (London, 1824).

McKay, Margaret, ed. *Dr Walker's Report on the Hebrides of 1764 and 1771*, (Edinburgh, 1862).

MacKenzie, Sir George Steuart, *General View of the Agriculture of the Counties of Ross and Cromarty* (London, 1813).

Mackenzie, Henry, ed., *Report of the Committee of the Highland Society of Scotland, appointed to inquire into the nature and authenticity of the Poems of Ossian* (Edinburgh, 1805).

MacLeod, Angus, ed., *Songs of Duncan Bàn Macintyre* (Scottish Gaelic Texts Society, Edinburgh, 1952).

Macneill, Nigel, ed., *The Literature of the Highlanders* (Inverness, 1892).

Macpherson, James, *Fragments of Ancient Poetry* (Edinburgh, 1760, reprinted 1979).

MacQueen, John and Scott, Tom, eds., *The Oxford Book of Scottish Verse* (Oxford, 1966, reprinted 1990).

Matheson, William, ed., *The Songs of John MacCodrum* (Scottish Gaelic Texts Society, Edinburgh, 1938).

Murray, A.K., *History of the Scottish Regiments in the British Army* (Glasgow, 1862).

Murray, Sarah, *A Companion and Useful Guide to the Beauties of Scotland* (Hawick, 1982).

Parliamentary Select Committee on the Education of the Poor: Digest of Returns to Circular Letter, &c., 1818.

Paton, Henry, ed., *The Lyon in Mourning, or, A Collection of speeches, letters, journals, etc., relative to the affairs of Prince Charles Edward Stuart, by Bishop Robert Forbes*, 3 vols. (Scottish History Society, Edinburgh, 1895–96).

Pennant, Thomas, *A Tour in Scotland* (Warrington, 1769).

Pennant, Thomas, *A Tour in Scotland and a Voyage to the Hebrides* (Warrington, 1774).

Pococke, Richard, *Tours in Scotland: 1747, 1750, 1760*, (Scottish History Society, Edinburgh, 1887).

Prize Essays and Transactions of the Highland Society of Scotland, 1st series (Edinburgh, 1799).

Report of the Committee of the General Assembly, for increasing the means of Education and Religious instruction in Scotland, particularly the Highlands and Islands. Submitted to the General Assembly, May 1829 (Edinburgh, 1829).

Rogers, Charles, ed., *Life and Songs of the Baroness Nairne with a memoir and poems of Carolina Oliphant the Younger* (Edinburgh, 1905).

Scott, Sir Walter, *The Lady of the Lake* (Edinburgh, 1810).

Scott, Sir Walter, *Waverley, or 'Tis Sixty Years Since*, Claire Lamont, ed. (Oxford, 1986).

Scott, Sir Walter, *The Lord of the Isles* (Edinburgh, 1815, reprinted 1877).

Scott, Sir Walter, *Rob Roy* (Edinburgh, 1830).

Scott, Sir Walter, *The Two Drovers and Other Stories*, Graham Tulloch, ed. (Oxford, 1987).

Sinclair, Sir John, *Analysis of the Statistical Account of Scotland* (Edinburgh, 1825, reprinted 1970).

The Statistical Account of Scotland, 1791–99 edited by Sir John Sinclair, D.J. Withrington and I.R. Grant, eds., 20 vols. (reprinted Wakefield, 1973–83).

The Sixth Annual Report of the Society for the Support of Gaelic Schools (Edinburgh, 1817).

Southey, Robert, *Journal of a Tour in Scotland in 1819* (London, 1929).

Statement as to the want of schools and catechists in the Highlands and Islands, by a committee of the General Assembly of the Church of Scotland (Edinburgh, 1825).

Stewart, Col. David of Garth, *Sketches of the Character, Manners, and Present State of the Highlanders of Scotland: with details of the military service of the Highland Regiments*, 2 vols. (Edinburgh, 1822).

Telford, Thomas, 'Survey and Report on the Coasts and Central Highlands of Scotland. Made by the Command of the Right Honourable the Lords Commissioners of His Majesty's Treasury, in the Autumn of 1802', Parliamentary Papers 1803, IV.

The Third Annual Report of the Calton & Bridgeton Association for Religious Purposes; with a Summary Account of the Societies aided from its funds (Glasgow, 1818).

Watt, James, 'Survey, Report, and Estimate', *House of Commons Sessional Papers of the Eighteenth Century – Reports and Papers*, vol. 53 (fisheries), 1785, appendix no. 27.

Wordsworth, Dorothy, *Recollections of a Tour Made in Scotland, A.D. 1803* (London, 1874).

(iv) Periodicals

Edinburgh Review, November 1814.
Scots Magazine, February 1756.
Blackwood's Edinburgh Magazine, May 1819.

II. SECONDARY SOURCES

(i) Reference

The Dictionary of National Biography, Sir Leslie Stephen and Sir Sidney Lee, eds. (Oxford, 1917, reprinted 1973).

A Dictionary of Scottish History, Gordon Donaldson and Robert S. Morpeth, eds. (Edinburgh, 1977).

The Companion to Gaelic Scotland, D.S. Thomson, ed. (Oxford, 1983).

The Concise Dictionary of National Biography, George Menary, ed. (Oxford, 2nd edition, 1906, reprinted 1979).

Scottish Population Statistics (including Webster's Analysis of Population 1755), James Gray Kyd, ed. (Edinburgh, 1975).

(ii) Theses

Macintyre, L.M., Walter Scott and the Highlands (University of Glasgow, Ph.D. thesis, 1976).

(iii) Commentaries

Adam, Frank, *The Clans, Septs and Regiments of the Scottish Highlands* (Edinburgh, 1934).

Barron, James, *The Northern Highlands in the Nineteenth Century*, 11 vols. (Inverness, 1903–13).

Bellesheim, Alphons, *History of the Catholic Church in Scotland*, translated by D. Oswald Hunter Blair, 4 vols. (Edinburgh, 1890).

Brander, Michael, *The Scottish Highlanders and their Regiments* (London, 1971).

Brown, P. Hume, *History of Scotland* (Cambridge, 1911).

Brydall, Robert, *Art in Scotland* (Edinburgh, 1889).

Calder, Jenni, *The Story of the Scottish Soldier, 1600–1914* (HMSO, 1987).

Campbell, Alastair of Airds, *The Highland Society of London, 1778–1978* (London, 1978).

Campbell, J.L., *Gaelic in Scottish Education and Life, Past, Present and Future* (Edinburgh, 1945).

Darragh, James, 'The Catholic Population of Scotland since the year 1680', *Innes Review* (Edinburgh, 1953), vol. IV.

Devine, T.M., 'The Failure of Radical Reform in Scotland in the late Eighteenth Century', in *Conflict and Stability in Scottish Society 1700–1850, Proceedings of the Scottish Historical Studies Seminar, University of Strathclyde, 1988–90*, T.M. Devine, ed. (Edinburgh, 1990).

Devine, T.M., 'Highland Migration to Lowland Scotland, 1760–1860', *Scottish Historical Review*, no. 63 (1983).

Dunbar, J.T., *Highland Costume* (Edinburgh, 1977).

Dunlop, Jean, *The British Fisheries Society, 1786–1893* (Edinburgh, 1978).

Drummond, A.L. and Bulloch, J., *The Scottish Church, 1688–1843* (Edinburgh, 1973).

Durkacz, V.E., *The Decline of the Celtic Languages* (Edinburgh, 1983).

Ferguson, William, 'The Problems of the Established Church in the West Highlands and Islands in the eighteenth century', *Records of the Scottish Church History Society* (Edinburgh, 1972), vol. XVII.

Ferguson, William, *Scotland: 1689 to the Present* (Edinburgh, 1965).

Fraser-Mackintosh, Charles, *Antiquarian Notes* (Inverness, 1897).

Gage, J.G., 'J.M.W. Turner', *The Thames and Hudson Encyclopedia of British Art*, David Bindman, ed. (London, 1985).

Gray, Malcolm, *The Highland Economy, 1750–1850* (Edinburgh, 1957).

Grimble, Ian, *The World of Rob Donn* (Edinburgh, 1979).

Jacob, H.E., *Felix Mendelssohn and his times* (London, 1959).

Henderson, Diana M., *Highland Soldier, 1820–1920* (Edinburgh, 1989).

Johnson, Christine, *Developments in the Roman Catholic Church in Scotland, 1789–1829* (Edinburgh, 1983).

Kaufman, Shima, *Mendelssohn* (London, 1934).

Macdonald, Roderick, 'The Highland District in 1764', *Innes Review* (Edinburgh, 1964).

MacDonnell, The Rev. Father, 'The Glengarry Fencibles', *Transactions of the Gaelic Society of Inverness* (Inverness, 1910), XXVI.

Macinnes, A.I., 'Scottish Gaeldom: The First Phase of Clearance', in *People and Society in Scotland*, I, T.M. Devine and Rosalind Mitchison, eds. (Edinburgh, 1988).

MacInnes, John, *The Evangelical Movement in the Highlands of Scotland, 1688 to 1800* (Aberdeen, 1951).

MacInnes, John, 'The Men', *Records of the Scottish Church History Society* (Glasgow, 1944), VIII.

MacInnes, John, 'Gaelic Religious Poetry, 1650–1850', *Records of the Scottish Church History Society* (Glasgow, 1950), X.

MacKay, D.M., *Trial of Simon, Lord Lovat of the '45* (Edinburgh, 1911).

Mackenzie, Alexander, *History of the Highland Clearances* (Inverness, 1883, reprinted 1986).

Maclean, J.P., *Settlements of Scotch Highlanders in America prior to the peace of 1783, together with notices of Highland Regiments and Biographical sketches* (Cleveland, Ohio, USA, 1900).

Macpherson, Alexander, *Glimpses of Church and Social Life in the Highlands in olden times* (Edinburgh and London, 1893).

Mason, John, Schools on the Forfeited Estates in the Highlands (unpublished typescript, SRO, 1949).

Mitchison, Rosalind, 'The Government in the Highlands, 1707–1745', in *Scotland in the Age of Improvement*, N.T. Phillipson and Rosalind Mitchison, eds. (Edinburgh, 1970).

Mitchison, Rosalind, *A History of Scotland* (2nd edition, London, 1982).

Moore, John Robert, 'Wordsworth's Unacknowledged Debt to Macpherson's Ossian', *Publications of the Modern Language Association of America* (1925), vol. 40.

Nenedic, Stana, 'Political Reform and the "Ordering" of Middle Class Protest', in *Conflict and Stability in Scottish Society, 1700–1850: Proceedings of the Scottish Historical Studies Seminar, University of Strathclyde 1988–90*, T.M. Devine, ed. (Edinburgh, 1990).

Prebble, John, *The Highland Clearances* (Harmondsworth, Middlesex, 1963).

Prebble, John, *Mutiny* (Harmondsworth, Middlesex, 1975).

Prebble, John, *The King's Jaunt* (London, 1988).

Smith, Annette, *Jacobite Estates of the Forty-Five* (Edinburgh, 1982).

Smout, T.C., *A History of the Scottish People, 1560–1830* (London, 1969, reprinted 1985).

Stafford, Fiona, *Sublime Savage* (Edinburgh, 1988).

Sutherland, Douglas, *The Argyll and Sutherland Highlanders* (London, 1969).

Thomson, D.S., *An Introduction to Gaelic Poetry* (London, 1974).

Wills, Virginia, 'The Gentleman Farmer and the Annexed Estates', in *Lairds and Improvement in the Scotland of the Enlightenment*, T.M. Devine, ed., Ninth Scottish Historical Conference, Edinburgh University 1978.

Withrington, D.J., 'The S.P.C.K. and Highland Schools in the Mid-Eighteenth Century', *Scottish Historical Review* (Edinburgh, 1962), vol. XLI, no. 132.

Wood, Stephen, *The Scottish Soldier* (Manchester, 1987).

Youngson, A.J., *After the Forty-Five* (Edinburgh, 1973).

Index

Act of Attainder, 21
Adam, R. J., 171
Africa, 93rd Highlanders in, 171–3
American War of Independence, 157–9, 180n
Anderson, the Rev. Dr. James, 34–35
Annexed Estates Board, 34, 42, 152–3
Annexing Act, 21–22
Anstruther, Col. Robert, 25
Ardchattan, parish of , 76
Ardnamurchan, 51
Argyll,
  2nd Duke of, 3, 6–7
  3rd Duke of, 3, 6–7, 26, 110
  5th Duke of, 161–2
Associate Presbytery, 81
Assynt, 48n

Bagpipes, 103, 110, 132
Ballachulish, 53, 102
Balnagowan, Rosses of, 13
Barra, Isle of, 54
  emigrants from, 165–6
  beathachadh boideach, 27
Beauly, 57
Blackadder, John, 42–3
Blair, Dr Hugh, 116–117
Board of Trustees for Manufactures and Fisheries,
  23–24, 45n
'Bonnie Prince Charlie', myth of, 135–7
Boswell, James, 64, 118
Bowman, John Eddowes, 102–3, 112
British Fisheries Society, 24, 37–8, 47n
Browne, James, 32, 155, 167, 178n
Bruce, Edmund, 12
  The Highlands of Scotland in 1750, 12–15
Buchanan, Dugald (Dughall Bochanan), 87–9
Burns, Robert, 135–6
Butter, Patrick, 78–9

Caledonian Canal (proposed), 24–5
Callander, 53
Cameron of Lochiel, Donald, 4, 181
Cameron, the Rev. John, 51, 91n
Campbell, Alexander, 159
Campbell, Clan, 8, 51–2
Campbell, John (1st Earl of Breadalbane), 150
Canna, Isle of, 55, 76
Carlyle, the Rev. Alexander, 70
Carswell, John, 85
Caterans, 10
Church of Scotland:
  Evangelical faction, 68
  General Assembly schools, 77–8
  Moderate faction, 68–9, 85
Clanranald, Donald MacDonald of, 4
Coigach, 22
Cope, General Sir John, 6
Cumberland, Duke of , 21, 98

Daniell, William,

Voyage Round Great Britain, 102
Deer forests, 48n
Deeside, Upper, 108
Disarming Acts:
  of 1716, 8
  of 1725, 8
  of 1746, 8–9
Douglas, Niel, 69–70, 164
Douglas, Thomas (5th Earl of Selkirk), 26–28, 40
Dundas, Henry, 161–2, 166
Dunlop, John (Lord Provost of Glasgow), 168
Dunoon, the Rev. David, 65
Dùthchas, 26, 144
Edgeworth, Maria, 122
Edinburgh Review, 124
Edinburgh Society for the Support of Gaelic Schools,
  73–4, 85
  Inverness and Glasgow auxiliaries, 74–5, 77, 85
Eigg, Isle of, 55, 76
Erskine, Sir Harry, 177
  'The Highland Character' (song), 177

Falconer, the Rev. Alexander, 66
Faujas de Saint Fond, Barthélemy, 112
Fea, James, 38
Fergusson, Adam, 47n
Fife, Earl of, 166
fisheries, encouragement of, 36–8
Forbes, Duncan (of Culloden), 6,7–9, 18n, 98
Forbes, Captain John, 22–23, 57–8
Forbes, Bishop Robert, 52–3
  The Lyon in Mourning, 52
Fort George, 9, 172
Fraser, Gen. Simon, 152

Gaelic language, 9, 53, 60, 63–4, 79, 132–4
Gairloch, 77, 159
Gallie, the Rev. Andrew, 35
George IV, visit to Scotland of 1822, 104, 127–9, 145
Girls, educational provision for, 9, 75, 78, 80
Glasgow, Highlanders in, 162, 167
Glencoe massacre, 14, 150
Glengarry, 165–9
  Macdonells of, 5, 19, 29n
  in Canada, 180n
Gordon, Elizabeth (Countess of Sutherland and
  Marchioness of Stafford), 28, 29
Grant, Anne, 139–143
Grant, Elizabeth, 143–6
  Memoirs of a Highland Lady, 143
Grant, Francis, 23
Grant, Sir John Peter (of Rothiemurchus), 128, 145
Guadaloupe, island of, 155

Haldane, James and Robert, 69
Hanway, Mary Anne, 105–6, 110
Harris, Isle of, 43, 65, 76
Heights of Abraham, Battle of, 153
Helmsdale, 79
Henderson, Diana, 165, 175–6
Heritable jurisdictions, 3–4

Heron, Robert, 100
Highland (independent) companies, 2
Highland dress, 112–3, 127–9, 176
Highland estates, reorganisation of, 182–3
Highland migration to Lowlands, 183
Highland regiments:
  statistics, 150
  Argyll Regiment, 150
  Lord Loudoun's Regiment, 163
  Glengarry Fencibles
    recruitment of 67, 165–69
    service of, 169
    emigration to Canada of, 169
  Strathspey Fencibles, 166–7
  Sutherland Fencibles,
    recruitment of, 169
    in Ireland, 169–70
  West Fencible Regiment, difficulty in recruiting for, 163
  42nd (Royal Highland) "Black Watch",
    foundation of, 3, 163
    mutiny of, 151
    in America, 154–5
    in Caribbean, 154
    in Ross-shire, 156
    in Ireland, 155
    and Lowland disturbances, 156
    recruiting problems of, 156–7
    in India, 160
  73rd (Perthshire), 179n
  78th (Fraser's), 151–3
  78th (Seaforth), 176
  79th (Cameron), 176–7
  92nd (Gordon), 177
  93rd (Sutherland) Highlanders,
    recruitment of, 169–171
    in southern Africa, 171–72
    conduct of, 171–74
    at Battle of New Orleans, 173
Highland Society of London, 37, 132–4
Highland Society of Scotland, 34, 134
  Ossian inquiry of, 118–9
Highlands, the,
  schools in, 77–8, 92n
  literacy rates in, 82
  evangelical missionaries in, 67–73
Hogg, James, 100, 101–2, 107, 137
Home, John, 15, 20n, 116
  History of the Rebellion in the Year 1745 (1802), 15–16
Honours of Scotland, 128
Hume, David, 117
Hyndman & Dick (Drs), report of, 58–60

India, Highlanders in, 134, 145, 160, 176, 179n
Inveraray Castle, 110
Inverness, 65, 69
Iona, resistance to conscription in, 164–5
Ireland, Highland troops in, 150, 152, 155, 169–70
Irvine, Dr Alexander, 72–3

Jacobite Rebellions
  of 1708, 2
  of 1715, 2
  of 1719, 2
  of 1745, and Government propaganda, 5–6
Johnson, Dr Samuel, 64, 97, 99, 104–5, 111–112, 118
Johnstone, James (Chevalier de Johnstone), 181

Kelly, George, 52
Killin (Lochtayside), 76
Kincardine (Ross-shire), 35
Kingussie, 78
Kintail, 66
Knox, John, 36
Knoydart, 14

Laggan (Strathspey), 139–41

Landseer, Sir Edwin, 139
Lewis, Isle of, 76, 79–80
Linen stations, 23–4
Loch, James, 28, 30–31
Lochiel, Donald Cameron of, 4, 181
Lockhart, John, and 'Celtification', 128
Lovat and Cromartie, disannexation of forfeited estate of, 153
Lowland plantations, proposed, 44, 48n

MacCodrum, John (Iain Mhic Fhearchair), 87
MacCulloch, Horatio, 139
MacCulloch, Dr John, 31
MacDonalds, the, 14
Macdonalds of Glencoe, 5, 150
MacDonald, Alexander (Alasdair Mac Mhaighstir Alasdair), 63, 86
Macdonald, Sir Alexander (Lord Macdonald), 87, 104–5
McDonald, Allan (of Kingsburgh), 158
MacDonald, the Rev. Anthony, 76
MacDonald, Colin (of Boisdale), 55–7
MacDonald, Bishop Hugh, 54–5
Macdonald, Sir James (of Sleat), 87, 104
MacDonald, the Rev. John, 81
MacDonell, Father Alexander, 165, 169, 180n
MacDonell, Alastair Ranaldson (of Glengarry), 165–9
MacDonell, Marjory Grant, 165
MacGregor, Rob Roy, 102, 120–1
Macintyre, Duncan Bàn (Donnachadh Bàn Mac-an-t-Saoir), 132–3
Macintyre, Lorn, 123
MacKay, Clan, 12–13, 66
Mackay, Rob Donn, 86
Mackenzie of Seaforth, 13
Mackenzie, George (of Dundonell), 26
MacKenzie, Sir George Steuart, 176
McLachlan, John, 51–2
MacLeod, Donald,
  Gloomy Memories of the Highlands (1840–41), 172
MacLeod, the Rev. John, 65
MacLeod, Lt Col Norman MacLeod (of Harris), 160
MacPhail, the Rev. William, 78
MacPherson, Clan (proposed massacre of), 153
Macpherson, James, 97, 99, 116–9, 133–4
MacPherson, Abbé Paul, 57
MacRae, Clan, 13–14
Mactavish, Lachlan, 38, 43
Martin, Martin,
  Description of the Western Isles of Scotland, 97
Matheson, Donald, 89
Mendelssohn, Felix, 137–8
  'Hebrides' Overture, 137–8
Menzies, Archibald, 42
Militia Act of 1797, resistance to, 162, 164
Mitchison, Rosalind, 7
Morar, 55
Morison, Roderick, 66
Morvern, 51
Muck, Isle of, 76
Muir of Ord, 53
Mull, resistance to conscription in, 164
Munro, Clan, 8, 13
Murray, Sarah, 106–7, 112

Na Daoine (The Men), 69,72, 85, 184
Nairne, Lady (Baroness Carolina), 136
New Orleans, Battle of (1815), 173
North Carolina, Highlanders in, 158–9
North Uist, 42–3, 87

Ogilvy, Walter (of Clova), 162
Oighreachd, 26
Ossian,
  'translations' of, 116–9, 133–4
  influence of, 119, 121, 138, 141–2
Oughton, Sir James Adolphus, 157

INDEX

Pennant, Thomas, 98, 105, 108–110
planned villages, 35–7, 47n
Pitt, William, and military recruitment, 153–4
Pococke, Bishop Richard, 98, 108
Pope, the Rev. Alexander, 86
Prebble, John, 129, 175

Raining's School, 78, 133
Reay, 4th Lord, 12–13
Red River (Canada), emigration to, 26
Relief Presbytery, missionary activities of, 69–70
Rhum, Isle of, 76
The Rise of the Present Unnatural Rebellion, 3
Roman Catholic Church, 12, 54–61, 66–7, 75–6, 78, 92n
Ross of Balnagown, 13
Rothiemurchus (Strathspey), 143–7
Runciman, Alexander, 138

St Kilda, 81–2
Schaw, Alexander, 58
Scott, Sir Walter,
  on Ossian, 121
  and the Clearances, 129–31
  correspondence of, 29, 122, 129–31
  and tourism, 97, 122, 138
  works of,
    "Highland Widow", 126–7
    "Lady of the Lake", 100, 121–3, 138
    "Lord of the Isles", 124
    Rob Roy, 102, 120, 124–6
    "Two Drovers" 127, 174
    Waverley, 123–4, 144–5,186
Scottish Episcopal Church, Non-jurors in the, 49–54
Sellar, Patrick, 28–9, 43–4
Shaw, the Rev. John, 74–5
Sinclair, Sir John, 36, 134
Skye, Isle of, 42, 80, 82–5
  military recruitment in, 160
Smout, T.C., 186
Sobieski brothers, 146
  Costumes of the Clans (1845), 146
  Vestiarium Scoticum (1842), 146
Society for Propagating the Gospel at Home, 84
Society in Scotland for Propagating Christian Knowledge
  (SSPCK), 50, 62–5, 78–80, 86, 133, 184
'Some Remarks on the Highland Clans', 10–12
South Uist, 55–56
Southey, Robert, 102, 107–8, 112–3
Spain, 2
Staffa, 137
Stafford, Marquis of, 28, 107
Stewart, the Rev. Alexander, 75
Stewart, the Rev. Charles, 162–3
Stewart, David (of Garth), 45, 151
  *Sketches of the Character, Manners, and Present State of
    the Highlanders of Scotland* (1822), 129
  on Black Watch mutiny of 1743, 151
  on the Forty-Five, 152
  on Highland character, 174–75
  on Sutherland clearances, 174
Stewarts of Appin, 51, 53
Stornoway, 79
Strathglass, clearance in, 165
Strathnaver, 86
Stuart, James (of Dunearn), 129
Stuart, Prince Charles Edward, caricature of, 5
Sutherland,
  'improvement' of, 29–31, 43–4, 107–8
  military recruitment in, 169–71
  tacksmen in, 170–71
  evictions of 1811, 172

tacks,
  on Argyll estate, 6–7
  auction of, 114n
Tawse, John, 79–80

Telford, Thomas, 19n, 25, 38–40
Ticonderoga, Battle of, 176
Thomson, D. S., 119
Tiree, 26
Toleration Act of 1712, 52
Tongue, Presbytery of, 85
Trossachs, the, 100–1
Turner, J.M.W., 139

Vesting Act, 21

Wade, General George, 2–3, 19n
Walker, the Rev. Dr. John, 32, 60–62
Washington, George, 159
Watt, James, 24
Wemyss, William, 169–71
Whisky, distillation of, 44, 109–110
William, Duke of York, and military recruitment, 161
Wolfe, Gen. James, 153
Wordsworth, Dorothy, 100–1
Wordsworth, William, 119–20
  'Rob Roy's Grave', 120

'Year of the Sheep' (1792), 141, 156
Young, William, 29